# Aloisia

THE MAKING OF A FRONTIER WOMAN

Also by Ella Benndorf:

RECIPE COLLECTION
Mom's Soup for You

BIOGRAPHY
Walter Benndorf, The Moulding of a German-Canadian

SHORT STORIES
Aloisia's New Beginnings
& Other Stories

# ALOISIA

## THE MAKING OF A FRONTIER WOMAN

Ella Benndorf

WhatWorks Media
Vancouver, Canada
Copyright © 2017 by Ella Benndorf

All rights reserved

Book layout by Michele Hall

*Photo on front cover: Aloisia at the age of 20 with Franz' writing in the background*

Throughout this book, we have used the symbol of the oak which represents patience, courage, strength and survival, wisdom and dignity. These are the very traits that the author feels embody her parents, Aloisia and Franz, who worked hard as pioneers and farmers in the new frontier of British Columbia.

ISBN-13: 978-1979595483

WhatWorks Media
Vancouver, Canada

*"Asked what love is, some reply:*

*It is only a wind whispering among the roses and dying away.*

*But often it is an inviolable seal that endures for life, endures till death.*

*God has fashioned it of many kinds*

*and seen it endure or perish."*

~ *Victoria* by Knut Hamsun


*"I realize today that nothing in the world is more distasteful to a man than to take a path that leads to himself."*

~ *Damian* by Hermann Hesse

Affectionately dedicated to Aloisia, my mother, who kept Franz' letters and then told her own stories of what happened during those times.

# Table of Contents

| | |
|---|---|
| Acknowledgments | 11 |
| Foreword | 15 |
| | |
| CHAPTER ONE: 1916-1919 | 22 |
| A Pause on the Stairwell, 1916 | 23 |
| Studying Is Always Interesting | 28 |
| Incoming Bees | 41 |
| The Spliced Cord | 49 |
| Strange Mail | 67 |
| Christmas in Ried | 71 |
| Waiting in Vain | 74 |
| Spring Was Late | 75 |
| Another Letter from Franz | 84 |
| Veterans | 86 |
| Manoeuvres | 94 |
| Our German Father | 96 |
| More Letters – "I Have Honey" | 98 |
| Letters Mailed From Scapa Flow | 100 |
| Reflections while a Prisoner in Scapa Flow | 102 |
| A Few Hours | 110 |
| | |
| CHAPTER TWO: 1919 -1922 | 112 |
| Franz Writes From Home | 113 |
| A Home of Her Own | 116 |
| Franz is Determined to Leave Germany | 120 |
| An Oak Leaf Falls | 122 |
| Unspoken Reproaches | 125 |
| The Versailles Treaty | 128 |
| Unsettled Times | 131 |
| Mangels | 147 |
| A Long Liaison | 149 |
| Being Practical | 151 |
| A Long Shadow | 160 |
| Letter From Argentina | 164 |
| Threshing | 168 |
| | |
| CHAPTER THREE: | 171 |
| 1923-1926 | 171 |

| | |
|---|---|
| A Quiet Sunday Afternoon | 172 |
| A Returned Friend | 178 |
| Letters After Aloisia Visits Franz | 186 |
| A Shot Is Fired | 198 |
| The Letters Say It All | 203 |
| Keeping the Connection | 215 |
| He Loves Me, He Loves Me Not | 221 |
| Bee Class in Ried | 227 |
| | |
| CHAPTER FOUR: | 233 |
| 1926-1927 | 233 |
| A Lark Was Singing | 234 |
| Letter From the Middle of Canada | 236 |
| The Four Leaf Clover | 239 |
| Pieces of Kindling | 247 |
| The Last Hayride | 255 |
| Even an Ocean | 258 |
| The Photo Album | 260 |
| Last Letter from Broadwater | 267 |
| Cast Iron | 270 |
| The Cookbook | 278 |
| Irish Crusaders | 286 |
| Buffaloes and Silk | 293 |
| A Fine Network | 305 |
| People Watching | 312 |
| The Scent of Lavender | 319 |
| Bluebird Mountain | 329 |
| Trix | 335 |
| The Fountain of Youth | 343 |
| Conclusion | 352 |
| | |
| Broadwater, The First Time In | 353 |
| Wild Cherries | 359 |
| Broadwater: The Last Time In | 371 |
| Epilogue | 386 |
| | |
| LOGGING AN ESCAPE FROM THE WILDERNESS: | 387 |
| Bibliography | 395 |
| | |
| About the Author | 396 |

# Acknowledgments

Many people have assisted in completing Aloisia. First, I wish to sincerely thank my cousin Paul for typing the forty-five letters my father wrote my mother between 1916 and 1927. Paul generously dispatched this large undertaking with his usual grace and accuracy. His work proved to be a catalyst for the entire adventure of writing *Aloisia: The Making of a Frontier Woman*. Paul also completed an extensive genealogy of the Schropp family, researched the origin of the Schropp name, and also typed out the genealogy for my father's side of the family.

I thank my cousin Oscar, for the graphic details describing the gunshot episode. My mother described this event many times but Oscar's written first-hand experience really made this scene come alive.

Thank you to my cousin Camilla Kraus for always encouraging my endeavours. The postcard her mother, Maria, wrote to my mother July 5, 1927, was the first mail my mother received after arriving in Canada.

I also thank my cousin Inge Kastenhofer, the granddaughter of Joseph Schropp, who gave me valuable documents and photographs for this book. I wish to thank her husband Franz, especially for driving me to another cousin, Maria Stecher, a daughter of Hans. Maria Stecher, though in her nineties, related personal anecdotes that filled in several gaps in Aloisia's chronicle.

My sincere gratitude to all my other cousins and their families for helping me in this search for my roots. I thank every one for your nourishment, both in body and spirit as we visited around bountiful tables laden with chocolate and strawberry tortes, coffee and the ever present whipping cream.

Dr. Hartmut Froeschle has always encouraged my endeavour to study my heritage. His extensive knowledge has been a great inspiration to me. I thank him, not only for his cheerful assistance to me personally, but also for being the catalyst for my study of German immigration and the contributions of German immigrants to countries around the world.

My sincere gratitude to the time-consuming work of Heidi Esser and Dr. Laurence Kitching for advice on the finer points of translating my father's letters.

Special thanks to my sister, Louise Bailey, who generously gave me my mother's original passport and important old correspondence and photographs from Bavaria. She was always patient when asked questions such as, "Did mother ever say where, exactly, where she saw the Doukhobour houses?"

Dr. Margriet Dogterom contributed a sense of humour, mixed with wisdom and encouragement, which definitely motivated me to complete Aloisia's story. In addition she shared the beekeeping expertise of her company, Beediverse. While we are on the subject of bees, I wish to thank Joe Gnilka, whose hives produce the best honey of the Kootenays, for describing the occurrence of swarming in such detail.

Robert D. Turner supplied invaluable information regarding the sternwheeler routes on the Columbia River/Arrow Lakes district of British Columbia. He generously gave permission to reproduce the picture of the Bonnington from his book, *Sternwheelers and Steam Tugs*.

I am thankful to Dr. Carolyn Mamchur, a gifted teacher of creative writing, whose inspiration first led me to putting the story of Aloisia in a written form so it could be shared with others.

My fellow members of New West Writers have been consistently helpful over the years. I sincerely thank the executive and all the members for their constructive criticism and encouragement. The opportunity to read sections of this novel at monthly meetings was invaluable. Of this group, I especially thank Marguerite Dolsen and Bill O'Connor who gave generously of their time and encouragement.

I am very thankful for the amazing proofreading skills of Denise Marasco and David Ward for his proofreading and cover advice.

Thank you to the patience of Dr. Vincent D'Oyley who insisted that I share more details of Aloisia's vital personality and that the cover design be adjusted to reflect this. It was a lesson, not only for the writing of this book, but for all of my writing, which I will always remember.

Bill Stephens shared his deep understanding of Canadian Pacific Railroad history, making my mother's journey across Canada in 1927 truly come alive. His wealth of knowledge and photographs gave me a deeper perspective of the journey of wheat from prairie swathes to the port of Vancouver.

Thank you to Helmut and Inge, Roland and Rainer Daniels who found and sent information about the Madden Hotel in Nelson where my parents spent their first few days of married life.

Hilda Stolz, who was born only a few years after my mother, gave me many details of farm life in Germany at the beginning of the twentieth century.

Many details of Aloisia's journey in the Arrow Lake Region of the Kootenays rely heavily on Edward Affleck's personal knowledge and assistance. My sincere gratitude for his generosity of time and his many publications giving a splendid and accurate portrayal of sternwheeler history in British Columbia.

Randy Puder's expertise in supplying an excellent computer and printer allowed me to transform my thoughts and ideas into hard copy. Thank you also, Randy, for following up on the installation with generous, consistent support.

My daughter, Celena, and my son, Eric, read the first drafts of Aloisia. Their comments gave me fresh insights and determination 'to dig deeper, become more honest and more real.' I also thank them both for their technical support whenever needed.

My husband, Walter, repeatedly provided invaluable details regarding obscure historical and geographical subjects. His memories from his childhood helped me understand many aspects of everyday German life.

The research librarians of Vancouver, New Westminster,

Coquitlam, Burnaby, Port Moody public libraries as well as the Canadian Pacific Railway Archives must be recognized. God bless them, every one!

Very special gratitude to Wen Lin who skillfully incorporated the suggestions of Dr. Margriet Dogterom and Dr. Vincent D'Oyley to design the cover. Thank you, Wen, not only for the beautiful cover but also for the careful copying of the illustrations. It has been a fun adventure working with Michele Hall of WhatWorks Media who is a Jill of all trades and was editor, layout artist, designer and publisher of my books.

My sincere gratitude for each contribution to the network that made the completion of *Aloisia: the Making of a Frontier Woman* possible.

Most of all I thank my father for writing such wonderful letters to my mother, and I thank my mother for preserving them with so much care.

# Foreword

Though at the time I was unaware of it, the seed for writing this novel was planted in the 1950s. I was only a teenager at the time, but I remember the incident as though it were yesterday. My mother and I were in the basement of her rooming house on 810 St. Andrews Street, New Westminster, British Columbia. Laundry was pegged on wash lines, its sweet scent mingling with earthy smells of sawdust and sacks of potatoes stored nearby. Contented noises were coming from the furnace.

We were moving boxes around—tidying up. She stopped for a moment and looked at an old pine chest pushed against the basement wall. It was a sturdy chest, reinforced with metal bands. I had never really noticed it before. It had black iron handles. My mother hesitated and then pulled it away from the wall. She lifted up the lid. First moving some of the contents aside, my mother gently took out a small package tied with a pale blue ribbon. Next to them was a thin booklet of some kind, browned with age, which she put back into the trunk.

Smiling at me rather shyly, she held up the package. "These are the letters from your father, the ones he wrote me before we were married." The gentleness in her voice was puzzling because my parent's difficult marriage had ended in separation just a few years before. I remembered the scene when the moving truck carrying her possessions left the farm. My mother and I were sitting in the cab. I was sitting next to the door. As the driver started the engine, my father held the door handle, wanting to say something to me. My mother ordered me to close the door. I can still feel the reluctant release of his hold and the awkwardness I felt turning my face away from him.

"Of course, they were written in German," her voice trailed off, "...you wouldn't be able to read them...." During the Second

World War, when I was growing up, the general Canadian public had an extreme aversion toward Germans; in order not to fan the prejudices against our family, my parents did not teach me my mother tongue. The elementary school teacher advised my parents not to speak German at home, ever.

Some of our neighbours were already spreading rumours; my father had set up a shortwave radio in our barn silo. He was communicating directly with Hitler.

This was ironic because, as a university student in Munich, my father had used his strong vocal chords to denounce Hitler and his party. My father was informed that, as a consequence of his loud opposition at meetings, he had been targeted by some of Hitler's supporters. (Many of Hitler's enemies were beaten up or found dead even in the early 1920's). In danger for his life, my father escaped over the Alps into Switzerland. He

***Schropp Family Portrait, 1897***
*With Maria shortly leaving for Africa, this was the last occasion the Schropp family could all be photographed together.*
*Back row: Franz, Emma, Maria, Peter, Paul*
*Centre: Dori, Alois, Victoria Schropp with baby Aloisia, Joseph Schropp, Joseph, Hans*
*Foreground: Otto and Ludwig*

stayed there for several weeks, finally coming home only long enough to pack up some belongings and emigrate to Argentina.

Regardless of the absurdity of the accusations, my parents complied with the teacher's request not to speak German at home; they didn't want any more trouble. My father tore down the silo.

With hands gnarled from a lifetime of hard work, my mother carefully pushed the package tied with blue ribbon back into the trunk again. She closed the lid.

In 1983, my mother died. It wasn't until 1991, after almost ten years had passed, that I came across this little package again. My mother's words came back to me. "These are the letters...."

I untied the blue ribbon. My father's letters were filed chronologically from 1916 to 1927 in small, white cardboard folders that had been neatly trimmed with pinking shears. They started right after he met my mother at a beekeeping course given at a college in Bavaria. After eleven years of correspondence my mother joined my father in British Columbia, Canada to become his wife. On the last folder, in my mother's handwriting, were the words, *Louise left with the ship the Old Country May 26, 1927.*

Though my father's handwriting appeared elegant with straight, evenly spaced lines and though as an adult I had studied German, I could not decipher the words as they were written in the old alphabet.

I phoned my cousin Paul in Augsburg and explained the problem. If he would type the letters, I would be able to read them. Paul agreed, and I immediately started mailing photocopies of the originals. He sent me the typed transcriptions by return mail. By October of 1991, when Paul had almost completed the typing, he included this note:

"The letters are getting more interesting all the time.... One can certainly imagine oneself back in the everyday needs and misery of those times. That each of your parents wanted to emigrate under such circumstances is fully understandable. Both had courage and enterprising spirits. One must also wonder how they managed it financially."

In December of the same year Paul mailed the last of my father's letters and included the following letter:

*December, 1991*

*Dear Ella!*

*I have typed out the letters to the best of my ability and now have a better understanding of your father's inner life. He had a very highly developed trust in God. His youth was not easy and the life with his parents should have been better. It doesn't surprise me that he didn't wish to stay at home and chose instead to look for some other course of action. He found that emigration was his only chance. He truly had a difficult time to find a girl to marry. Your mother, Louise, was such a far distance away from him and because of the circumstances of those times he could not possibly get to know her better or more quickly. That they both, despite all these difficulties, managed to get married can only be looked upon as destiny.*

*When I was twenty-two years old I married my dear Hilda. It was during the war. There were very few career opportunities so, during the first years of marriage, I took courses to be a social worker. And during those uncertain times, while I was studying, our son Heine was born. Until now Hilda and I have stayed together both in good times and in bad. We understand each other very well and have a married life with which we are content. Even at our age we are still happy.*

*This is what we wish for you and Walter and hope that both of you can, in the best of health, still have wonderful, peaceful and happy years together. With these thoughts we wish you a merry Christmas and a Happy New Year from Paul and Hilda.*

With all of my father's letters to my mother in typewritten form, I could now read them and get some insight into my father's upbringing, beliefs, aspirations, life as a naval signaller, and pioneering experiences in Argentina and Canada. The letters, often referring to questions my mother asked him, also revealed much about her. I am grateful she did not destroy them (even the one she was specifically asked to burn). In fact, the letters proved so interesting, that I decided to translate them into English so the rest of our family could also read them and get a glimpse into their heritage.

But something was missing – my mother's story told from her own perspective. Fortunately, when I was growing up on the farm, she had shared many anecdotes while we worked together picking strawberries, raspberries or beans. My mother's voice always grew soft and nostalgic when speaking about her happy childhood in Ried. "Of course," she often said, "we may have been considered poor by today's standards, but it was organized poverty." She always emphasized the word 'organized'. "We all had to pull our weight. We always had enough to eat."

Although Aloisia's childhood was secure and happy, even as a young girl she was taught how to arrange herself comfortably for any job so she would not tire and could stay at the task longer. Bowls needed for food preparation, for instance, were to be arranged around her or on her lap in a convenient way.

*The village of Ried, Germany*

The few seconds required arranging tools properly would quickly be regained when the work proceeded efficiently. If a chair was required, she was reminded gently but firmly not to sit on the edge of the seat as though ready to escape out the back door to play. She would be there awhile.

There were many rules in the Schropp family about work. Some rules were explicit, others implicit, learned by example, an encouraging nod or a disapproving frown. Don't step over the work, do something with it. Never go anywhere with your hands empty. And once you have an article in your hand, don't put it down, so that you would have to pick it up once again. That just takes more time. Finish the job. Today these concepts are called the science of ergonomics or office efficiency. Then it was called being practical.

The Schropps were a prime example of how a large family could progress if everyone did their share, if no moment was wasted. When Aloisia audaciously started somersaulting in the field or learning how to ride a bike, her mother disapproved. She had enough boys. There were more useful ways a little girl could use her energy, like watching the geese, feeding the chickens and the pigs, washing the dishes, and hoeing the garden. And she could help carry things to the train station when relatives were leaving. Aloisia shouldn't be a tomboy. "By the way, you could crush the egg shells and feed them to the chickens."

When my mother became elderly and too frail to walk, she lived in a German Canadian Care Home. Though I already had written down many of my mother's stories, I took this opportunity to fill in some gaps by asking her questions. Some questions were relatively straight forward, such as the one about the appearance of red hair in the Schropp family. Others were 'how to questions' such as, "How did you make sauerkraut?" or "How did you make that wonderful tomato soup?" I also formulated questions about the war years and the reasons she finally left her beloved homeland. Other questions were more personal. Her responses are included in this book.

Mother used to smile when she saw me writing down her answers. "What are you going to do with all that information, write a book?" At the time I just laughed at the idea. "Maybe!

It's so interesting!" without ever thinking for a moment that I would ever do just that.

It was not until many years later that I realised just how much information I had gathered about my mother's life, certainly enough to write some chapters to fit between my father's chronologically arranged letters. Information about my mother would also have the advantage of adding a new perspective to my father's letters. Virtually every event and anecdote in this book, be it my father's good bye salute, the sandwich episode in the train or the story of the cloverleaf tablecloth, is authentic and based directly on my mother's transcripts.

Half a century has now passed since my mother first opened that chest in the basement. So much has taken place since then. The house at 810 St. Andrews Street in New Westminster, where mother first pointed out those letters so long ago, no longer stands; an apartment building rises in its place. I have gathered together many of the household articles my mother brought to Canada as a bride and I placed them in her old pine chest, which now stands in our guest bedroom.

The navy uniform, which my father wore when he stood on the platform of the Freising train station and silently saluted my mother good-bye in 1916, is carefully packed away in the same room. Aloisia's Excella sewing machine, refinished by master craftsman George Skene (as was the trunk), is ready for use as it once was in the Old Country.

The letters tracing my parent's courtship extended just over a period of eleven years. I hope you will enjoy discovering, as I did, how Aloisia and Franz first met and how the relationship developed until my mother became his bride on June 11, 1927.

# CHAPTER ONE: 1916-1919

## FROM BEEKEEPING TO SCAPA FLOW

# A Pause on the Stairwell, 1916

Victoria Schropp was forty-two years old and had not had a child for three years. She thought her family was complete. When Victoria discovered she had conceived again, an old woman down the lane comforted her with a prophecy. "Don't worry, you will have a girl and she will be a blessing to you. She will care for you in your old age and one day she will close your eyes."

Aloisia was born on August 20, 1896, a warm summer day. The younger Schropp children asked why the church bells were ringing. When they were told that another baby had arrived in the family they plugged their ears and shouted. "Stop the bells! Not another baby! Stop the bells!"

But baby Aloisia had already arrived. Aloisia Schropp was baptized a few days later in the Catholic Church across the lane. It was where all of her twelve older brothers and sisters had also been baptized.

That was almost twenty years ago. Now Aloisia, the last of the children of Joseph and Victoria Schropp, had grown up to be a strong young woman.

Aloisia rested her hand on the stair railing worn smooth by generations of students. Through the open window, purple wisteria blossoms dangled from grey twisted vines and permeated the air with a fragrant, spicy aroma. Aloisia, however, was concentrating at a map framed to the wall. As the sound of some footsteps approached up the stairs, Aloisia moved to make room, keeping her eyes firmly fixed on the left side of the map. The steps stopped behind her. There was a muffled cough. Aloisia turned around.

A young man, whom she recognized from her class, was standing before her. He was well built and little above average height. He had dark brown, almost black hair, and hazel eyes. "Good morning, Miss Schropp. May I introduce myself?" he said, bowing slightly from the waist. "Baumgartner, Franz Baumgartner, from Pocking," he said, holding out his hand.

Aloisia shook his hand. "Aloisia Schropp," she said, giving a small nod. She wondered, as when she had first noticed him in class, why he was taking this course. From his erect bearing she wouldn't have assessed him for a farm boy. But then he must be, or he wouldn't be at an agricultural college learning about bees.

Aloisia was used to greeting people. Even as a little girl, she often was sent to welcome visitors arriving at the nearby Moedishofen train station. The neighbours always laughed, "Even if nobody in the whole village has someone to meet at the station, there would always be someone coming to the Schropps." There was a Schwabian proverb that visitors just rob you of time and cost money. But this saying could not be applied to the hospitable Schropp family.

Usually the guests were Aloisia's brothers and their families. Or they might be other relatives and friends from nearby towns and cities. Whichever the case, there would be parcels for Aloisia to carry.

When Aloisia grew older she liked hearing news from the city and finding out the latest fashions in skirts, dresses and blouses. She had started to sew for others and was becoming a trained seamstress, so these details were important to her.

Before the war, when the economy was booming, a trip to the Schropp farm was usually light-hearted, a carefree excursion in the country for her nephews and nieces, with just a peek into the cow barn or the horse stable. The children might gather dandelions and feed them to the rabbits.

Or maybe they would go inside the coop to gather eggs from the laying boxes. In the spring, when the chickens were laying heavily, there would be enough in the basket to ensure the smell of crepes coming from the kitchen soon after.

In summer, visitors would go to the garden beside the house and pick pailfuls of raspberries or gooseberries. Aloisia's brothers helped with seasonal chores in the field like planting and harvesting. But those were happy, carefree days in comparison to the present times.

Hunger was now common in the cities. Relatives were usually looking for food to take home: a few eggs, some potatoes or apples, maybe a bit of fat for rendering, a pail of milk, a bunch of parsley – anything. And why shouldn't they expect something from their parent's farm after their many years of hard work, getting up before dawn and working until dark? They were always taught that the farm was an insurance policy, something that the whole family could depend on if times got tough like they were now.

"Pleased to meet you," Aloisia added, "Isn't Pocking near the Austrian border, near Braunau?" She felt a wisp of hair touch her forehead, but she caught her impulse to tuck it back into her bun for then he would surely notice all the freckles on the back of her hand. She detested her red hair and the freckles that came with it. The fact that Emma and two others in her family had the same red hair did not lighten her burden. Why couldn't she have had flaxen coloured hair like so many others in her village?

"Yes," Franz gestured towards the map, "But our farm is not really in Pocking. It's out of the way – no village nearby – but that's the closest city. Our place wouldn't be marked on anything but a local map. But you seemed to be looking for some place special? Perhaps I can help you? Geography is one of my favourite subjects."

"Oh, Geography used to be my favourite subject too," Aloisia said, remembering how she had been the only one in her class who had memorized all the countries of the world, and their capitals, too. "But once you are out of school there's not much chance to keep it up. Too much work to do, especially now, with the war."

Franz's eyes observed her carefully. "Yes, I heard that you were a hard worker."

Aloisia was surprised that her reputation had travelled so far as to reach Freising, which, though still in Bavaria, was a long way from home. "Really?" She laughed softly, embarrassed, yet inwardly pleased. "Where did you hear that?"

"Oh, someone," Franz smiled. "Anyway, nobody would have to tell me. Your hands give you away. They don't belong to a lazy person. By your accent I would say your farm is here in Bavaria."

A barely perceptible frown crossed Aloisia's forehead. "Yes, I'm from Ried. It's just a small village... near Munich," she added, glancing down at her hands. Just this morning she had noticed how they had become much softer in the few days she had been away from the farm. Of course, the calluses were still there and her fingernails were short and practical.

It was true that at home her neighbours often commented that she worked like a man. What compliment could be greater when times were so tough? There was no excuse for idleness. In October, after the potato picking and gleaning, she had a hard time getting her hands clean before she visited her sister Emma and Maria, her niece, in Munich.

Even so, Aloisia prided herself in giving the impression of a city girl. She always took care to walk erectly and cross her ankles when she sat down. Maria, though three years younger than Aloisia, was very smart and even she said Aloisia would not be taken for a country girl because of how she walked and sat. And Aloisia was so slim. Such words were music to Aloisia's ears, the greatest compliment she could get.

Franz's voice cut into Aloisia's thoughts. "You should be proud to be a hard worker. I asked Father Klassen which of the women here, just confidentially, had the best character, and was smart too. And he pointed you out." His words carried up and down the stairwell.

Aloisia blushed and wished he would speak more softly. She glanced out the open window framed with blooming wisteria to the courtyard below. Maybe his voice could be heard even there.

"Class is starting. I have to go," Aloisia said, seeking a gentle disengagement.

"Yes, we'd better go," Franz echoed.

Aloisia held up her skirt and started up the stairs to the second floor landing.

Franz followed. "Would you like to visit the city with me sometime?"

Aloisia turned and looked at him. Though she was used to talking to men – after all she had eight older brothers, not to mention their friends – this was different. This man was a total stranger, not from her village or even the same district. She hesitated, not knowing what to say.

Franz's voice interrupted her thoughts. "Did you know that Freising is the very oldest town between Bavaria and South Tyrol? It's full of culture, museums and cathedrals and art galleries. There's more to this place than just this college, you know."

Aloisia did want to see the city. She looked down at the floor.

"Two priests are arranging a tour," Franz added.

"Oh, then that would be very nice," Aloisia answered, glancing up at him. "I'm sure some of the other women would like to come too."

Franz smiled. "Of course," he nodded.

# Studying Is Always Interesting

Their teacher, Mr. Blumental, a neatly dressed, short man with a kind face, bustled into the classroom. Some rolled up charts were tucked under his arm. The students who were not already seated walked to their benches. There were about forty altogether, but none from Aloisia's district. They were all older – and married.

Except for Franz, whom she now heard sliding into the bench behind her. He didn't seem married. She gave herself a mental tug for being selfish – some would even call it sinful – for thinking about available bachelors when her country was in the middle of a war. Besides, she was only nineteen years old and her father was sick.

She must concentrate to get as much out of this trip as possible. If the war went on, who knew when she could leave the farm again? By the second day she had learned many of her fellow students' names. By the third day her curiosity had led her to discover where most of the halls and doors led.

Blumental turned out to be a gifted educator, the best she had ever had. Aloisia had completed all of her seven years of education in the two room school of Ried which, if the truth be known, served as a training ground for new teachers. It was generally known that getting a teaching position in Ried was considered a stepping stone towards getting better city positions in the future. The women often got married. One way or the other, Ried had a difficult time keeping good teachers. The village children took advantage of the situation, making discipline a constant problem – and learning difficult.

Occasionally, the teacher, if having to leave the class for some reason, would ask Aloisia to supervise the other pupils. As soon as the teacher was out of sight, however, Aloisia joined the others in running around the room and sitting in the teacher's chair. Only when the lookout gave the signal did everything turn back to some semblance of order.

If parents found out that their child was misbehaving at school there would be more punishment at home. The children, however, didn't tell on each other and this led to life long friendships and bonding. The only time parents discovered what went on in the classrooms was if the teacher came to the house. Then the children were very quiet, embodiments of the motto, *Children should be seen but not heard* (unless they were spoken to first, that is.)

Once, when the inspector came to the school, he seriously wondered about the teacher's ability; the children couldn't answer his questions. But then he realized that the teacher must have covered the curriculum because Aloisia seemed to know all the answers. When he was convinced that the village children were simply slow learners, he directed his questions only to Aloisia in order to find out how much of the curriculum the teacher had covered. To the relief of the teacher, Aloisia answered all his questions satisfactorily.

Finally the inspector asked, "Who was Alfred Nobel and what did he invent?"Aloisia was stumped; she had never heard of that name. She muttered something to that effect.

"Of course! Dynamite! That's what Nobel was famous for. He was a Swedish chemist and engineer. But more important than that, as far as I'm concerned, is the fact that he founded the Nobel Peace Prize. It doesn't matter how many things you know about. If you don't know how to keep peace, it's all for nothing."

Aloisia's classmates knew Aloisia had not answered the question but had mumbled that she didn't know the answer. But the children sensed the inspector was on a pet topic of his and shouldn't be distracted. They focused their eyes on him, ready to ask questions if he should run out of material. Yes, the Ried children may have been slow in some things but they were experts in wasting time in the classroom if the opportunity arose.

"Yes, when Alfred Nobel died in 1896," the inspector continued, "He left enough money to establish an international peace prize every year for the person – or organization, for that matter – contributing the most for peace during the previous year." The inspector was on a roll. "Some of you in this class must have been born in that year. Put up your hands if you were born in 1896."

Several students put up their hands and so did Aloisia.

"Well, well," he said, pointing to them and smiling broadly, "You are all lucky because you will always be able to remember when the Nobel Peace Prize was started."

The children nodded their heads encouragingly and the inspector responded to their enthusiasm.

"Have you heard of the Red Cross? The founder of that organization got the prize just a few years ago. He was Swiss and so he chose the emblem of the Swiss flag, but reversed it so it was a red cross on a white background, for his organization's symbol."

The Ried children stared at the inspector with admiration.

"Then there was the man who founded the first French peace society. And one year the peace prize went to an organization called *The Permanent International Peace Bureau*. You wouldn't remember, but some of your fathers fought in the Franco-Prussian War, and still have the scars to show for it, if they came home at all. Yes, the idea of building peace is really spreading, thank God. I think it is high time we honour efforts for peace instead of which country conquered which country and when. What do you think?"

The children nodded in agreement and smiled back.

Aloisia was relieved her ignorance had gone unnoticed by both her teacher and the inspector. For some time she earnestly believed this episode taught the lesson that people assume the best if your reputation is good.

Later, however, she realized that the inspector only brought up this question as an excuse to talk about a pet subject. He probably knew that nobody would know the name Alfred Nobel. Having a captive audience simply gave him an opportunity to preach about something he strongly felt was lacking from the school curriculum.

## *The Making of a Frontier Woman*

Now those school days seemed a long time ago and as unreal as a faded dream. Aloisia remembered one of her teachers warning the class when there were complaints about excessive homework, "if you think you are having a difficult time now, just wait until you grow up. Then you'll know what hardship is." And she had been right.

Here in Freising, the students were adults who knew the importance of learning. Blumental made the course interesting for everybody, whether they were beginners in beekeeping or, had some experience, like Aloisia had gained when she helped her father.

Blumental also pointed out that now was not the only time in history when honey had become scarce. Manuscripts from renaissance times, when wars ravaged Europe, revealed great shortages too. Many beehives were destroyed or neglected as a consequence of advancing armies continually forcing peasants to flee back and forth across the countryside.

He said that bees had been domesticated since ancient times and were even referred to in ancient literature of Egypt and India. A 20,000 years old fossilised bee had been found right in Germany, in the next province! It seems that Virgil (a poet of whom Aloisia had never heard), helped tend the hives on his father's farm near Mantua in Italy and even wrote about them.

Blumental's voice rose and fell, accelerated and slowed. Sometimes he gestured widely with his arms. At other times he leaned forward with his hands on his desk and in almost a whisper shared some fact that was unknown to most people.

He explained how important honey was for improving the living standard of pioneers in the New World. He pointed to a large globe in the corner of the room and told the story about a German settler in the Great Lakes region of Canada who made arrangements with a Moravian mission in the eastern United States to buy a hive of bees. An Indian from that mission carried them to the homesteader all the way on his back!

A hand went up. "What kind of a container did the Indian use for carrying the bees?"

Blumetal smiled. "Your guess is as good as mine. Maybe a

box made out of birch bark, maybe a leather bag. Maybe the missionaries made something out of wood."

Blumental unrolled his charts showing the four stages in the life cycle of a bee: egg, larva, pupa and adult. He explained the difference between worker bees and drones. Only the strongest drone could fly high enough to fertilise the queen on her maiden flight.

The queen, he said, was responsible for swarming. He described what provoked her to fly away from her hive and how the worker bees would all follow. When she landed they formed a huge living ball around her. It was a sight to behold! If you were lucky, the swarm settled on a nearby tree and better yet, on a low branch of a nearby tree. Then one person could hold a bee bag while another shook the branch so the bees would drop in. This was a job that needed two people. The bag could then be carried to the prepared hive and the bees were gently dumped in.

If nobody noticed that a hive had swarmed, bee scouts would fly off looking for a new permanent home. When they found a suitable site they would return to get the approval of more scouts. Finally, by using bee language, there would be a strange humming, different from before, a contented humming of consensus. Truly! You could tell how happy the bees were by the sound they made. Then the whole ball loosened up and lifted off in a sort of constellation and travelled slowly, always keeping together, until the new location was reached.

The trick was for the beekeeper to get them back into one of your own hives before the scouts led the hives too far away. Sometimes things didn't turn out quite that way, however. You would have to chase your bees all across the countryside and then look on helplessly as they flew up to a high branch of a cherry tree. Then you had to wait until they swarmed again, to a location the beekeeper could reach.

Before taking this course, Aloisia had somehow been under the impression that using the smoker made bees drowsy and too tired to sting. Did her father know, as she now was learning, that in fact the smoke made bees feel their home was in danger? They gorged themselves with honey so they could carry it away but when gorged their stinger couldn't reach around their abdomens to make contact with a victim. Of course, when the smoker was being used, incoming bees could still pose a problem.

How do you protect yourself from stings? Could you really die from them? What would alleviate the swelling? Did a bee always die after stinging someone?

And what about supers? When are they added? And diseases? How are they detected? And then what do you do?

Blumental had promised his students they would discover the answers to all these questions and more. Each student would learn how to start a hive, collect the honey and get the bees through the first year.

He now leaned forward and his voice took on a more sympathetic tone. It was understandable that some of the graduates might feel a little nervous at times. That was only natural. "But just remember," he said, "You will know more about bees than most of your friends and neighbours." He promised to send each home with instructions and, of course, they had their notes.

He looked around at his class proudly. "You should also keep contact with other apiarists," he said. "Yes, by the time you're finished this course you can consider yourselves apiarists, and apiarists always share information. There's always something new to learn." He himself was still acquiring knowledge, he said.

At first, Aloisia had wondered why this course had to be two weeks long. Ever since she could remember, her father had looked after the bees on their farm and she had taken his knowledge for granted, not realising the skill and labour involved.

But since last summer her father wasn't feeling well. Nobody knew what the matter was; he simply had no appetite. Her mother plied him with all his favourite dishes: liver with onions, scrambled calf's brains, beef broth with a raw egg beaten in. She gave him hot camomile and linden blossom tea to sip. Nothing seemed to help. Cancer was suspected. He was almost seventy.

## Aloisia

The honey from last year was now nearly used up and government rationing was in full effect. Sugar was virtually impossible to obtain, even if you had money. Though the war had caused the government to shut down many programs, such classes as this one, which Aloisia was attending, were considered essential to alleviate the sugar shortage.

Since her brother, Ludwig, was building up his own farm in Untermeitingen, and the other Schropp sons had left years ago to make their own way in the nearby cities of Augsburg and Munich, Aloisia was really the only one left who could take advantage of these classes. Anyway, she liked finding out about new things. As a bonus she would get to travel past Munich railroad station for the first time in her life and see Freising, a city of which she had so often heard.

Before she left home the rye and barley had been seeded. The potatoes were in too. Delicate rows of radishes, peas and lettuce were starting to show in the vegetable garden and would soon need weeding. When Aloisia got home again she would have to make up for lost time but who knew how long the war might go on? Times could even get worse.

Keeping bees was important if Aloisia's mother wanted to continue giving honey to her grown-up children and their families when they came home to visit. At Christmas, relatives and neighbours would again say, "Ah, your gingerbread is so delicious! Did you use your own honey?" Aloisia and her mother would be able to smile and nod. They might even have extra to sell! And honeycomb was so good to chew!

Taking this course reminded Aloisia of the time she took the train to a nearby cloister to learn spinning because wool yarn was scarce. Aloisia's mother was good at spinning but she wanted Aloisia to learn from the nuns. Now Aloisia and her sister Dori were knitting men's socks, women's stockings and gloves from the wool cut, carded and spun from their own sheep. The money for that course had come from a few marks saved from her dressmaking, sewing shirts and turning collars. Sometimes she got a few young girls together and taught them how to use a wooden egg for darning or she gave lessons on needlework or knitting.

## The Making of a Frontier Woman

This beekeeping course was considered so important that the government had promised to reimburse the tuition if all lessons were completed and attendance was satisfactory. The only cost was time and work. You just had to fill out the proper forms. Hard work and persistence could get you anywhere.

These qualities were abundant in Aloisia. And as she worked, she planned, and as she planned, she worked. Much time and energy could be saved with good organisation. There was a saying that some people knocked over more with their rear ends than they accomplished with their hands, but that certainly did not apply to Aloisia.

*Maria, now Sister Clothilde, top row, third from left in Capetown, South Africa*

Aloisia knew her duty, just as clearly as years before her oldest sister, Maria, had known her duty. Maria had chosen to become a nun. It was considered a blessing in a family, the respected family, if the eldest entered the church.

Peter, the eldest son, could not join the priesthood. As a teenager he had a terrible accident while helping neighbours cut firewood. He got his left hand in the way of the band saw. Several fingers were cut off and the Church did not accept people with physical defects. Maybe Peter didn't have a vocation anyway. Aloisia didn't know or dare to ask. It was a delicate subject. He looked after their sheep with their dog Butsie.

## *Aloisia*

For Maria it was clear. She always wanted to become a nun. Everybody in the family said so, even the neighbours. She had no deformities and was in perfect health. But money was needed, enough money to pay for the dowry required to be a bride of Christ. If, however, she went into a cloister in Africa, rather than in Europe, no dowry was required except a supply of undershirts and bloomers to last a lifetime. Maria could sew these herself. She also needed two pairs of shoes. These, she would have to buy. That was enough of a financial burden.

Maria wanted to go to Africa anyway. That's what she told everybody. She wanted to follow in the footsteps of her mother's two sisters. When her aunts left for South Africa, Aloisia's mother cried. Maria told her she shouldn't because one day she would become a nun too. Maria was just a little girl when she said this, but now it was as she had foretold. It was settled.

In the summer of 1897 Aloisia's mother arranged for a photographer to come. With Maria leaving for Africa and Aloisia definitely being her last born, this would be the only chance her whole family could be together in a family portrait.

When the day came, the photographer laid down a large canvas on the ground outside the front door of the farmhouse. On it he placed chairs, benches, chairs and a small table covered with a chequered cloth. Two wicker stands, holding carefully tended geraniums and trailing fuchsias (her mother's pride and joy), made an excellent frame for the grouping. He set up his camera.

But little Otto and Ludwig were suddenly missing. Their names were called. Where could they be? The family fanned out and looked in the house, in the barn, in the outhouse, in the stable, everywhere. Finally they were spotted hiding behind some bushes in the garden. They could not be coaxed out.

"What's the matter? What is the matter?" Mother asked.

"The devil," they each sobbed, pointing at the photographer in his black cloak. "The devil...."

It took awhile before it was discovered what had gotten into their heads. An older sibling had told Otto and Ludwig that the strange man in black was the devil. By the time they could be convinced that the strange man was just going to take a picture, there was no time for them to be changed into their Sunday suits or to polish their shoes properly. They sat on the two little stools waiting for them and the photographer placed a pot of geraniums at their feet. Otto and Ludwig looked bravely, yet apprehensively, towards the camera.

The family portrait turned out well. The next generation of Schropp men looked self-assured and responsible. The boys with polished shoes and the girls with garnet or cameo broaches carefully pinned to their bodices, were arranged according to the photographer's instructions. Father casually had his right arm resting on the blue and white tablecloth as though he had not a care in the world. Mother held baby Aloisia on her lap. All were in their Sunday clothes – except little Otto and Ludwig sitting in the front.

In the centre of the back row stood Maria. She had large eyes, a high forehead, dark hair and radiant smile. Holding onto her arm was Emma, not looking pleased, obviously very much aware that she would soon be losing her sister to the dark continent of Africa – forever.

The family photograph was hung in the Schropp living room and repeatedly prompted stories of Maria's beauty, virtue and intelligence. Maria became an idol, not only for Emma, but also for Aloisia. She grew up dreaming of meeting Maria, of getting to know Maria in Africa. That is what everyone called her, Maria in Africa.

Maria was stationed in Johannesburg and was trained to be a teacher. At the age 33 she was coming back from a village where she had been teaching young children when she was caught in a thunderstorm. She contracted tuberculosis and was admitted into a Cape Town hospital. In 1906 Maria died. Aloisia was twelve years old when her dream of meeting Maria faded into the night. In the meantime Emma had married and given birth to a little girl whom she named Maria, after Maria in Africa.

Maria in Africa had done her duty and now Aloisia would

do hers. Everyone in the family did their duty. That's what the Schropps were known for, doing what had to be done, completing the job at hand once it was started. There was a saying in the Schropp family, "If you say 'A' you had to say 'B'." In other words, once you started a job you had to work on it until it was done. You had to complete it – and not interrupt it with side issues like the scarcity of bachelors or marriage.

Now Aloisia was certain she could feel Franz's eyes penetrating the back of her neck. Probably he was counting her freckles. During the winter some of them disappeared but they always returned in the spring with the first rays of sunshine. If only she had black hair, or blond hair or brown hair like her mother and father and Maria and Emma and Ludwig and....

Blumental continued following the outline he had distributed on the first day of classes. He never mentioned the war effort or fighting for the Fatherland. He talked about how bees increased the pollination of fruit trees and therefore increased the crop of cherries, apples, prunes and pears. More fruit resulted in more cherry pies, plum jam and apple cider, in short, more food. He handed out some of his wife's recipes that used honey as a sweetener. Honey was healthier than sugar anyway, he said.

*Franz Baumgartner, age 20, 1916*

Blumental spoke about the beautiful old city of Nuremberg, famous in medieval times for gingerbread, not only because it was located at the end of a major spice route from the east, but also because of the number of beekeepers living in the surrounding forests. He described the old hives woven from reeds and the superiority of the modern square hives made of wood. He even handed out blueprints of new, improved supers, covers and frames so that when the students got back home they could have them made by their local carpenter. He wrote the addresses on the blackboard of places where wax sheets could be purchased for a reasonable price. He promised to give each graduate enough wax sheets to fill one hive. They were included in the course. They were light, but fragile. If wrapped between layers of paper and cardboard, they could be transported home quite safely. Of course, one couldn't sit on them.

Blumental explained how honey could vary in colour, taste and aroma, exactly like wine, beer or fruit juice. Apiarists could create a different flavour by placing their hives in the middle of a clover field or at the edge of an evergreen forest. He himself had tasted acacia honey from Hungary and Italy. It was lighter in colour and had a thinner consistency. It was his personal favourite, though not everybody's.

In the early spring, Blumental said his bees collected pollen and nectar from the pine-covered hill behind his own home. Because some people prefer the taste of pine honey, he removed that honey from the hives before the bees went to other sources.

Aloisia knew her father's bees collected most of their nectar from wild flower meadows around the Schropp farm and, of course, their orchard. She visualised their fruit trees burdened more than ever with golden pears and her favourite Gravenstein apples. She would have to keep her eyes open for forked poles to support the heavily laden branches. The smell of prune jam and dried apple slices seemed to be wafting by her already, prune cakes and cherry cakes with streusel on top for celebrating name days and holy days.

Thinking of these treats made her glad it was time for lunch. Before they slid out of their benches, Blumental explained that in the afternoon they would actually be working with bees, hands on. His enthusiasm was infectious. It seemed bees were all he thought about, all that was worth thinking about. Aloisia just hoped they wouldn't sting her.

She walked towards the door, giving friendly nods to the other women in the class. Then Franz was at her side again. Could they eat together? Aloisia hesitated. She had assumed she would be eating with the other women, as on previous days.

*Aloisia*

What would her older sister, Emma, advise? It's never wrong to be friendly, her mother would say. That is what Emma would say too. And who knows what benefit could arise from this connection? After all, he was very polite. What excuse could she have?

"That would be very nice," Aloisia said. "We could do a little studying together."

"Studying is always interesting. I love it," Franz said.

# Incoming Bees

Aloisia and Franz crossed the sunny, cobblestone courtyard and turned along a sidewalk leading to some restaurants. They noticed one with window boxes of pink geraniums and settled themselves at a corner table, outside. Some children were playing in the lane beside them, their laughter mingling with the clatter of pots from the kitchen.

On such a warm June day it was hard to believe that somewhere people were being wounded and killed or getting a notice that a loved one was missing or wounded – or worse. And here she was in Freising sitting beside a very handsome man and eating bread dumplings with sauerkraut and drinking a beer.

"So, Miss Schropp," Franz looked at Aloisia intently, "What was so interesting this morning?"

"I beg your pardon?"

"On that map you were looking at...by the stairwell."

"Oh, my brother...my brother has been sent to the front in France. In his last letter from Arras, he said that we only needed one more push to end the war. He hoped to be home in time for the birth of his fourth child. His wife is worried sick about getting bad news from the front."

"Always one more push," Franz shook his head. "I'll bet the French and British troops are hearing the same lies. The push at Verdun has been going on since January. And then there's the Somme. And who will win after it's all over? Not the common people. Not the common people on either side, I can tell you. We're far from reaching egalitarianism."

Aloisia gave a puzzled look, wondering at the strange word and its meaning.

"Equality for all."

"Ah," Aloisia nodded.

"The politicians claim that Jutland was the greatest naval battle of all time. Hypocrites! They're all hypocrites. Do you know how many men were lost in those two days off the coast of Denmark?"

Aloisia shook her head. How could she know?

"Sure the British lost their flagship and many men, but we lost a lot of ships too. Our flagship suffered tremendous damage and our government hasn't told us how many of our men got killed. Maybe it was thousands, but they don't want to tell us for awhile. It wouldn't be good for our spirits."

"Really?" Aloisia looked at him intently. She didn't want to seem ignorant, but then curiosity overcame her. "How do you know all this?"

Franz lowered his voice. "I'm in the navy and I read the columns in the newspapers, not just the headlines. This one writer, Hesse..."

"Hesse?"

"Yes, Hermann Hesse. He's written some fantastic articles against the war. I saw one in the *Allgemeine*, or maybe it was some other newspaper. I can't remember now, I read so many. Anyway, he's an internationalist and against militarism and excessive patriotism. Of course, anyone who takes a critical attitude towards the war has got to be careful."

Aloisia listened carefully. He talked fairly quickly and used words not in her everyday vocabulary.

Franz leaned over and lowered his voice even more. "At times like this you aren't supposed to think too much." He looked around communicating with his eyes that care should be taken. "It's bad enough being torpedoed by the enemy without having your own government questioning you. At times like this, freedom of speech is herded into a smaller and smaller corner."

"Then...," she couldn't help asking, "Then why are you in the navy if...what I mean to say is...if you're so against it all?"

"Discretion, you might say, discretion. I knew my turn for conscription was coming up, so I enlisted. That way I got a little choice with my future." He emphasised the word 'little'. "Yes, it's funny how yesterday somebody here in Freising referred to me as 'young man' just because I'm probably the youngest male taking this course, I guess. But it's galling. I'm old enough to be enlisted and get killed."

Aloisia liked Franz's manner of speaking, his thoughtful, penetrating eyes, his solid build. He was so knowledgeable, so sure of himself. And he talked about much more interesting subjects than the farm boys back home.

"So," Franz continued, " I'm in the navy and getting a fantastic training, more than anything your brother would get as a soldier. But there's a lot of political unrest in the navy. Won't get into that. I guess your brother waited too long and was conscripted, or maybe he wanted to stay on land?"

Aloisia shook her head and bit her lip.

"Ah," Franz sighed. "You said he has children. Of course, he wouldn't want to leave them any sooner than necessary. Maybe he thought the war would end and then he wouldn't have to go at all."

"Yes, it was hard on him when he went back to the front last time. He said good-bye as though...," Aloisia's voice wavered. But then she took a deep breath and continued. "He talked to each of us in person, thanked them for whatever they had done for him in the past."

"Don't worry," Franz shook his head in sympathy.

Aloisia was sure he started to reach his hand out to comfort her, but maybe she was wrong.

"Many feel they won't come back. We're all cannon fodder either way. I've been thinking to take another course when my basic training is complete. My instructors say I would make a good signaller. I have good eyesight and a loud voice for shouting and my marks are good. Then at least I'll know what's going on. I'll get the news first. Still," he said looking directly into Aloisia's eyes, "It's not much safer being a sailor. It's all over for a lot of our men. I'm just lucky I hadn't finished my training or it might have been me drowning off Jutland. I've spoken with some sailors who watched their friends disappear. They can't get over it."

Aloisia nodded sympathetically. "It's terrible, just terrible."

"Well," Franz continued, "I guess we all have to die sometime, but it would be best from old age."

Aloisia smiled and took the chance on changing the subject to a lighter topic, "How is it that you are taking a course on beekeeping?"

"Well, when I attended agricultural college it wasn't on the curriculum, so now I'm rounding out my knowledge. And those big shots, the armament builders and the munitions salesmen…" Franz was obviously going to keep talking about the war. "It's really unconscionable. They'll be relaxing in their board rooms in their wingback chairs, drinking some choice wine and celebrating." Franz raised his right hand as though giving a toast, "Prosit! Cheers! Sante! To 1916! The most profit ever!"

Aloisia didn't know what kind of a room a boardroom was, though she thought she had heard the expression before. Wingback chairs were obviously for men who flew aeroplanes but she didn't want to sound ignorant by asking. 'Unconscionable' obviously had something to do with not having a conscience. Yes, she could figure things out. After all, in school she was always the smartest in her class.

Franz pierced the last piece of a dumpling with his fork. "In wartime, certain people make a lot of money and those certain people have connections to their friends in government. We commoners have not a clue to the machinations going on behind the scenes. What we hear and see in the news is only a fraction of the whole story." Tilting his plate towards him, he soaked up the rest of the sauerkraut sauce.

As he ate, Aloisia observed his fine lips and strong jaw. She admired his dark hair and brown eyes. So, he'd been to agricultural college. That's quite an accomplishment for such a young man. Nobody from her village had ever gone to an agricultural college. Maybe it was there that he picked up those strange words such as 'unconscionable'. And though he spoke the local dialect with Aloisia, she had overheard him speaking high German with a priest.

## The Making of a Frontier Woman

All this intrigued Aloisia and she found it refreshing to have someone paying attention to her. She had grown up hearing comments such as, 'women shouldn't have opinions' and 'a woman doesn't have any value until she is 17 years old.' Aloisia didn't notice much change of attitude even after her seventeenth birthday. The expression that children should be seen but not heard was equally applied to women, proper women that is, women who knew their place was in the kitchen, in the church and with the children.

She wanted to say something that would make a favourable impression on him. "Everyone in our whole family was against this war. We grew up with our father telling us how futile it all is. There are still families mourning losses from the Franco-Prussian War, so why would anybody with any common sense want to enlist? Just for another death in the family? And then there are other families who know they have an ancestor who got killed in a war, and when you ask them which war or which relative, they're not sure. They say, 'I've forgotten.' Can you imagine?'"

Franz nodded. "You see? You give your life for your country and people don't even remember which war. And now we're being asked to give our lives again." He leaned closer, "You know Blumental, our teacher? Notice how he seems in a daze sometimes, looks out the window?"

Aloisia said she had noticed that too. She didn't want to seem unaware. Not Aloisia who noticed everything.

"When he saw on my registration that I was on leave from my base at Wilhelmshaven, he told me his son's missing in Verdun. He thinks he'll show up any day, but he's probably at the bottom of a mortar hole. Just another statistic."

Aloisia cringed. "Who ever thought there would be times like this? For heaven's sake, who ever wanted a war anyway?"

"For heaven's sake? What a strange expression! What has this to do with heaven?" Franz looked at her with a puzzled, or was it a critical look? "It's more the other place."

"I mean, we were doing so well," Aloisia said, twisting a strand of hair back into her bun. She remembered the gloom that pervaded their home when war was announced. "My father always says everyone was so well off before this war that hardly anybody bothered with keeping bees. Nobody wanted to run after swarms and do the extracting. It's good we can come here and learn how it all goes, just in case the war goes on. Who knows when a truce will be worked out?"

"Yes, our economy was booming until grasping for power changed all that. You know the royal families of Great Britain and Germany are jealous of each other, jealous of each other's fleets, just like children with their toys."

Aloisia thought of how she could turn the topic away from the subject of war again. She hated talking about war even though it now affected every minute of her day, one way or another. "I'm a little surprised your family doesn't need you at home. It was quite difficult for me to get away. I had to get all the seeding done."

"Well, to be honest, since coming back from agricultural college with all my new ideas, my family is sort of glad to have a rest from me. Not my mother so much. It's more my father. We're sort of estranged right now. He just can't get it into his head how things could be. Well," Franz hesitated, trying to find the best word, "Not really estranged, if you know what I mean. But I like everything immaculate and that really gets on his nerves. Then my father shouts, 'cleaning and sweeping doesn't bring money into the house.'"

Aloisia laughed. "They always say that at my home too! But we still have to keep everything clean, including shining the brass handle on our front door every Saturday."

Franz nodded. "That's good." He drank up the last of his beer and put the mug down on the table firmly. "I don't hold the purse strings yet, but being the eldest, I will get the farm one day. Then things will change. Until then, and that could be a long time off because my parents are only in their 50s now, I have to compromise. Or give in, I should say. As it is, I'll get two weeks furlough at harvesting time. That's when they'll really need me. My younger brothers are at home anyway."

Aloisia thought how a man with his shoulders could pitch a lot of hay, stook a lot of wheat. As for family problems?

Well, they had plenty of their own. Only, being the youngest in her family, she would never get the farm, regardless of how hard she worked.

She had anticipated seeing him during supper or breakfast the next morning but he wasn't anywhere to be seen. Now the photographer had arrived to take pictures of the graduating class. He was positioning everyone on and behind benches. In the background the wisteria vine was covered with dangling, fragrant blossoms. Some sparrows were ruffling themselves in the freshly raked sand of the courtyard. Everything was almost ready.

But where was Franz? She had decided which topic she would bring up when she saw him again. She knew a little about grafting, but maybe he could give her some tips. With a name like his, which meant tree gardener, he should. Yes, she would ask him about grafting scions on apple trees when he showed up.

Suddenly, she heard her name called. It was Franz's voice. But when she turned around she barely recognised his face. It was puffed up and covered with red blotches.

"My God! What's happened?"

"The bees got me. Should have seen me before. I could hardly open my eyes."

"Didn't you wear a head net?"

Franz shook his head. "I was helping Blumental with a swarm. You know, he doesn't use a hat or anything. At home, he says, he sometimes only wears a bathing suit. He just smokes a cigar and that seems to quiet them. If you're afraid, they smell it. So I thought, I'm not afraid. I'll take it slow and easy. But they attacked me anyway."

Aloisia laughed. "I guess it must have been some incoming bees."

"It's really not a joke," Franz frowned. "I could have been killed you know." Then his eyes softened. "Better than being stung by bullets though. At least I'll recover. Which side of my face is best for the camera?"

Aloisia looked at one side of his face to the other. "It might be the left side, but...it really is hard to tell. Yes, maybe the left."

# The Spliced Cord

After getting the photograph taken, many in the class decided to go down to the Isar River where there were supposed to be good and reasonably priced places to eat.

Franz remained at Aloisia's side until they found a small restaurant. They seated themselves at a corner table and made their order. Soon they were enjoying noodle soup with a few slivers of pork floating on top. The waiter brought mugs of apple cider, placing them on the pewter coasters in front of them.

"Let's talk about pleasant things now. I'll be in the middle of the war all too soon. Let's talk about your family."

Aloisia gave a little sigh. "That could take quite a long time. What about your family?" She reached into her bag and pulled out a navy blue sock she was knitting. "Tell me about your farm."

"Ah, we live in a beautiful area near the Austrian border. We've rolling land, fruit trees, everything. Our farm once belonged to one of the many little kingdoms that existed before they unified. A princess fell in love with a forester whose name was Baumgartner. Maybe there was a shortage of men because of the wars or maybe it was true love. Anyway, they got married, brought up their family in the forester's home and we still live in that same house today." He took a deep breath. "There. You have it in a nutshell!"

Aloisia's eyes opened wide. "What a story!"

"So, would you like to hear more?"

Aloisia took a sip of her cider and nodded.

"Well," Franz took a deep breath, "I know that one day some of Napoleon's officers came through our area on horseback. That was 1812. They conscripted every able-bodied male. 'You and you and you.'" Franz punctuated each 'you' with a jab of his finger at different parts of the red and white chequered tablecloth.

"Oh, that's so cruel!" Aloisia lifted her hands to her face.

"Not any more cruel than what's happening today. The British are famous for it. I don't call them British. I call them Brutish. How any nation could be called civilised, yet consistently be so greedy, is difficult to fathom. They would actually kidnap young men, just knock them out or get them drunk, and when they came to they were already at sea. But to be fair, it happened everywhere."

Aloisia didn't know much about the British except that there was considerable intermarriage between their royal families and those of Germany – or had been. For instance their Prince Albert had married Queen Victoria and he had even given her a German Christmas tree the first year they were married.

Aloisia had heard that English cooking was completely tasteless, but there was no crime in that. It was just sort of sad.

Some years ago, before the war broke out, she had seen an English woman knitting on the train. The way she did it, twisting the wool around her needle each time a stitch was made, was really a waste of time, maybe a brutish waste of time, but that wasn't her business.

Of course, now she remembered that Peter, or was it one of her other brothers, had heard of a shepherd in England who castrated lambs with his teeth. He also left one of his thumb nails grow very long for digging maggots out of sheep's hides. In times of war, it seems stories such as these circulate a lot. Probably the other side has stories of their own about Germans.

"Anyway," Franz continued, "My great-great grandfather, the forester, was in his early thirties when Napoleon's army marched through my valley. He was just the right age so he got grabbed. And before you knew it, he was marching with the French army to Moscow." Franz raised his eyebrows to see if Aloisia understood, "To conquer Russia, you know."

"Yes," Aloisia reassured him, "I learned about that in school."

"Good. You can see paintings of it everywhere, but what many people don't realise is that most of Napoleon's army weren't even French. They were conscripts from the countries his army defeated and passed through. Anyway, this ancestor of mine had quite a sense of humour and our family history has it that he often played the part of a storyteller for Napoleon and his officers."

Aloisia frowned.

"You're wondering about such an occupation," Franz said noticing her questioning look. "Have you ever had the opportunity to listen to a real storyteller?"

Aloisia shook her head and thought. The idea of adults having time to tell stories, let alone to listen to them, was difficult to imagine. She thought of their priest who sometimes told his parishioners a story based on a parable from the Bible. He had to do that because otherwise how would people learn? Non-clergy were not allowed to read the bible; they would only get confused.

Of course, there were children's stories like *Hansel and Gretel, Rumpelstilskin* and *Cinderella.* Sometimes, when her father had his family gathered around the kitchen table, he talked of being in the occupation force in France after the Franco-Prussian War. He had wonderful memories of the French people and made a point of learning as many French words as possible while stationed there. When he got home, he married her mother and later taught his children how to count in French. He also taught them the colours: rouge for red, bleu for blue, noir for black and so on. Her father often said, and Aloisia could hear his voice even now, that the French are people, like the English and the Germans, and nothing, not even the picturesque Alsace, was worth shedding blood over. Does that count as a story?

The conversation at mealtimes was only about work: work that was finished, work that was being done, work that was planned for tomorrow. Work, work and more work. Lately there was often talk about the neighbours' sons. Had there been any news from Karl. Was he still listed as missing. What injuries did Fritz have? Who was the latest to be killed in action? How were the boys doing in the neighbouring villages?

She shook her head again. "No, I can't say that I understand what you mean."

"Can't think of anything?" Franz asked. "Well, you've missed something. There's a lot of skill and training involved. A real storyteller has such a keen mind that he can entertain for hours. When you listen you can forget about everything."

Aloisia looked at Franz as she reached into her bag for her knitting. She took out a new ball of wool and joined the yarn together by overlapping the two ends. Franz was quite a good storyteller himself. She certainly forgot everything else when she listened to him.

"Well, getting back to Napoleon," Franz continued, "He thought when he got his troops to Moscow they could spend a cosy winter there. The Russians, however, had burned the city and carried off all the food, leaving just ashes and empty cellars. So he had no choice but to turn round and come home. But by then winter had set in with freezing winds and snow. Few of his soldiers ever saw their native land again. If they didn't die of cold or hunger, they were picked off by snipers."

"Picked off? What do you mean, picked off?" Aloisia had gained enough self-confidence to ask.

"Ambushed, shot one by one by snipers. Out of 550,000 men, only 20,000 got back alive. I doubt that anyone was in the mood for stories on that long march back." Franz drew his fine, dark brows together and, fixing his eyes on some distant object, half closed his eyes.

Aloisia had come to realise that he had that mannerism when he was deep in thought or trying to find the right word. Now it seemed he was thinking he had been in that battle himself and was imagining his ancestor coming around the last bend on the road home. She kept on knitting, hoping he would continue.

Franz opened his eyes. "My great-great grand-father was the only man from our entire area to come back. According to family history, he was a walking skeleton when he finally dragged himself back home on Christmas Day, 1812. He must have had a strong constitution and a lot of luck on top of it."

"Yes, he must have been very strong."

"And lucky," Franz added. "More than anything, lucky."

## Aloisia

"Only one out of thirty came back," Aloisia said.

"What?" said Franz.

"If only 20,000 came back that would be one out of thirty. Or maybe three and a half for every hundred that went."

"Yes, yes, that would be about right," Franz nodded, "You're obviously good in arithmetic too!"

Aloisia was pleased that she had impressed him. In fact she had memorised the times tables to 25 times 25. She was proud of that, but didn't mention it now.

"And my ancestor," Franz continued grimly, "Was one of the halves. According what my mother told me, he didn't lose his sense of humour. He would be telling jokes while picking worms out of his skin and bones."

Aloisia cringed.

"Yes, he would sit on his stoop making jokes as he was pulling them out. They were white worms of some kind. That's the story my mother heard. I think she said his flesh was frozen and it started to rot right on him. He only made it home to die with his family."

Aloisia's face was even paler than usual. She put her knitting down.

"It's quite a story, isn't it? And it's true too. So, now it's your turn."

Aloisia sighed. "I don't have any subject to talk about. I don't have anything so…so interesting. Our family is very ordinary. As far as I know we have no princess in our ancestry. But my parents always say we can be very content that we don't have any black sheep in our family either. Not one. Nobody became famous, but nobody became infamous either."

"And how long have you had your farm?" Franz prodded.

"Oh, that must be over 25 years. I have never thought to ask. But I know that when father bought our house it had been a school. No princess ever lived in it long ago like in yours. My father and mother gradually fixed it up and made it into a wonderful family home. And now, we just finished building a retirement house for my parents, right in the garden behind.

*The Making of a Frontier Woman*

But prisoners of war are living in it right now."

"Well, having no black sheep is a good start," Franz smiled. "How many are there in your family? You could tell me that."

Aloisia looked at him and smiled. "Well, I'm from a family of thirteen."

Franz nodded approvingly. "I don't think you are lacking for subject matter there. You can tell me about your brothers and sisters."

Aloisia could never remember going through such an exercise before. Nobody had ever seemed that interested. But then, in her little village of Ried, everybody knew. Everybody knew everything about everybody.

"Well, first there's two girls," Aloisia started, taking up her knitting again, "The oldest, Maria, became a nun in Africa. She died there. Sister Clotilde was her name. Emma comes next. She lives in Munich. When Maria left for Africa, Emma went to work in Ausburg, as a housekeeper for a rich family. It wasn't long before she was introduced to a good-looking young man called Christian Scheufele. The two got married soon after and they had a little girl. Emma named her Maria, after her sister who became a nun. Even today Emma talks about how smart and beautiful Maria was but Emma's Maria is just as beautiful and intelligent and spiritual as the Maria who went to Africa. Everyone in our family says so."

"Emma's husband, Christian, had a good job with the railroad. But in 1910 he had a terrible accident. Somehow he knocked his head on something when he was checking under a train and without realising it, stretched out his legs just as the train began to move. He lost both legs. Anyway, to make a long story short, now he and Emma are rich."

"Rich?" Franz said, "How can somebody lose both legs and be rich?"

"I know," Aloisia said, "It seems strange but that's how life is. The railroad compensated Christian, and on top of it, because of his severe disability, he was given priority to lease a kiosk in Munich's main railroad station. It was amazing how many people found money for cigarettes after the war started even when there was hardly money for food."

"That's what happens," Franz nodded, "Smoking is sort of an addiction. And then?"

"Well, after Emma came a little boy, Joseph. But he only lived five days. Then came Peter, who lost three fingers from his left hand when he was cutting firewood. He's gradually taking over the farm, but he mostly tends the sheep."

"Then," she looked up from her knitting, "There's a Franz, like you."

Franz nodded enthusiastically, "It's a very good name. My second name is good too, Xavier. After the saint who…"

"Yes, I know," Aloisia continued not wanting to get on to the subject of how that saint was martyred by being shot through with arrows.

"And then there was another Joseph but we call him Sepp for short, so he is not mixed up with my father, who is also a Joseph Schropp. Then came Paul. He has brown hair like Emma and Maria. It's lucky that he has something the matter with his thigh so he can't be conscripted."

"Johann is the one who's fighting near Arras right now. We call him Hans. He has three little girls, like I told you and was just home this month on a few days leave."

"Then comes Victoria. She has the same name as my mother so we call her Dori. She's eight years older than me and helps on the farm too, but she's not strong like mother or me."

Aloisia thought of how Dori often seemed to be ill and had to lie down with a hot brick or water bottle on her stomach. She didn't mention the details to Franz, nor that some in the family often said Dori was only pretending to be sick because, after all, she still had an appetite. One of the Schropp rules was that if you could eat, you should be able to work.

Franz swallowed another sip of apple cider, "Then?"

"Three boys: Alois, Otto and Ludwig. They used to like playing tricks on me. I could usually tell by the twinkle in their eyes when were up to some mischief. Now Ludwig has his own farm and Otto and Alois both are in Munich. Otto is a policeman and Alois is a civil servant there. What more can I tell you? They are all doing well."

"So you're the youngest?"

"Yes, I'm number thirteen."

"And your grandparents, the Schropp name? No history?"

"The Schropp name? I believe it goes back a long way in our area and my father's mother, Maria, was from the Meitinger family who for generations owned a prosperous farm. Really, it was almost an estate with the buildings arranged around a large courtyard."

Franz leaned his elbows on the table, "And who gave you the red hair?"

Aloisia felt her muscles stiffen; red hair was not her favourite subject. None of her father's ancestors had red hair. It must have come from her mother's side.

"Well?" Franz was looking at her, waiting.

Aloisia knew that her grandmother, Afra Voelk, had conceived the child who was now Aloisia's mother, out of wedlock. When the child was born, Afra baptised her Victoria, after the Queen of England. The father claimed the child was not his, so would not be responsible for support in any way. Afra charged the father in a paternity suit, swearing an oath before a judge in the Zusmarsshausen court that he was the only man with whom she had ever slept. Afra won the case.

But a man who can tell a lie like that is no husband material. And from what Aloisia heard, the father was reluctant to get married anyway. Afra married another man and went on to have a wonderful family. Afra's aunt and uncle wanted to adopt Victoria. They could not have children and had a little farm nearby. Victoria grew up under their loving care, developing into an intelligent, beautiful young woman.

Joseph Schropp, who lived in a nearby village, fell in love with her. As soon as he came home from the occupation forces after the Franco-Prussian War, the two got married. Joseph moved to the little farm. When the aunt and uncle died, they willed their small farm to Victoria and Joseph. They in turn sold it to make a down payment on the old schoolhouse in the centre of Ried.

## Aloisia

Aloisia had found this all out from someone who made her promise never to tell anyone. Since that time, Aloisia often suspected that her mother's biological father had red hair. Maybe that is how it popped up in their family so suddenly.

Once, in a round about way, Aloisia tried to bring up the subject of her mother's father. Her mother looked at Aloisia with astonishment and said, "Aloisia, Aloisia. You are sometimes too curious about things. Let sleeping dogs lie. Have you not enough to do with the present? That you have time to waste by poking around in the past! Are you out of work to do?"

Aloisia never brought up that topic again. And she certainly was not going to tell Franz all this. It wasn't his business. Actually, it wasn't anybody's business....

"We don't know," Aloisia shrugged Franz's question off. "There hasn't been red hair in our family for generations and now it popped up in eight of the Schropp children."

The jingle, which the redheaded Schropps used to shout back when taunted, flashed through her mind:

Rot ist fein,
> Red is refined,

Blond ist Gemein.
> Blond is nothing special.

Schwarz kann jede sein
> Anything at all

Drecksem (Drecksau) sein
> Can have black hair.

But that was too vulgar to tell Franz. And it would be sort of an insult to his black hair.

Instead she blurted, "It's just a mystery to everybody. I hate it!"

Franz shook his head disapprovingly. "You shouldn't hate what God has given you."

Franz seemed to be a very, very devout Catholic. Even more than she was. What could she say to put herself in a good light again? Something about their church would be good.

"Our home is right across from the church. If you go out our front door and just turn a little to the left, there it is. It's the most elaborate in the whole district because once some rich prince got lost in the forest nearby and made an oath that if he ever found his way out again he would build a church for people to make a pilgrimage to, and he kept his word. He commissioned the carving of the main altar and purchased rare relics for the side altars. And the priest comes to our house for dinner all the time."

When Aloisia finally stopped talking, Franz's raised eyebrows and smile confirmed that she was on the right path.

"And I sing alto in the church choir."

"Really?" He was impressed. His smile lingered on his lips. He didn't notice her abrupt change of topic, or if he did notice, he made no comment.

Aloisia didn't mention that if one went out their front door and turned a few steps to the right, instead of the left, one would be in the local tavern. The singing coming from there was quite a different kind and certainly not in Latin.

"Let's go for a walk," Franz said. "There are some lovely paths around here. I explored them yesterday. We could walk through town along the Isar river or go up into the forest."

"If you don't mind, I'd love to walk into the forest. I'm a little homesick for trees, having sat in class all week."

Franz agreed. He opened the side door of the small restaurant and they walked out to the sidewalk leading to the forest. Soon white daisies, red poppies and blue cornflowers were edging their footpath. A farmer was starting to cut hay in a nearby meadow. Two butterflies fluttered in the warm breeze across their path. Franz remained quiet.

"Isn't June a wonderful month?" Aloisia asked randomly, trying to sound casual, yet searching for something to say.

"Yes," he gave no further response for a moment, "And now we'll soon be off in our different directions. I'll be shipping out soon. Who knows if we'll see each other again. You're interesting to talk to, as interesting as any man. But...but that's the way life is."

He looked over at Aloisia, her hands busily knitting even while she was walking. Not everyone was able to do this without dropping stitches. But Aloisia could. She was already on her second pair of socks since coming to Freising. Another student in her class had admired her even knitting and asked if she had ever tried making a sweater. Knit sweaters were a new idea becoming popular in the cities. Aloisia shook her head. As in most German households, the motto for women was 'Never have idle hands' and that included not wasting time on frivolous new ideas.

"I wonder," Franz asked, "Could I ask you a favour?"

Aloisia suspected what he was going to ask. She had already considered giving Franz a pair of socks. After all, she knit them for the Russian and Serbian prisoners of war working on their farm. The prisoners always called her parents 'our German Father' and 'our German Mother.' And they loved her socks. Why shouldn't she knit a pair for one of her country's seamen?

His voice interrupted her thoughts, "Would you write to me?"

Aloisia was taken aback. She acted as though she had not heard his question. They had come to a timber bridge over a rushing stream. There was a little wooden gate where people could slip through, but not cows.

"Should we keep going?" Franz asked, his hand already touching the stile.

"Sure," Aloisia said. "If you like."

They passed through.

"So, will you?"

"I, ah...," Aloisia stammered. The idea of corresponding with someone was strange to her. And she would have to buy postage stamps, which were not cheap. "I...I don't think so. We've only been acquainted for a few days. We don't really know each other."

"How can we get to know each other better if we don't correspond? Lots of women write to the men who are fighting for their country. My family hardly writes me. They're so busy and…well, they don't write much. I bet your letters would be interesting. Just tell me what you're up to and how the world is going on where there is solid ground under your feet."

Aloisia said nothing.

"Anyway, Blumental said we students should correspond with each other once class is over. You could tell me how you're making out with your bees. What do you think of that?"

Aloisia looked around as a slight breeze rustled some leaves overhead and from far away the mating call of a cuckoo pierced the suspended silence, and then called again. "Hear that?" Aloisia said looking off into the surrounding birches and firs. "Usually you don't hear cuckoos anymore in June. This area reminds me so much of our forest at home. A forest means a lot more than just firewood, you know."

"You know," Franz mimicked her voice, "When you're away from home it means so much to get a letter. You could address it to our farm and my mother would forward it to whichever ship I get stationed on. She'll know. If I keep getting good marks on my examinations my superiors already told me I could be on our flagship, Frederick the Great. But," he shrugged, "Nothing is certain." He said nothing for a moment. "Or I could write you first."

"No, don't write me," Aloisia said, quickly winding her yarn back around the ball and pushing her needles into the sock. "What will my family think, only being away for a couple of days and getting strange mail. The postman would see it too."

"Of course, that's his job. He can't deliver mail unless he looks at the address. And it won't be a couple of days, it will be a couple of weeks."

Aloisia shook her head as she pushed her knitting deep down into the large side pocket of her skirt. She thought of how her mother had impressed on all of the family that it takes a lifetime to build a good reputation but only one false step to lose it. The poor girl in her village who was not allowed to go into the church because she had had three children out of wedlock flashed through her mind. And her mother had told her other stories….

## *Aloisia*

"You don't understand. Everybody knows everybody in Ried. It must be the same in your village. Strange mail coming to me would...."

"Yes? Would what?"

"You know, cause rumours."

Franz stood in front of Aloisia and put a hand on her shoulder. "You're not a school girl any more. May I ask you something?"

Aloisia felt uneasy, her heart was pounding strangely. She nodded.

Franz looked deep into her eyes, "How old are you?"

Aloisia was afraid she might be older than Franz, but she looked down at her feet and answered honestly. "Twenty. I'll be twenty, in August, just after the Assumption of the Blessed Virgin Mary. This is the first time I've been farther away from home than Munich." She didn't know why she added all that information.

"And how far is your village from Munich?" Franz continued.

"Sixty kilometres. I go there sometimes to visit my sister and Maria."

"Well, I'm older," his broad smile showed his fine teeth, "I was twenty just last month. And I can assure you I have been a lot farther from home than sixty kilometres. You should listen to me."

They had come to a vantage point from where they could see the well-groomed Freising city landscape and the manicured valleys with red rooftops of villages far in the distance. The church bells were ringing the Angelus. Aloisia felt her decision to write or not to write was important, a fork in a road.

If she said no, well, that would be the end of it. Another of her mother's remonstrations winged through her mind. 'It's better to keep doors open. Keep doors open. Don't close them unless you're very sure. And then if you think you must close a door, be gentle, always gentle. One day you might change your mind. And remember, you can't get help from someone you've hurt.'

"I...I guess I could," Aloisia said somewhat less reluctantly this time, "But...," then she thought if he never wrote back, that would be that. Nobody would even have to know that she wrote him a letter. She remained silent, trying to balance taking a risk, with the risk of losing an opportunity.

"What is it?"

"I...well, I guess it would be better, if you do, to please send greetings to my older sister, Dori. Then she might add a few lines to my letter when I write back. That would be better, I think."

Franz said that could be done and now they had to shake hands to make it binding. He shook her hand slowly and firmly, looking solemnly into her eyes. Afterwards, he stepped away from her and whistled a plaintive two-noted birdcall, like a cuckoo calling. Aloisia smiled encouragingly. Franz happened to have a piece of rope in his pocket and deftly demonstrated how he could splice the ends together to form a loop. "If I had another rope I could make another loop and link them together," he said with an enigmatic smile.

Aloisia pointed to the sunset streaked with orange and crimson. "We had better get back. Evening red...."

"...morning grey, sends the traveller on his way," Franz completed the old axiom. "We should have a good day for travelling tomorrow."

They walked back by the last light of the day. It was almost dark when they got to the college. They had missed the evening devotions.

The last day of the course had come; classes would finish at noon. Aloisia worked carefully on her hair as she prepared herself for the morning class. She formed one long braid, trying hard to catch every strand of her fine hair. Then she took a few strands from her brush and deftly twirled them around the end of the braid. Pulling her braid back and circling it into a bun, she fastened it with long hairpins.

She didn't think Franz had seen her when she arrived in Freising but now, on her departure, she really wanted to look her best. He would see the tailored suit she had sewn during the previous winter when she realised she would be taking this trip.

She had ridden her brother's bicycle all the way to Fischau

to buy the fabric. Her mother didn't approve of Aloisia learning to ride a bike – it wasn't considered proper for girls to ride on handlebars either or skip rope, for that matter. Those activities were for boys and she had enough boys in the family already. And the fact that those activities were now happening in the big cities did not affect her. She didn't want Aloisia to make a loose impression on the neighbours.

Aloisia secretly learned anyway, but Peter scolded her when he discovered her practising figure eights in the back lane. Gradually, however, the family got used to the idea; knowing how to ride a bike sometimes came in very handy.

After all, the world was changing. Sometimes, on hot summer days, Aloisia even waded into a stream, lifting her skirt right up to her knees. She knew that city girls wore bathing suits, even showing some leg up to the knee. They even went to public beaches like that, where there were men around. But that was unheard of for a village girl.

When Aloisia rode to Fischau to buy her suit fabric, she saw many other women who had travelled there to buy good quality clothing and yard goods at reasonable prices. Many Jews had stores in that town and frugal purchasers could make purchases not readily available elsewhere – and make a good deal. Notions such as white woven cotton buttons for duvets, embroidery thread in every colour, sewing machine needles, darning needles and knitting needles. Everything could be found in Fischau, even findings for sewing homemade garter belts, corsets and brassieres. There were white handkerchiefs for use in church. There was damask for bed linen.

There was a greater demand these days for darker colours. The table with indigo headscarves was always well picked over. Behind the counter, where bolts of black crape were stored, clerks served ashen, sallow-faced women with lustreless eyes.

Tucked away in one corner of the shop that Aloisia entered were sewing, knitting and crocheting patterns. There were fashion magazines available too. Even if one couldn't afford to buy them, you could leaf through the pages for ideas.

Some articles, however, seemed completely ridiculous now. Berlin needlepoint, for instance, was made from Bohemian beads and brightly tufted wool. (The article said the beads and tapestry wool were manufactured in Berlin and thus the name). Who could imagine wasting time making needlepoint cushions so fancy that they couldn't even be sat on, let alone leaned on! The Victorian times must have been quite decadent. Again, the war had changed all that.

Aloisia spotted the finely woven wool fabric for her suit on a remnant table. The material had subdued blue and green threads running through a grey background. It was very good quality and would wear well. She had calculated with the saleslady how, by carefully laying out the skirt and jacket pattern, she could make herself a complete suit. Being not as robust as other girls, was now to Aloisia's advantage. There was enough material to make two tucks in the front bodice, and making the skirt a touch shorter saved fabric too. You could just see her ankles, but Emma had told her that the shorter length had been acceptable in Munich for some time now and wearing the new length would no longer raise eyebrows in Ried.

Aloisia and Franz walked together to the Freising station. Franz was wearing his navy uniform. Aloisia's train was already waiting. His would leave shortly after and bring him directly to his naval base at Wilhelmshaven.

Aloisia lifted her skirt a little and, holding the carefully packed parcel of wax sheets in one hand, her suitcase in the other, she carefully climbed the steps into the train. She spotted a space and, squeezing past knees and baggage, sat down on the wooden bench.

Through the open window she heard a plaintive two-noted birdcall.

She looked out and saw Franz standing at attention, his navy uniform suiting him so well. She waved.

He put his right hand to his forehead and saluted.

Aloisia smiled and waved again. Steam swirled past her window. With a hiss and a jerk her train pulled out of the station.

Aloisia sat back in her seat and pulled a sock out of her knitting bag. She started to cast off stitches to shape the toe. What could Franz see in her? As Dori had told her often enough,

## Aloisia

Aloisia was a beanpole. She, herself, admitted hardly being able to keep a skirt up over her hips.

She had red hair. It was not bright red but too red, even with the greatest generosity, to be called auburn. Her eyes were sea green.

As for her face, it was small, long, perhaps even classic. But freckles covered her fine white skin all summer. Even in winter they never completely disappeared from her hands and wrists. Her nose was straight and unremarkable in every way except that it was so unremarkable, neither turned up nor hooked, nostrils neither pinched nor flared. It was, however, a perfect example of 'the Schropp nose' and had become, by association with her hardworking and honest ancestry, a sign of respectability and good character.

Aloisia's erect bearing, her habit of always crossing her ankles when sitting, her soft voice, all gave the impression of a city girl rather than a farm girl. Upon first seeing her, perhaps when she was taking communion, she gave an almost delicate impression, especially when contrasted with the stockier, more buxom girls common in her village. If, however, one followed Aloisia's footsteps during the course of the week, you would soon get a different impression. She not only had the knowledge to handle most jobs a man could do, she had the will and the strength to do them too.

Aloisia finished the sock, found its mate in her bag and pulled the two together. She picked up her needles again and cast on stitches for another sock. She would try to have the pearl two, plain two ribbing done before she arrived at the Moedishofen station.

When she got home and talked things over with Peter, weeding, hilling, cutting hay would be prioritized. Had her father's health improved while she was gone? Had there been another letter from Hans? She wondered if Goldy, her favourite cow, had calved.

Franz must be on his train by now. If she wrote, would he really write back? How long should she wait before writing? Aloisia remembered and could still feel his firm handshake as she promised to write.

She shook her head trying to rid herself of the seriousness of the situation. After all, he was fighting for the fatherland. Many girls corresponded with men in the service.

Aloisia worried a little about Franz's outspoken manner. It might lead him into trouble one day. Not that what he said wasn't true, it was just how he said it. And even when he talked softly, his voice carried....

A shadow crossed her window. She looked out and saw a crow, cawing, flapping its wings and looking in at her as though trying to get her attention. Everyone knew this was a bad omen; someone in the family was going to die or had already died. Aloisia quickly turned away pretending she had not seen it, knowing it was too late.

If the double white lilacs on the road home from the station were still blooming, she would pick a few branches for her mother. She could handle that and still not crush her sheets of wax.

# Strange Mail

*Wilhelmshaven*
*October 17, 1916*

*Dear Miss Luise!*
*Received your letter of October 8 that my mother forwarded to Wilhelmshaven. I was very happy to get it. Thank you very much. Am a seaman since October 1. How are you doing these days? Hopefully well.*

*We will not be able to leave our barracks until we are fully trained and that won't be for at least several weeks. Then we will soon be on a ship.*

*Would you by any chance be able to send me a few pounds of butter by C.O.D. to my address? I would gladly pay you two marks a pound and even more. Please write me as soon as possible regarding this. We have a lot of work, but it is not too heavy. I do miss home cooking, but I guess I will get used to the food soon.*

*How are things going with you? How are the bees doing? I am surprised that you still haven't got your money back from the government for completing the beekeeping course. In this respect I have been more fortunate. Hope to hear from you soon.*

*Many cordial regards!*

*Your Franz Baumgartner*

*Wilhelmshaven,*
*October 29, 1916.*

*Dear Miss Schropp!*

## The Making of a Frontier Woman

*Received your letter of October 22 and really enjoyed your news. Please excuse me for taking so long to answer. Part of the reason is that I am very busy these days but I also wanted to wait for your parcel. Yesterday, to my great pleasure, the package arrived and I thank you so much. The butter is top quality and the apples were wonderful too. Again, my deepest*

# 1916

*thanks. Am very sorry that I cannot send your four marks by mail because here at the naval base of Wilhelmshaven all the letters must be left open for the post office. For this reason I wonder if I could send the amount owing as a money order or as a registered letter which also would work. Please answer as soon as possible.*

*If you send butter again it would be wonderful and I could pay 2 marks 20 for it. You could send as much as you liked. The packaging was pretty good, but it would be even better if each single pound could be packed individually again, so each separate pound would stay nice and clean. I would be very happy if you could send me butter again and don't worry about getting paid.*

*Everything is going quite well here and I hope the same goes for you. The food is very good here, better than at Freising, but of course there are some restrictions. My best wishes to you and also to your sister.*

*Aloisia*

*Your devoted Franz Baumgartner*

*Please include the price of the butter.*

---

*Wilhelmshaven,
November 26, 1916.*

*Dear Luise!*
*Your package arrived the day before yesterday and made me very happy. I was surprised to get such top quality butter and also want to thank you from the bottom of my heart for the good apples. For important reasons I wish to wait until next week to send the money because then I can do it myself.*

*I am fine and in excellent health. This week we are being inspected and then we will probably be assigned to our ship, unless my application for leave to work on our farm is granted. I am very curious if they will allow me to go home. It is actually nicer here than at home. In the meantime, please don't send me any more butter as I don't know yet if I will be here or on leave.*

*You certainly had to wait a long time before you got your tuition paid back from Freising. As far as I can remember, I received only about 25 marks.*

*I finally have a photograph of our squadron and I can fulfil your wish. The uniforms we are wearing are probably not to your taste. In peacetime, the complete training was done in these but they were totally white. Right after our enlistment our uniforms were dyed grey because they were too hard to wash and soap is scarce.*

*We are now finished learning embroidery and sewing so we can label and mend our uniforms. We also know how to carefully put away our laundry. The front edges of our shelves are decorated with lace, exactly like a German woman would do to proudly show off her linen cupboard. We have learned how to keep everything meticulously clean. When we come*

*back home we will be different people.*
*Hearty greetings,*
*Franz Baumgartner*

*Lumber hauling with oxen in front of Schropp farmhouse.*
*Peter, Aloisia, father and mother.*

# Christmas in Ried

Four Sundays before Christmas Aloisia's mother hung the Advent calendar on the wall in the living area. It had been brought as a gift from one of her sons before the war but was still as good as new. After Christmas each year, she carefully closed each door and window cutout to hide the rocking horses, wise men and other surprises hidden behind them. She placed the calendar between two dampened pieces of light cardboard and ironed over it gently. When she lifted up the cardboard, the doors and windows looked as though they had never been used. Every year during the four weeks of advent all the tiny pictures were once again revealed.

The last of the four red candles on the Advent wreath had been lit last Sunday. Christmas preparations were almost complete. A well-shaped fir had been cut from the Schropp forest. It was now standing behind the house in a large enamel pot filled with water.

*Franz's squadron 1916; Franz is second from right on middle row*

In the cellar, the reddest, firmest apples, including the least blemished loden green Russets, were set aside for the holiday season. Spicy gingerbread cookies were stored in tin boxes that had tight lids. Dori and Aloisia declared the choir was ready to sing the Latin High Mass at midnight.

Snow had gradually crept down to the lower elevations on the Bavarian Alps. Soft, gentle flakes covered the surrounding countryside and the farmyards of Ried. Shrieks of excited laughter came from the narrow lane leading from the main village road into the Schropp's yard. Three children, their pockets holding a few candies left over from St. Nicholas's visit, pushed and rode their sleighs down past the manure pile to the path leading to the back fields.

When they were out of sight, a small bird flew to an exposed piece of turf in the yard. Soon, several other birds joined the first.

Despite this peaceful scene, war was still raging in Europe. Many men would not be home for Christmas or, for that matter, ever. The good news was that all the mumbling about peace seemed to be finally becoming a reality. Recently, Chancellor von Bethmann Hollweg had announced Germany's willingness to negotiate for peace. There had been cheers both inside the parliament building and from the throngs of people outside on the adjoining streets. The German newspapers were headlining and analysing his words.

The Chancellor admitted in his speech that the situation had been serious. Romania had entered the war to roll up the German positions in the east as well as those of Germany's allies. At the same time the grand offensive on the Somme was intended to pierce the German western front. Renewed Italian attacks had threatened to paralyse Austria-Hungary.

"Yes, the situation had been serious, but with God's help German troops shaped conditions to give security more complete than ever before. The western front was also safe. Not only does it stand, it is fitted out with larger reserves of men and material than before."

The Chancellor praised Field Marshall von Hindenburg for making possible what was previously thought impossible, the capture of the hostile capital of Bucharest.

In Romania, great stocks of grain, victuals, oil, and other goods fell into German hands and their transport has already begun. In spite of scarcity, Germans had enough supplies to live on. So now security was beyond question.

"But," the Chancellor continued, "Germany's strength had not made it deaf to its responsibility before God, before the German people and before humanity. In August 1914, enemies challenged Germany's superiority. Former declarations concerning readiness for peace were evaded by the adversaries. Now Germany has advanced one step further. Today, again, Germany raises the question of peace, which is a question of humanity. If the enemies decline to end the war," he said, "Then even in the smallest homes every German heart will burn in sacred wrath against enemies, who are unwilling to stop human slaughter in order that their plans of conquest and annihilation may continue...."

On the evening of the 24th Aloisia's father and Peter fitted the fir into a wooden stand and brought it into the house. He placed it in the corner of the living room where the spinning wheel often stood. Then, as was the custom, they closed the door until the family would be invited in after returning from midnight mass.

While Aloisia moved the flickering kerosene lamps from hook to hook along the barn wall as the milking progressed, her mother clamped the tin candle holders to the sturdiest branches, twisting and tilting them for the most advantageous effect. Later, while the rest of the family was at midnight mass and admiring the hand carved nativity scene for the first time that year, Aloisia's mother carefully unpacked straw stars from between layers of paper and lifted fragile coloured glass balls out of small partitioned cardboard boxes. These heirlooms had come from her mother and had been in her family for generations.

The pieces of lead tinsel were getting shorter and more brittle from years of handling. But there was enough to give the tree a pretty effect. Especially dear to Victoria was the snow globe her husband to be had brought home from his occupation in France so many years ago. She gave it a little shake and set it on a little side table as she did every year at this time. The snow spiralled around a Paris scene and settled quietly once again.

She put it down and hung dried apple rings from some of the branches. Surely, the war would be over soon.

# Waiting in Vain

## 1917

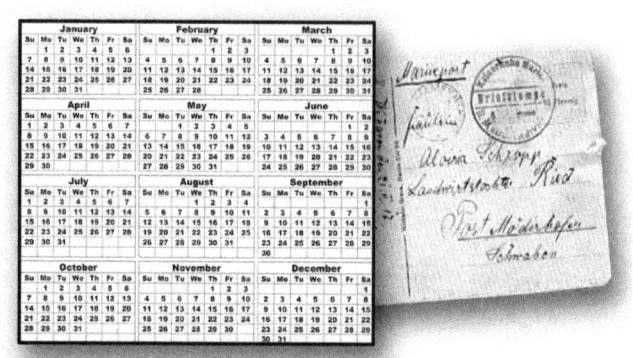

*Wilhelmshaven,
February 21, 1917*

*Dear Aloisia!*

*Am waiting in vain for your answer. Did you get the money? I hope so. Please write me.*

*I am pretty good and I hope you are the same. How are your bees doing? I will probably be getting a special leave. I am now with the signalling company and will soon pass the examination.*

*Many best wishes from your beekeeping colleague.*

*Franz Baumgartner
Wilhelmshaven.*

# Spring Was Late

Aloisia's father was very ill, lying down most of the time. He liked to have Victoria, whom he had married over forty years ago, close at hand and whenever he woke up, she was sitting there beside him, darning socks or stitching with bright red embroidery thread a sampler with the words, 'A Stitch in Time Saves Nine.' They had weathered many storms together.

Sometimes he would be on the downstairs couch, propped up on large eiderdown cushions. On these occasions, Victoria put pieces of birch into the stove so there would be more heat. The old mother cat was often beside him, purring loudly as he gently stroked her – unless she was beside Victoria watching the wool being pulled into the spinning wheel.

*Aloisia's mother, Victoria, spinning wool in farmhouse.*

Joseph watched his Victoria card wool or sort through her seed box. Often she would be folding and cutting newspapers for the outhouse just outside the door. Or, with her big black scissors, she would cut wide strips from old cotton garments and wind them into large balls for the rug weaver to pick up.

And there were always boiled potatoes to peel. Usually she cooked a big pot of them each week. Some were eaten the first day, each one at the table peeling their own. On the succeeding days, Victoria would peel and slice them up for frying, or cut them into small pieces for making potato salad. Sometimes she grated them for making potato pancakes. Mashed potatoes made with butter and milk were a luxury reserved for Easter or some other special occasion.

Sometimes Victoria was liquifying honey so she could refill it into smaller containers for their grown-up children and their grandchildren. She reminded Joseph of their names to cheer him. She never could do it in order of the grandchildren's age but rather by the ages of her own children: Emma's Maria; Franz's Franz, Oscar and Frieda; Joseph's Otto and Paul's Klara and Paul. Then there were the four daughters of Hans and Luise: Resi, Finny, Maria, and little Emma who was born after Hans was killed in France. Otto and Gusta had two daughters, Luise and Elsa. Ludwig and Margriet had two sons, Ludwig and Alfred.

The Schropp parents were proud of how their sons had succeeded with their jobs in the city. And they still came home when they could to help with planting or harvesting. With the war still raging, however, life was getting harder and harder on the farm. Most of the Schropp boys had been conscripted. They were seldom home with their families, let alone getting leave for helping on the family farm even though the parents were elderly and Peter had a maimed hand. The ten prisoners of war quartered in the house in the back garden were generally not familiar with German farming know-how and were no replacement for the Schropp sons.

Women were now expected to take the places of men. They could do jobs for which they were previously not considered capable or strong enough. Aloisia was pivotal to keeping the farm running. The prisoners often took a shovel or sack from her shoulders. "You work too hard," they said. "It is too heavy."

Aloisia had to milk the cows every morning and evening. Preparing slops for the pigs, pitching hay down from the loft for the animals and forking fresh straw down were only some of the daily chores. Manure had to be scraped into the gutter, shovelled onto a wheelbarrow which, rain, sleet or snow, had to be pushed out the barn door, up the wooden plank on the manure pile and dumped.

The pig stalls had to be cleaned, the chicken pens too. Then there were the droppings from the pigeon cages up in the attic. Once in awhile these also had to be scraped together into metal tubs and carried down to the manure pile.

Other jobs took their turn in the centuries old schedule of farm management. Each chore had to be carefully, but quickly, completed so the next job could begin.

In late winter (this year it was March because January and February were so cold), but before warmer weather would make other chores a priority, Aloisia had pruned the fruit trees. This usually took only a few days during a stretch of clear winter weather but this year there were constant interruptions of sleet and snow. Sometimes she kept pruning even though it started drizzling again but one couldn't keep working for long with rain dribbling down her neck and arms.

Often there was some early harvesting before the late planting but neither was possible this year. There was no block of sunny weather, only cold rain and more cold rain.

Finally, the weather changed. The snow melted; a warm sun dried the fields. Aloisia harnessed their two oxen and forked the steaming manure from the manure pile onto a wagon. Switch in hand, she drove the team out to the Schropp fields around the village. Once there, she pitched the heavy clumps onto the ground where it remained until the oxen chain harrowed the fields. Of course, some manure was forked onto the vegetable beds and around the bases of the fruit trees and lilac bushes.

On a sunny, warm day, when one could almost hear the clover crying for food, liquid manure was drained out of the storage vat under the manure pile into the tank wagon and sprayed over the fields, which, when treated in this way, yielded three good crops a year. You could smell that good ammonia smell for kilometres around!

Moving her hand like shaking a baby's rattle and again reaching her hand into the deep sheet metal tray tied around her waist, Aloisia dusted lime over the vegetable plot and around the gooseberries and red currants growing beside the house. It was simple, if you knew the correct technique. And while Aloisia had lime in the tray, she spread some under the chicken roosts. It cut down the smell and was good for the compost where most of the chicken manure went because it was too strong to be applied directly on the ground. The plants would burn.

Aloisia also knew how to shape her hand for planting seeds: a fist like a closed funnel for vegetable seeds such as lettuce and spinach, the thumb and first two fingers for legumes, and fingers continually moving like an opening and closing fan for grains. The evenness of the growing seedlings as they appeared above the earth, would later prove her skill.

Seeding time was also calving time. Each calf which she helped bring safely into the world had to be fed – and weaned. One had to be selected for slaughter if there was to be Wiener Schnitzel at Easter. She would help with butchering too.

The oxen must pull the tank wagon of liquid manure across the fields of sprouting grass and clover. Has that already been done? Well, it must be done again if three cuttings were to be harvested. Everything was a must. And spring was so late.

Aloisia, her cloth covered forehead firmly pressed against a cow's flank, could often be found sitting on the three-legged stool, stripping the last milk from an udder. Occasionally she gave the meowing cat a squirt.

At such times Aloisia had time to think. Blumental's words echoed in her mind about wintering bees. She thought of the previous fall when she had finished harvesting the honey. She had carefully tied burlap sacking around all the hives to prepare them for winter.

This winter had been colder than usual, colder than the farmer's almanac had predicted. Even though her father had planted a thick boxwood hedge on the north side of the hives, giving them some protection from stiff breezes and harsh winter winds, there was no balmy winter day that would give an excuse for removing the cover from a hive. Blumental had warned never to be tempted by curiosity.

Some mornings were sunny but still very cold. Aloisia noticed what appeared to be chicken feathers beside the woodpile and looked for fox tracks in the snow. But it was just hoarfrost caused by expanding ice in a wet piece of wood. Though the sun had come out, the hoarfrost was proof that the temperature during the night had dropped below freezing.

Finally the days grew lighter and finches were twittering in the sunny edges of the forest. Little rivulets carried the snow water away from the forests and meadows. The pungent smell of freshly ploughed and harrowed earth was in the air. It was truly spring and certainly too late for yet another cold spell. She untied the sacking from around the hives. It wasn't long before the bees peeked out and flew to the golden hazelnut catkins and the open place down by the stream where the sun shone brightly on the pussy willows.

Aloisia noticed two little boys picking some pussy willow branches down by the stream's edge. Blumental's pleading voice came into Aloisia's mind. 'On a warm spring day, a bee's first visit is to the pussy willows and they're protected by law because the bees need them. The pussy willow catkins are the bee's first food.' He had repeated the message in several different ways.

Aloisia went up to the boys and quietly told them that pussy willows were for the bees.

The boys looked at her and at then at each other. They shrugged. They were just picking them for their mothers, they said.

Aloisia said that was very nice but there was actually a law against picking them.

The boys gave her disbelieving looks. Suddenly, they ran off, leaving their willow branches lying on the ground. Aloisia picked them up and pushed them deep into the marshy ground. They would probably root in no time.

She realised that she must have sounded like Blumental. Yes, if times were different, if there had been no war she might have been able to get a higher education and become a teacher like him. After all, she was always the best in the class. But the thought of her ever becoming a teacher was completely out of the question. She was needed on the farm.

More than the musical sound of her teacher's voice, Aloisia

remembered the strong voice of someone else. And his last name had a much nicer ring to it than Schropp, which always reminded her of a scrub brush for some reason. In a way it was a suitable name for her because, if she wasn't working out in the field or in the barn, she was inside the house, scrubbing.

The photograph taken at Freising College had finally arrived in the post. She was pleased with the picture; the hat suited her face. But Franz's face was swollen from bee stings despite turning his better side to the camera. Even so, he was still the best looking man in the picture.

When Aloisia wrapped and sent the butter, packing in a few Russets nobody would miss, Franz paid for them as soon as mail delivery from his ship would allow it.

Aloisia thought that might be the end of their correspondence. She had not written back. She didn't want to seem forward. Even though it did not go unnoticed that Franz had reverted to using her formal baptismal name of Aloisia rather than the familiar Luise, he made it clear he was waiting for another letter.

How strange life was! Who could have imagined a year ago that she would be writing to a man, a seaman of all things! Her family found it strange, if not alarming, when the postman delivered his first letter. What could it mean?

But the world was changing. The needs of war were taking priority over the established customs of what was considered ladylike. Women should not only knit socks; they should support the military effort in factories. Some no longer felt they had to clasp their hands and bow their heads modestly when men were around. They could even point their finger at things and offer ideas about subjects other than the care of children or the kitchen.

The suffragette movement had been active in Europe, especially Germany, even before the turn of the century but so far it had not been able to get the vote for women. Even America, which was supposed to be so advanced in humanitarian concerns, had no success. Many Swiss people thought the idea of equality for women was a sure sign of moral decay. Certainly it was not necessary to burden the women with more to think about when the men were quite capable of running things.

But if women proved their equality in times of need, would they not finally get the vote when the war was over? In Great Britain and the United States, women were having their hair bobbed. In Germany most women felt that was going too far; women were not going to cut off their braids even if now they often ploughed the fields. But if the British royal family could renounce their German names and cut off relatives just like that, then cutting hair shouldn't be a big issue.

There were complaints about newspaper articles discussing the futility of war. Some were by Hermann Hesse, the writer Franz had mentioned. The government said Hesse's kind of thinking was an embarrassment to their beloved country – and dangerous. A good citizen was either for their country or against it. There was nothing in between.

The common people bit their lips and struggled on. There was more talk of possible peace negotiations....

Aloisia often had second thoughts about what she said to Franz. Perhaps she should have mentioned that she knew all the countries in the world, and their capitals too! Certainly, it would have been better if she had not been so emphatic about hating her red hair.

But Franz was writing her despite this missing information. There had been four letters and he had remembered to send greetings to Dori – once. His handwriting was elegant but Dori had mocked Aloisia about getting mail from a seaman. Aloisia explained that Franz had only asked her to send butter and he had paid her right away. He wrote her a letter even before Christmas, thanking her.

Now months had passed and she found herself thinking of Franz while in the kitchen slipping skins off cooked beets or rubbing the tongs of their wooden handled cutlery with fine sand or while turning up the wick of a coal oil lamp. Aloisia was both embarrassed and pleased when she read in Franz's last letter that he was waiting for a letter from her, in vain. Those words did not sound platonic. The effort she had put into composing her letters had been worthwhile.

She remembered his firm handshake, the sign of an honest, sincere and good character. That is what her family always said about strong handshakes. And Franz's handshake was definitely firm, perhaps too firm, but that may have come with his strong build.

Anyway, she really shouldn't judge. Franz was probably busy remembering the freckles on her face. But no, neither her red hair, nor her freckles, nor her small face (which she often wished were rounder) seemed to bother him. He said she should be thankful for what God had given her. At the time, she had taken those words as an admonition. Instead, he may have meant it as a compliment.

She thought of the rolling foothills near the Austrian Alps where his family lived. When would he inherit the farm? She remembered how they parted. She could still see him in his navy uniform, standing at attention and gravely saluting to her as her train pulled away.

She really must answer Franz. After all, he was fighting for the homeland. He seemed lonely – and he was so interesting.

What should she write? That her bees got through the winter and were now collecting nectar and pollen from the meadows around her farm? That would be nice for him to read. And she would explain that she had ordered the village carpenter to build five new hives using the modern design from Freising. Franz would be impressed.

She would not write about Hans, at least not this time. He had died in an Arras field hospital. It was his death the black crow had signalled.

When her brother, the other Franz, came home on leave he explained the details. Hans had just eaten lunch and walked outside for some reason. A sniper shot him in the stomach. Hans didn't have a chance of surviving. Franz brought home a photograph of himself standing beside his brother's grave. It was the month of June. There were many flowers on the grave.

On the very next day, a bomb landed on Hans' grave and blew it up. Because of all the fighting that followed in the area after neither his grave nor his coffin could be found again.

## The Making of a Frontier Woman

No, she wouldn't write that. She would keep the letter as light as possible, complimenting Franz on becoming a signaller and asking him how he liked his new position. Yes, that would be best. And she would ask Franz for a photograph of himself if he could spare one.

It was Sunday. Aloisia had heard that Schmid, the son of the village mayor, was home on a few days leave from the navy. He would probably be up in the choir loft because before the war he was a tenor. After church, when everybody was congregating in the yard, she hoped to have an opportunity to ask him a few things about navy life. That would give her some other ideas of what to write Franz.

Then, before going into the house, she would pick some Rapunzel, now beginning to leaf out so nicely. It would go well with the noon meal of potatoes, applesauce and the boiling hen she had killed and cleaned the day before. The broth had turned out so good, even though she only used the tiniest part of a bay leaf because that spice was hard to get now. Tomorrow she would use that broth to make bread dumpling soup.

After doing the dishes she would slip up to the farmhouse attic where the pigeons were kept. She would write Franz on some lined paper still saved from her school days. It was so peaceful there; she wouldn't be disturbed.

Later, after her evening chores were completed and the milking pails scrubbed, she would go up to her bedroom and copy the letter onto good paper.

On Monday, she would slip it into her skirt pocket before delivering the milk to the dairy and hand it directly to the postman. The next twenty-four hours all planned out. She was a real Schropp.

# Another Letter from Franz

"Where's Aloisia?" Oscar asked Peter.

"She'll be back in a minute. She's just gone to bring some radishes to the priest's housekeeper."

Oscar walked towards the rectory and, sure enough, Aloisia was already coming back. He reached under his jacket and pulled out an envelope. "I think it's from Baumgartner."

Aloisia gave Oscar a hug and pushed the envelope deep into the pocket of her skirt. Franz had replied quickly this time. She quickly walked into the stable, broke the seal and read the letter.

*On the billowing waves:*
*May 26, 1917.*

*Dear Luise!*

*Received your dear letter yesterday with pleasure. My sincere thanks. I am very well. Just want to quickly tell you that I probably will get work leave in the next few days. The weather here is heavenly. You will have to be satisfied with these few details for the time being. I have my hands full trying to arrange my leave because we have so much duty on the signalling bridge. More next time. Please forgive my haste. My sincere best wishes.*

*Your beekeeping colleague,*

*F.B. naval signaller*

## The Making of a Frontier Woman

She read it again a pushed it deep into her pocket. As she fed oats to their horse, touching his soft nose, the words 'pleasure', 'forgive', 'sincere', and 'more next time' caressed her mind.

But, as she emptied the slops into the pig trough, she wondered at the letter's shortness. In the hen house, as her fingers scraped the bottom of the tin pail holding the last of the wheat, she wondered if she would ever see Franz alive again. How did the mail make it to shore with enemy ships all around?

Whatever the case, Franz seemed busy. He did not send the photograph she had requested. But she liked the way he signed the letter, *Your beekeeping colleague*.

*Beekeeping class in Freising where Aloisia (second row from top, first on left) and Franz Baumgartner (back row, second from right) met in June 1916*

# Veterans

On Sunday afternoons a few old cronies got together for a beer over at the inn. They were veterans from the Franco-Prussian War. Aloisia's father, the youngest of the group, was now completely bedridden and could no longer join them. Aloisia asked if she shouldn't at least go over after her chores and bring his greetings. He agreed.

When Aloisia walked into the inn, three of her father's cronies, their walking sticks hanging on the nearby coat rack, were sitting at their regular corner table. One of them noticed her right away.

"Well, well," he said, waving his pretzel, "Here's the young lady who never walks, she just runs!"

"You'll be sorry one day for overdoing it, you know," one of the others piped in as he shifted his wooden leg to a more comfortable position under the table.

"I used to think like you," the third one added, "I thought I could finally finish all the work but instead the work has finished me. Ha, ha." He waved a fly away from his beer, "You'll be sorry later in life if you don't slow down."

"He's right," the other two chimed in, alternately shaking their heads and giving each other knowing looks.

"Yes," the one with the wooden leg said, "Didn't you have a breakdown awhile back when you were building that house in the back, where the Russians are staying now?"

Aloisia smiled and shrugged.

"Oh well, young people never learn that work never goes away," he sighed. "And how's your father doing?"

"Not that good. He's in a lot of pain," Aloisia said, "But he asked me to send you his best regards. That's why I came."

They asked her to bring their best wishes back to her father.

## The Making of a Frontier Woman

Maybe they could come over and visit him?

"Maybe some other time," Aloisia answered, "If he's feeling better."

They repeated their greetings for him and invited her for a drink. The cronies reminisced how in council meetings her father always had the best ideas in the village. And he knew how to get consensus even from those who were at first opposed or didn't understand all the issues. How old was her father now? Only sixty-eight years?

The waiter came and they ordered a small light beer for Aloisia.

"And how is your mother? Still busy as ever?"

Aloisia assumed the question referred to her mother's midwifery. Her mother always helped people in need and that especially included women in confinement. She didn't get overly anxious about colds, measles, mumps or even chicken pox. Gargling with warm salt water cured many a sore throat. Applying mustard plasters and sweating under piles of featherbeds were standard cures with which she had successfully raised all her children. When it came to a woman's confinement, however, she had no end of sympathy. Though Victoria had no formal training, people said she was as good as any midwife.

Sometimes, in the middle of the night, there would be a clattering on the Schropp's master bedroom window. A neighbour had thrown some pebbles as a signal that the time had come for another birth in the village. Her mother would quietly get out of bed, dress (she usually had her things laid out as she knew the approximate time of deliveries), and slip out the door. When dawn broke, Joseph often awoke to find she was still not home.

That is to what the veterans were probably referring. Aloisia didn't want to get into those details. Lately there had been no calls for help in the middle of the night; the neighbours knew Victoria's husband needed all of her attention....

"She's fine, thank you. My mother spends a lot of time looking after my father. Does a lot of spinning these days. That way she's virtually always with him."

They nodded to show they understood. They sent greetings to her mother too.

The conversation then drifted back to what they were apparently discussing before Aloisia walked in, specifically, the difference between battleships, cruisers, destroyers and U-boats. They talked about vessels being requisitioned for naval service. Most important were a series of freighters and passenger ships being converted into auxiliary cruisers. Fishing trawlers were now turned into patrol ships for reconnaissance work.

Aloisia asked, as casually as she could, in which category Frederick the Great would be. She found out it was in the battleship category but she couldn't understand the reason they gave and felt to shy to ask them to repeat their explanation. That would seem to be a little pushy.

Soon the veterans were talking about how the navy had to keep its whereabouts secret and, in case the mail was intercepted, the crew had to be vague in the few letters they did write.

Of course, Aloisia thought, that made sense. That is why Franz had written, *'On the Billowing Waves.'*

"Surely a peaceful settlement must be made soon," said the one who had been quiet so far, busy cleaning his teeth with a toothpick.

*Peter with sheepdog, Butsy, in Ried*

## The Making of a Frontier Woman

The conversation shifted to Rasputin, the Russian monk. According to newspapers he had become too influential in the court of Czar Nicholas II. It was said Rasputin had eyes like burning coals but the Czarina didn't seem to mind, ha, ha. The veteran with the wooden leg said he had read there was some hanky-panky going on between the two of them.

"You mean between the Czar's wife and that monk?" said one veteran.

"Yes, you idiot. Who in the devil's name did you think I meant? Rasputin and the Czar? Ha, ha!"

Aloisia bowed her head and blushed.

"Hey, we have a lady present. Watch your language!"

"Oh excuse me. Excuse me, I forgot."

Apparently nobody liked Rasputin. Somebody had tried to poison him, but the attempt had failed. Then somebody shot at him. That was supposed to be good. Czar Nicholas II had been forced to abdicate. He and his family had to leave their Petersburg palace and move to an estate in the country. That was going too far.

The veterans started talking about Germany's astounding technical advances displayed years ago at World Exhibitions in Brussels and London. Hadn't that been amazing? The Germans were leading in everything! More inventions could hardly be imagined.

"Well," laughed one, "Don't forget about pop-up books. My wife has a whole collection of Lothar Meggendorfer books and when my great grandchildren come, she lets them look at the doll house book where the table and chairs all fold up. It's all three dimensional! There's a boy playing a piano and doors that open and you can see a woman and her child feeding pigeons and chickens...."

"Ha, those books are probably more interesting for you than the grandchildren," said the one who had asked about Aloisia's mother. "But aren't grandchildren a great excuse for collecting things we wish we had?"

Everyone laughed, enjoying the moment.

"Let's be serious," said the one with the wooden leg. "All the German cities are now connected with railroads. The city of Leipzig has the most modern train station in all Europe! Those steam engines are so fast! And then there are the amazing Zeppelin's air raids and U-boat attacks. And completing the Kiel Canal! What an engineering feat that was, ships not having to go round Denmark anymore. Straight from the North Sea to the Baltic!"

"You mean the Kaiser-Wilhelm Canal," said the veteran who had spoken about the pop-up books. "That's the official name they gave it when it was opened. The British, they call it the Kiel Canal."

"Okay, okay, we all know what we're talking about."

"And," continued the one who was now wiping pretzel crumbs off his moustache, "Don't forget the sickness insurance that Bismark introduced way back in the eighties. There was a first in the world! And there was Bach. What would the world do without his music?" he added, shaking his finger at the others. "And now there's Albert Schweitzer saving lives in the French Congo. And already in the middle of the last century, Siemens developed the first electric streetcar."

Everyone nodded in agreement.

"And Dr. Oetker," Aloisia said, wanting to contribute to the conversation. "Before he invented baking powder my mother said only eggs were used for leavening cakes. You used to beat and beat forever, my mother always says."

The men looked at Aloisia, appreciating this added point to their list of firsts for their country.

Baron von Richthofen and his red Fokker triplane was the topic that came up next. His name appeared in every German newspaper either above or below his photographs. He usually was wearing a scarf. He had a sincere, boyish face. According to reporter's claims, he was a true hero and yet very shy when interviewed. He had shot down so many enemy planes that now he had been awarded honours for being the highest scoring German alive – the ace of aces.

Such stories were supposed to keep the spirits of the masses up, said the veteran who had removed the crumbs from his moustache only to have them settle in his beard. He nudged one of his cronies with his elbow and gave Aloisia a knowing look.

All acknowledged how difficult it was to keep spirits up when many young men were among the official numbers of 'those who would not come home again'. High and low masses were offered up regularly for sons of local farmers. Candles were lit.

In April, America, the world's richest and leading industrial power, had declared war on Germany. What business of theirs was this war anyway? Didn't they have enough to do chasing their gangsters?

The men asked Aloisia about her brother, Ludwig, and his farm in Untermeitingen. How was he doing? Working hard? He's lucky he didn't have to go to war. At least farmers aren't starving.

One of them felt this was the time to tell the tired joke about farmers carpeting their barns with Persian rugs; city dwellers were bartering their most precious possessions to get food.

Aloisia thought of the beautiful linen tablecloth, richly embroidered with pink and purple clover blossoms and soft green leaves, the one her mother exchanged for half a pound of butter.

The British blockade was effectively cutting off food supplies; there was now starvation in all German cities. Those who had flour and sugar set aside when the war began, had now used up their stocks. Elderly men and women were lining up to exchange potato peelings for firewood.

Before the war it was only considered proper for little boys to run out on the streets to pick up horse dung. Now women of all ages were going out with pails to bring home some nourishment for their tiny garden plots built against apartment walls where flowers used to grow.

Chicken feet, which were always thrown away before the war were boiled to make a broth and were worth chewing. Malnourished mothers were succumbing to various illnesses as they tried to keep their children healthy.

"And how are your bees doing?"

## *Aloisia*

"Fine, fine," she answered. It was a blessing that Aloisia had increased the number of her beehives. Blumental had said you couldn't get rich with bees, but honey certainly makes life with virtually no sugar more bearable.

Aloisia rose to leave. The veteran who had talked about pop-up books and sickness insurance walked with her to the door and quietly asked if she couldn't spare any honey next fall.

"Oh, it's really all promised to family members," Aloisia said. Then she remembered how he had given her three large spools of string last year and how handy they had been for many jobs around the farm. "But I'll see," she added. "I think I could spare a jar or two."

As Aloisia walked outside again, she heard some gramophone music. The Blue Danube was playing. She thought of how Franz in his last letter had given his location as 'on the billowing waves' wherever that was. Was he on the North Sea or the Baltic?

Did he have any idea of the hardships being endured on land? Being a signaller, he must get news one way or another. He must also know how proud the German people were of their fleet.

Schmid had told her that Frederick the Great was called a flagship because the admiral used it as his headquarters. It was so big that messengers often used roller skates to get around. She assumed it must be the largest and most modern of their fleet – or was it? Those veterans would have known. She had forgotten to ask them. But her interest might have aroused suspicion. Maybe they already knew that she was corresponding with its signaller but if they did, they didn't say anything

Aloisia thought of the last letter she had written so carefully to Franz. It was both interesting and cheerful. The first draft had been completed in the attic, encouraged by the cooing pigeons. Yes, she would find time to write Franz again even though it was such a busy time of the year and she was thankful for fields lying fallow. Who knows if he would survive the war? She should tell Franz that her bee population had increased so much that more supers were added.

She would also write that their church choir was learning a new mass. Concentration on the new score helped to keep one's mind off the hardships of everyday life. Should she write that this new mass would not require bass singers? The only bass singer left could sing in the baritone section, which was missing two men. They were recovering in hospitals somewhere.

Surely, the war could not go on much longer. When she was in school she had memorised the beginning and ending of many wars. The American Civil War was 1861 to 1865. The Franco-Prussian War was 1870 to 1871. The Boer war in Africa was 1899 to 1902. Aloisia had heard that the Kaiser had promised to bring Britain to its knees by the end of June and then a truce would be drawn up. No war lasts forever. It just seems that way when you're living through it.

# Manoeuvres

Aloisia hoped Franz would answer her letter by Christmas. Now another year had begun and it was already the end of January. She had not heard from him in half a year. Though there was talk of an imminent breakthrough in peace negotiations, war was still raging.

Hans' widow, Luise, who lived a little way out of the village, with her four daughters Resi, Finny, Maria and little baby Emma whose red hair at birth showed no signs of changing colour. Sometimes Aloisia carried her portable Excella sewing machine to Luise's place so she could keep her company. Life went on.

Today was Saturday. Aloisia was home getting ready for Sunday. As she swept the front yard she kept a lookout for a bicycle rider in dark blue carrying a large bag behind the seat. The postman was a little late today. Finally, as she was shining the brass latch on the front door, she saw him.

The postman saw Aloisia too. He rode into the yard and leaned his bicycle against the linden tree. He tipped his hat and then reached into his leather bag. He had a twinkle in his eye as he pulled out an envelope and handed it to her.

Aloisia recognised Franz's handwriting. He was alive. As usual, the address said:

> *Miss Aloisia Schropp*
> *Farmer's daughter*
> *Ried Post Office*
> *Moedishofen*
> *Schwabia*

She looked around and the quickly slipped the envelope under her apron and into her side pocket. She gave the latch a final rub with a clean cloth and then, with steps slower than usual, she casually walked into the stable and closed the door. She stopped by a window where the pale winter sun gave some light. She opened the letter.

## The Making of a Frontier Woman

*Fortress Hospital, Wilhelmshaven,*
*December 29, 1917*

*Dear friend!*

*Received your letter. Thank you. You will probably wonder why you haven't received a letter for so long. I was on the Baltic Sea the entire time doing manoeuvres. As I had to be on the signal watch both night and day I thought I would wait until Christmas to do my writing.*

*Unfortunately, I got sick on the 24th of December and am now in the hospital. I have hardly any pain. Otherwise everything is fine.*

*Sincerely,*

*Your friend, F.B.*

---

Aloisia shook her head in disbelief. It was hard to believe that Franz was so busy he had to be sick in hospital before finding time to write. And what kind of an ending was 'Your friend, F.B.'? Certainly not warm like the previous one. The letter seemed very official and distant. What was she supposed to think? Or was he just so weak that he couldn't say more? Had the war taken away all his emotions?

Schmid had written his family during the same time. Of course, maybe Schmid could somehow get mail out because of his location and Franz couldn't. No, the only real excuse Franz could have had for not writing in such a long time was that he was dead. But, since he wasn't, well there was no excuse at all. Or was he really that ill?

Aloisia was now embarrassed she had asked him for his picture. She wouldn't write back immediately. That would really be making a fool of herself. And when she did write, she would make it clear that their relationship was only platonic. She certainly would not ask for his picture, ever again.

She had more important things to think about, anyway.

# Our German Father

*Guard with Russian and Serb prisoners in front of "the house in the garden" where they were quartered.*

The doctor said Aloisia's father had cancer. He had lost so much weight that his body was barely visible under the bed covers. Finally, the pain became so intense that the family doctor was called to his bedside. Was there nothing more that could be done?

After talking with him for awhile about the pain, the doctor said, "I think I have something here that will help you," and then took his hand. "My dear Mr. Schropp, We've been friends for a long time. I've witnessed how you have raised a wonderful family that you can be proud of. You have built up a farm that could be an example to any farmer. On top of all that, you always worked for the community."

Aloisia's father smiled feebly as his wife looked on.

"And," the doctor added, giving his hand a squeeze, " I always remember how you said to me once that anything worthwhile doing, was worth organizing. I've told so many people about your wise words. Your wife has been a good nurse for you. She has done everything she can."

Joseph Schropp nodded weakly.

The doctor withdrew his hand. "I'm going to give you something so you can sleep. It will take away your pain." The doctor reached into his black leather medical bag. He took out a syringe and held it up to the light of the window. Then he gently lifted the bed covers and gave him an injection. He stroked his old friend's head and then turned to Mrs. Schropp. "Mrs. Schropp, your dear husband will sleep peacefully now."

She wrung her hands and nodded in speechless gratitude.

Within a few minutes the pain seemed to melt away. Aloisia's father breathed easier and soon fell into a deep sleep. He never woke up. The date was January 26, 1918.

The Russian and Serbian prisoners were still being quartered on the Schropp farm. When Joseph Schropp died they wept. "We have lost our German Father." They asked if they could have the honour of digging the grave in the churchyard for him.

# More Letters – "I Have Honey"

## 1918

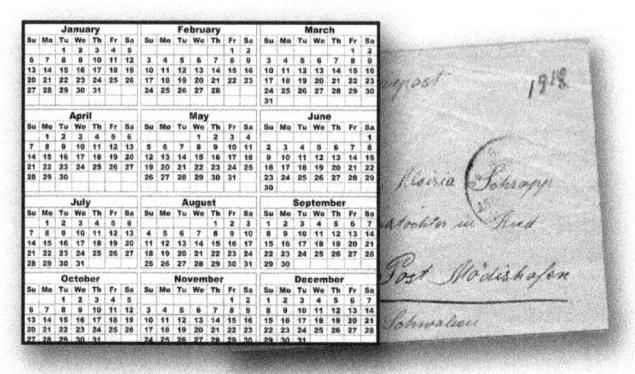

*Frederick the Great,*
*August 18, 1918*

*My dear friend!*

*I am waiting for a letter from you in vain or didn't you get my last letter? Please don't be angry. If I have offended you, please be frank and tell me to explain myself. This uncertainty is an oppressive feeling. Be good and share your pain with me. If you haven't any time because of all your work, then at least send me a postcard. I know that at this time of year there is no end of work to do.*

*Just have come back from fourteen days leave to help with the harvesting. I arrived home exactly at the right time and we got everything finished by the time my leave was over. All is in order. Even though our hayloft was enlarged, it was again filled to the top.*

*Everything is going well with the bees. I have honey and also have been able to keep the swarms.*

*Unfortunately, I cannot send any photographs as I still have to get copies. It would be wonderful if I could get a picture of you and your sister, Dori. How are you doing these days? I am well and I hope you are too.*

*I am looking forward to a letter from you in the near future and remain yours sincerely in friendship,*

*F.B.*

---

S.M.S. Frederick the Great (Military postcard),
September 4, 1918

Dear Luise!

*Oh, how businesslike and cold it is when you address me with the word, 'esteemed'. The whole world seems just a little sadder than it already is. At present it seems even more irksome as I am not supposed to ask about your personal state of affairs. Why don't you write me anymore about how things are going with you? It's strange that you always tell me what I already had in mind to ask you. You are a little bit angry with me aren't you? If so, just tell me.*

*Everything is going well with me. Right now I have an opportunity to accompany a group which is studying the management of large farms in the province of Schleswig-Holstein.*

*Best wishes in friendship to you and also Dori.*

*F.B.*

# Letters Mailed From Scapa Flow

*Frederick the Great,*
*November 8, 1918*

*Dear Luise!*

*Many thanks for your letter, which I was very happy to receive. I will gladly fulfil the wishes you expressed in your letter when things have settled down. Because of the great unrest here, I have my doubts if you will even receive this letter. We have been aimlessly drifting around for weeks now. There is much confusion and we cannot enter any port. At present we are looking for provisions and I wonder if we will be allowed to get bread or potatoes in any harbour. We have been without meat for days and have no idea what is going on in the world. Such circumstances cannot last and it would be terrible if they did. I am doing quite well for myself as I have put aside tobacco and foodstuffs. I also will find my way through in the future—if I am still alive. But it's not that bad yet and maybe on the way home from the war I will drop by and visit you. Probably you will not recognise me anymore. I am enclosing my photograph even though you might not receive this letter. Hopefully the situation will alter in a way that makes it better than we have it at the moment.*

*I remain with many sincere greetings to both you and your sister.*

*In friendship,*

*Fr. Baumgartner*

## The Making of a Frontier Woman

*Dear Luise!*

*I wanted to send the enclosed poem long ago. I don't think you have it yet. Please judge it kindly. In fact a dream is the real origin of this poem. It suits the two of us so well and if it will be fulfilled, then the longing of two hearts will be quieted in one regard.*

*With sincere greetings,*

*Hope to see you again, Franz*

*Aloisia with visiting child, Peter, father and mother on steps of newly completed "house in the garden".*

# Reflections while a Prisoner in Scapa Flow

(Seelenstimmung aus meiner Internierung in Skapa Flow)

Ach, wie treibt heisses Sehnen
*Oh, how passionate yearning drives*

Die Gedanken hin und her.
*My thoughts hither and fro.*

Weite Wasserwellen trennen
*High waves still separate me*

Mich doch von des Glueckes Meer.
*From the sea of happiness.*

*Franz mailed this photograph to Aloisia from Scapa Flow, Scotland on November 8, 1918.*
*"I am enclosing my photograph even though you might not receive this letter."*

Nicht die Heimat, nicht die Fremde
*Not my own or foreign country*

Weder Fruhlingsreiz noch Gold
*Not springtime's charm or gold,*

Sucht mein Sinnen, meine Lippen
*Oh my lips may they kiss*

O, kuessten sie das Brauetchen hold
*Only my sweet bride.*


Ja, ein Frauchen will ich finden!
*Yes, I want to find a dear wife.*

Sehe ich wieder sie im Traum
*I see her once again in my dreams,*

Wie sie duftet, mich umschlinget
*How lovely she smells hugging me*

Anmutsvoll in Hochzeitraum.
*Charmingly in the bridal chamber.*

## The Making of a Frontier Woman

Und dann liebend mir zur Seite
*And then, lovingly at my side,*

Laesst vergessen alle Welt
*She makes me forget the whole world*

Mit ihrer Torheit, leeren Weite
*With its folly, empty expanses*

Wo sich alles dreht ums Geld.
*Where everything revolves around money.*

Golden sind die Haare Dein,
*Golden is your hair,*

Blau dein himlisch Augenpaar,
*Blue your heavenly eyes.*

Noch bist du erst im Traume mein
*'Til now you are mine only in my dreams*

Mit deiner Liebe treu und wahr.
*With your love so faithful and true.*

Ach wo haelt sie sich verborgen?
*Oh where is she hiding?*

Ob sie wohl schon lebt und schafft
*Is she already living and toiling*

Fuer ein gluecklich Eheleben
*For a happy wedded life*

Wie ich, mit frohen Jugendkraft?
*Like me with joyful, youthful strength?*

Ob auch sie gleich mir im Streite
*Does she struggle just as I do*

Mit der eigenen Natur
*With her own nature,*

Den Versucher treibt ins Weite
*Driving temptation far away*

Nur aus Lieb zum Liebsten nur?
*Keeping herself only for her beloved?*

## Aloisia

Ob auch sie gleich mir beschwoeret
*If she, like me, prays*

Jeden Tag und jede Stund
*Every day and every hour*

Das mich keine je betoeret
*That no woman ever seduces me*

Und ich stark bleib und gesund?
*That I remain healthy and strong*

Denn zum Lebendsbund auf Erden
*For our marriage here on earth*

Muss man tapfer, fromm und treu
*One must remain brave, devout and faithful,*

Kaempfer sein und Sieger bleiben
*Be a warrior and a victor.*

Gottes Segen sei dabei.
*With God's blessing!*

Ja, auch sie traegt Sehnsuchtsschmerz
*Yes, she too is filled with yearning*

Hoffen und ein Liebesgluehn
*Hope and love's desire.*

Die wird unsre treuen Herzen
*Will draw our faithful hearts*

Magnetisch zueinander ziehen.
*To each other like a magnet.*

Dieser Glaube, dieses Hoffen
*This belief, this hope,*

Dass ein Maedchen meiner denkt
*That a girl thinks about me*

Haelt den schoensten Hafen offen
*Keeps the most beautiful open harbour*

Wohin unser Lebensschifflein lenkt.
*To where our small lifeboat sails.*

# 1919

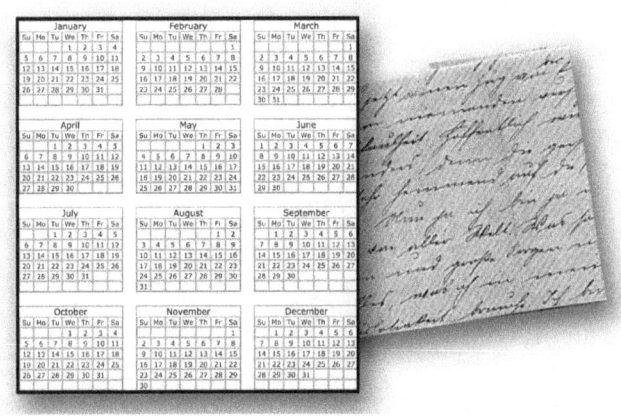

*Scapa Flow,*
*February 20, 1919*

*My dear friend!*

*I received your dear card on the same day your letter from my home arrived. My sincere thanks for both of them. I regret to say that once again you let me wait such a long time to hear anything from you and now today you give me the distressing news that you really don't want to stay at home any more. Furthermore, it seems that you have really changed, rushing all over the place in these unsettled times, like a real adventurer.*

*You will certainly lead the whole operation for the priest you mentioned and organise like a real administrator. One should not underestimate you in anything.*

*I was really anxious to visit you on my way home but if you won't even be there, that will be a little difficult. Please write me regarding this. You could have sent along the photograph, which I have been looking forward to for such a long time or do you think that your promise is so old that it has already expired?*

*You asking whether I don't have any more interest in dumb Swabian girls really hurt me. In these things I am very sensitive. For me all people are equal*

## Aloisia

*because I look at them from a completely different perspective than most people do. I can understand all people and forgive all, but I myself am usually not understood.*

*If I don't answer all your questions it is not for lack of good intentions, but because of shortage of time as the post office closes in fifteen minutes. I will answer all your questions when I answer your next letter, in which I hope to find your photo.*

*I send you the sincerest friendly greetings,*

*Baumgartner*

*Scapa Flow,*
*April 18, 1919*

*My dearest friend!*
*Have received your letter with photo a long time ago and thank you so much. Today I also received your second card and that reminded me again of my negligence. Please forgive me. Lately I have just had so much to do.*

*Last week I moved and now live by myself in a small room. It is very comfortable. Besides my bed I also have a nice chesterfield and hot water heat. You should see how beautiful and comfortable it is here! Have also an attractive writing desk and writing chair to go with it. I would be content if one day in the future I will have such a comfortable and practical set up again.*

*Above the writing desk I have a large carved holder for postcards. Always the prettiest picture postcards go in there and because it is already full the worst*

Photo that Aloisia sent to Franz Scapa Flow, 1919

*ones must come out to make room for the new ones. Today, again, one had to be taken down. Pretty soon comrades will come along and judge which one should come down next. You may laugh at our childlike amusement but we have our fun with it. What else can we do with our free time? We visit back and forth and tease each other.*

*I have a picture of a stout young woman on display beside your photo. Some say you are too skinny for a country girl and I tell them you are a beekeeper and always have to run after swarming bees. But what do sailors know about beekeeping? And, to tell the truth, you had to work too hard during that damned long war when there were no men around to help. You have written me about that several times and I can see it by looking at your picture. I myself am almost as heavy again as I was at Freising. Well, maybe we will see each other soon. I would really be delighted if there would be an opportunity on my return. Then I will take a small beekeeping course from you and review all that I have forgotten.*

*Just now I had to break off my letter for an hour. A water tap was left open in the kitchenette and when the water was turned on again the room flooded. There was no one else but myself because the others went dancing but I stayed behind so I could write. That was quite some fun. Two comrades and I carried the water away. We were barefoot and the water went all the way up to our ankles. We had the gramophone playing 'Stormy is the Night and the Waves Were High'. It is only a pity about wasting all that beautiful fresh water because we have to buy it. Of course it was nobody's fault. We didn't argue about who was to blame as we are almost used to these floods.*

*Today is Good Friday and, can you believe it, we ate meat three times! But it is not our fault. Easter will be celebrated in a wonderful way. In the evening there will be a stage play called the 'The Enforced Holiday'. There will be, among others, five girls on stage. It will be wonderful. Our theatre group is really a sensation.*

## Aloisia

*Every fourteen days a new program.*

*I hope to get an answer from you soon and greet you heartily,*

*Franz Baumgartner*

---

*Scapa Flow,
May 16, 1919*

*My dear Luise!*

*I started this letter which you see here many times but it never amounted to anything. I now possess a trait, which formerly I could never understand when I saw it in others—laziness in writing. Hopefully this will soon change because mental lethargy suppresses people's productivity. I am, of course, interned and shut off from the whole world. So there is little reason for me to have big ideas or for that matter, great sorrows. I have enough food because I have been very frugal. I am healthy and feel better every day. That is how easily one gets used to one's fate. Most of the others here are very discontented, nervous and what not else. I have not had a letter from anybody for fourteen days. It could be that the newly implemented interruption of postal services is to blame. Hopefully I'll get mail in the next few days.*

*How is everything going with you? Here one doesn't see the terrible forces in the world but neither can I see the beauty of nature. I am just amazed that I can remain so calm. How wonderful it will be when we come back home again!*

*It will take me a long time though because I want to stay awhile at each of the places where I have been invited. How happy my parents, brothers and sisters and especially my mother will be when they see me again healthy in both body and soul. For my mother's sake especially I will stay at home for a couple of weeks. Then I'll visit my friend from school who lives in a forested area of Bavaria. He invited me to spend my holidays in the beautiful forests and the romantic mountaintops of his area. I am really looking forward to it because I have been there once before. I know the whole family and some of the village's inhabitants. It will be a wonderful time among the locals.*

*I am like you and don't know what I am going to do in the future either. I have thrown out the idea of becoming an agricultural civil servant. During these unstable times, I neither want to harass people nor do I wish to take advantage of them. I would rather become a small farmer myself.*

*Of course, I could also take over the family farm. You can see that worries about the future are not of much importance to me right now.*

*Dear Luise! I have to bring up an old question and please, finally give me an exact answer. It is about your invitation, which I would really like to accept if I only knew how you and your family would feel about it. You never refer to this and the fact that in your last letter you said that as far as you are concerned, nothing would stand in the way, still doesn't satisfy me. Please answer this question in detail in your next letter and tell me specifically how it would really be if I ever had the honour of visiting you and if there wouldn't be prejudices against a sailor. Perhaps those few hours would only ruin everything. Even a negative reply will not influence our friendship.*

*I wish you greetings from far away,*

*Franz Baumgartner*

# A Few Hours

At the war's end, the German fleet was supposed to be interred in a neutral port but instead had been escorted across the North Sea to the barren east coast of Scotland. Aloisia had found out that the landscape in Scapa Flow was dreary and barren because of the prevailing winds. Even though little vegetation could grow, the German sailors would have liked to go on shore. That, of course, was not allowed. When Aloisia received Franz's last letters from Scapa Flow, the flowers on the linden trees were just beginning to open in Ried. Surely he would be back in Bavaria in time to see them in full bloom.

Before the peace treaty was ready to sign, many drafts had to be made because the victorious countries were haggling over the war booty. Just one of the many prizes fought over were the ships of the German fleet. There were the battle cruisers Seydlitz, Moltke, Von der Tann, Derfflinger and the battleships such as the Kaiser, Prinz Regent, Kaiserin, and Frederick the Great. Then there were cruisers and destroyers. There seemed to be an endless controversy over which country should get which ships.

In the beginning of June of 1919, the sailors on these ships were no longer ordered to keep the fleet in a state of readiness for sea. There was a reduction of crews to the care-and-maintenance level. Those sailors who wished to be repatriated had an opportunity to leave.

On June 21 sailors still left on these ships were given instructions by a coded secret signal to bolt the hatches open. Their Admiral, Ludwig von Reuter, had given orders to scuttle all the ships interred at Scapa Flow. At first, the British didn't realize what was happening and they fired on the German sailors escaping the sinking ships on lifeboats. Several were wounded and killed. It was in all the German newspapers.

## The Making of a Frontier Woman

Aloisia wondered what had become of Franz. She had not heard from him since the middle of May. Had he been one of the sailors who returned home before the scuttling? Or was he in the group that came home after the scuttling? Maybe he was among those shot at by the British. He may have been wounded or even dead.

The blossoms on the linden tree would soon be too wilted to pick.

The war was over. All of Aloisia's brothers came home again, except Hans. The three brothers of Sepp's wife, Anna, didn't. Neither did many others.

# CHAPTER TWO: 1919 -1922
## UNSETTLED TIMES-ARGENTINA

# Franz Writes From Home

*Eggersham,*
*July 17, 1919*

*My dear friend!*

*Greetings from home! Why do you doubt that I am still alive when you have my letter in your hands? I have been home since June 23. Since then I have had so many demands put on me that, despite my best intentions, I haven't been able to write you until now. However, if I remember correctly, but I could be wrong, I have already notified you of my being here and you have probably already received my letter, unless it has been lost. I have not run away from my work. After all, I am supposed to be on holidays! By the way, I still haven't made firm plans for the future. I am very behind in my writing. It is not easy to get used to it. Due to the long war and internment I am not as mentally alert as before. Your inquiry about my mother pleased her very much. As she is completely inundated with work, she handed your letter over for me to answer. I accept your dear invitation with pleasure and will surprise you one day.*

*Many greetings from my mother and especially from your friend Franz.*

*So far everything is going well here and I hope everything is fine with you and your family. Please give them my best regards on my behalf.*

## The Making of a Frontier Woman

*Eggersham,
August 24, 1919*

*My dear friends, Aloisia and Dori!*

*Many thanks for your well meaning letter which I was happy to receive. You belong to those few who not only mean well but have also answered my questions in a realistic way. Even so, under the circumstances, I am still undecided how much I can use your advice regarding staying home and taking over my parent's farm.*

*In regards to religion, our outlook is exactly the same, except I cannot penetrate so deeply into the holy mysteries. I am happier to have the mercy given to me to remain faithful to my old observations, despite the many dangers the world offers, especially to young people.*

*I think back to my youth when the inhuman circumstances and treatment became unbearable and how, with no support from any side, I attended agricultural college. It was difficult, terribly difficult. At home there was disorder, lack of cleanliness, disharmony in the family, no love, no heart, only the good mother, for whom I felt so terribly sorry because of her overwhelming financial problems. Then, oh I had better not start. I can only say that I was so happy to be away and in the navy.*

*In the navy, I have learned to expect more from life, at least in comparison to the circumstances at home. I want everything to be at least halfway clean, orderly, etc. so I don't have to feel ashamed of myself as before. But that means that I had to be my own housekeeper. I have just finished making my bed, tidied up, dusted, and scrubbed the floor. Otherwise, I would just have to come back to what I left behind. There are still socks to wash, underwear to mend, and shoes to shine. Then the joys of Sunday are completed except—I would rather not write about that.*

*Otherwise, I am in good spirits, because I do what I think is right. If I didn't do that, I would go under. But sometimes I have doubts and if I am not right in something, please tell me. Am I in some things too stern or strict? Am I too sensitive in some things or too harsh?*

*I send hearty greetings. Please write me as soon as possible. An early response is awaited by your friend, Franz*

# A Home of Her Own

Aloisia studied Franz's letter carefully. What should she write back? Though she had never seen his farm, it seemed only sensible that he should stay there and take it over one day. Now that there was finally peace, he must be patient. Family life is never all easy; she had her own problems.

To be sure, a man with his intelligence and training could get a government job with the Department of Agriculture or immigrate to some underdeveloped colony of Britain or France for that matter. A strong young man with his skills, (she remembered him mentioning in Freising that he had even learned welding), had been to agricultural college, and even looked after all his own housework, would certainly succeed as a pioneer anywhere in the world. But to be able to take over a large farm handed to you on a platter? That was not to be thrown away lightly.

Why did he ask in his letter if he were too strict? How could she know? She hardly knew him. Obviously he was concerned about it. But if there is so much work, and fall was that time of year when there was really no end of work to do, one had to be strict. There was no time for indulgence and permissiveness. Maybe that was what he meant.

And what did he mean by 'the joys of Sunday'? That could only mean he had a girlfriend. Curiosity gnawed at her. Should she casually ask what he meant by that expression?

Years ago, Aloisia's parents had decided to build themselves a retirement home in the back garden, just down the lane. The front door and the steps leading to it were in the centre of the house, of course. It had a small entrance hall. On the left there was a kitchen with a corner table. On the right, doors to a small living room and bedroom. From the hall there would be stairs leading to a second floor with three small bedrooms. And of course, a house wasn't a house without a cellar for

## Aloisia

their very own handy store of potatoes, carrots and apples and sauerkraut. The retirement house had everything they needed.

Aloisia knew the house well. After all, she had helped construct it when she was fourteen years old. At the time, building was a new experience for her and she enjoyed the challenge. Aloisia helped dig the cellar, loading the soil onto the wheelbarrow, pushing it and unloading it where it could be stored until it was needed to build a flowerbed or fill low spots in the fields.

Aloisia helped cut the timbers. When the proper time came, Aloisia also carried tubs filled with bricks and mortar up the ladder to the scaffolding. Finally, she carried tiles for the roof.

While the house was being built, the seasons could not be ignored: spring planting, the weeding of peas, beans and spinach in summer, the harvesting of beets in autumn. Only aches, pains and feelings were discounted for if every effort were not made, a loan would have to be made from a moneylender. And that was usually the beginning of the end.

After the house was stuccoed outside and whitewashed inside, shutters painted, Aloisia collapsed from exhaustion. She slept almost night and day for a week but it took nearly two months for her to get back most of her usual strength. It had all been too much; her body couldn't take the strain. With all the excitement of the building project, she hadn't realised she was overexerting herself. The neighbours weren't surprised; they had tried to tell her but she had just laughed away their warnings

Just when the retirement house was completed, however, war was declared. The government leased the new house for lodging prisoners of war. Now the prisoners had gone back to their homes in Russia and Serbia. It was the end of a time that would never come again. Her father had died and the prisoners had asked to dig the grave for 'their German Father'. Sometimes Aloisia still imagined she could still hear the tremulous music of zithers and mandolins carried on the evening air.

Peter was forty years old and finally getting married. He and his wife, Mina, decided that this would be the right time for Aloisia and Dori to move out to the house in the garden.

Flowering shrubs were growing all around it. What more could two spinsters want? Long ago Aloisia's older brothers and sisters had decided that it would be best if Aloisia should not get married, but stay on the farm. Vegetables and fruit from the orchard and potatoes could come from Peter's garden. After all, they were still one family.

Dori was delicate and always seemed to be, well, not what you could call sickly, but frail. The two sisters would be good company for each other. They didn't need to get married. And with those two on the farm there would always be a reason for the older siblings who were establishing families in surrounding cities of Munich, Augsburg, Donawoerth and Wassertruedingen to have access to some fresh farm produce. After all they had worked hard growing up and had been painfully frugal so father could pay off his mortgage first on the farm and then on a small forest. It was well worth the trip home to get a head of cabbage, a few eggs or a pail of milk or honey. They brought their own containers.

After some years, it became apparent that Peter and his wife, Mina, could not have children. There was talk that one of Mina's nieces might come to live with her and Peter. Who knows where that could lead, perhaps to adoption? That situation could cause the Schropp farm to gradually slip into stranger's hands. That was how the threat was always expressed—slip into stranger's hands. Ottiel—that was the niece's name—could inherit the farm some day and then some lucky man would marry her and get everything. It would prove awkward for the Schropp siblings to get produce from the farm they had worked so hard to build up – and pay off. One had to look ahead. One should see the writing on the wall. If Aloisia and Dori would still be on the farm there would be less chance of losing that connection.

If times had been different the two sisters would be getting married. But so many men never came back from the war. With a cosy arrangement like this they wouldn't have to get married anyway. They had everything they needed. And Peter had help for the farm.

Aloisia hoped that with both she and her sister having more

space, there would be fewer problems between them. In fact, the two of them were lucky. How many young women had such an enviable situation? Everyone in the family said it was a very practical idea.

Aloisia painted all the walls. She scrubbed the wood floors and polished them with a special paste made of beeswax and turpentine until they softly reflected the sunlight coming in through the windows.

The sisters used a cart to move their belongings out of what now was Peter and Mina's home to the house in the garden. The slope was slightly down hill so it was easy.

Aloisia slipped the finger of a cotton glove over the curtain rods to prevent them from tearing the old mended lace curtains as she pulled them on. For her own bedroom she made curtains from new material received in exchange for teaching sewing at a neighbourhood village.

When everything was finished she looked around. It was beautiful. The duvets for the feather beds were freshly washed and she stuffed the large square goose and chicken feather pillows into pillowcases she had embroidered herself. On the wall above a little table, hung a thick calendar showing one scene for every three days. She had washed the woven floor mats and hung them over a wooden stile during the last hot days of summer. Now they were fresh and clean and made the area next to her bed warmer for the coming winter.

She would sit down at that table and write a letter to Franz telling him about her new home and her new bedroom.

# Franz is Determined to Leave Germany

*Eggersham,*
*September 15, 1919*

*My dear friend, Luise!*

*Thank you for your dear letter waiting for me after being away for a fortnight. Don't feel too sorry about my terrible situation. I have already resigned myself to my fate and cannot cry anymore, as in the past. The situation is the way it is. Because of the bad experiences I had since returning from Scapa Flow, it is much easier to leave my homeland as it has become its own grave digger of morality and manners. I have been working on going to Argentina for the last two days at the emigration department in Berlin and very likely will be leaving in the not too distant future. I met a young salesman there who has the same opinion as I have. We are both going to work together as partners.*

*On the way home, on the fast train between Berlin and Munich, I met the brother-in-law of the nephew of the famous former agriculturist and author, Schultz-Lupitz. This nephew owns extensive stretches of land and I could probably work as a helper on a large plantation or Estanzsia if I wanted to. The brother-in-law is going to forward further information to me when he gets to Argentina. If my plans work out, I will not take on anything which is against my material well being, let alone my eternal salvation.*

*In Germany, one has to really struggle if he wishes to pull himself out of poverty in an honest manner. And wealthy I certainly am not. The struggle for existence in Germany can become so all consuming that one can be in danger of losing one's clear conscience and then be left with nothing. Look how I have fared so far. Even before my military service, I quickly left a position offered to me because the whole enterprise*

## Aloisia

*was based on a dishonest foundation. In the military I was mistreated because I wasn't bad enough to join the others, a thought which my reasoning refused. At home I experienced one disappointment after the other. Now I am unemployed, possess only the money I saved in the navy, because I had to struggle against opposition to go to agricultural college even though I had to pay the expenses myself. I could go on for hours but I'm not going to because if I do, there won't be time left for me to prepare for my mission. I am just going to try Argentina out. If it's worse there than here I can always come back. In order to rob you of any possibilities of talking me out of this, I should tell you that Argentina is totally Catholic and many Jesuits and Franciscans are working there as teachers.*

*But that's enough talk about emigrating; for now I'm still here. To come back to your letter, I see that you don't take my words as seriously as they were meant to be. Or are you only joking when you write that you are not bothered by people's gossip? You sneaky character. Tell me, why do you always write about your niece, Maria? You are making me so curious that eventually I will want to see her. Best of wishes to Victoria.*

*Your friend, Franz Baumgartner*

*Please answer as soon as possible. But don't get too excited. I am still here.*

# An Oak Leaf Falls

Autumn had arrived, the season for mushrooms of all kinds. Named according to where they were found, their shape, or how they tasted (Pfefferlinge were said to taste as though they had been sprinkled with a little pepper), they now filled the pathways around Ried with their wonderful fragrance. The year's last cutting of hay was drying in winnows. Though the earth radiated back the warmth and fragrances of summer days, cool breezes rustled the remaining blossoms of the linden trees, many of which had been collected and stored for making tea in the winter. A few clusters of black elderberries, which villagers could not reach and birds had not yet found, were glistening among on high branches. Hazelnuts still reached out from forest edges to ripen in the autumn sunshine. The Octoberfest was again underway in Munich, but the farmers in Ried didn't have time for carousels and looking at the famous black Rappen draught horses that pulled the beer wagons.

It was Sunday. There was no need for an umbrella as the rain had virtually stopped and the gusts of wind would have probably have blown it inside out. Brown leaves, which last night's rain had shaken down, were being scattered like small birds across the pathway where Aloisia and Schmid were making their way to their favourite bench under an oak tree. Some children were building a leaf fort. The sky was almost clear. From this vantage point, framed by golden larches, they could see their homes, their church where they both sang in the choir and the school they both once attended. A narrow road softly curved across the rolling hills to other villages and towns. Today, no workers were on the fields; the last haystacks of the season rested quietly.

Only the occasional leaf falling on the forest floor reminded Aloisia that time was passing. She reached into her pocket and took out her watch.

"Let's stay just a little longer," Schmid said, his arm tightening around her shoulders, "It may be raining next Sunday."

Aloisia smiled. "We'll wait for the next leaf to fall and then we really will have to go. We'll see each other again at the dance tonight."

They looked up into the dark green canopy above. Soon a solitary bronze leaf from some high branch spiralled slowly downward. The oak leaf, well-known symbol of strength, peace and consultation, landed right at their feet. It was like a sign from God, a blessing on their love and mutual devotion. They had known each other for so long.

When the war started in 1914, Schmid was the perfect age for conscription, twenty-four. He joined the navy. Aloisia was only eighteen at the time. They had a nodding acquaintance before he left, seeing each other in the choir where they both sang on Sundays and Holy Days but also during the weekly choir practices.

When he came home from the war, Aloisia asked him about his navy experiences. Schmid was glad to talk to someone who asked such provocative questions. Their nodding acquaintance turned into a friendship and then more. He explained about the boiler room where Aloisia had heard men had to shovel coal into the furnace all day and night. That had nothing to do with being a sailor, Schmid answered. There was another crew for those things, another crew for the kitchen work and laundry too. The navy had enough to do navigating into proper positions for targeting the enemy not to mention escaping from being targets of the enemy.

"And what about the signallers," Aloisia asked. "What do they do?"

"Oh, they are in the lookouts. They have to climb a rope ladder to the top of the masthead."

"And wasn't it cold or stormy up there?"

"Well, the crow's nest gives some sort of protection."

"Crow's nest?" Aloisia smiled.

"Yes, it's sort of a shelter and it's high up like a crow's nest on top of a tree and they have a good view of everything up there."

"And how do they signal, Schmid, from way up there?"

"They have to take a special courses to learn the flag alphabet. They can also signal with lights if they take more courses."

"Isn't it lonely being up there?"

"I guess the men who take that job find out soon enough in training if they can take it. Not everyone can be a signaller, you know. You have to have very sharp eyesight and a loud voice for shouting."

"Can't they use binoculars or a megaphone?"

"Sure, but you have to have good eyes and strong vocal chords too."

Schmid had heard that the local mailman occasionally delivered a letter addressed to Aloisia from a Franz Baumgartner, but Aloisia explained that the letters were simply an exchange about beekeeping, a continuation of a platonic friendship which had started at the Freising experimental college in 1916.

At first when Aloisia started spending time with Schmid, her family didn't take it seriously. The two, however, enjoyed each other's company; they talked things over. It was too late for the family to deflect this liaison. Who would have thought that the mayor's son would be attracted to Aloisia. She was too thin and her red hair was certainly no asset. He had so many other chances.

On Sundays, when the collection plate was being passed around the choir loft, Aloisia always smiled at Schmid who sang in the tenor section. He always smiled back – and winked.

Of course this was not a time to get married. They both were responsible. Aloisia's mother was sick. Savings had been wiped out by the runaway inflation. They would have to start saving, again. There was no question of them marrying into the house at the back. Dori would make life miserable. Schmid wouldn't have liked that situation anyway. Aloisia and Schmid were sensible. There was no alternative right now but to wait.

# Unspoken Reproaches

*Eggersham,*
*November 11, 1919*

*My dear friend Luise and Victoria!*

*Forgive me that my letters have been so short lately. Today, I will try to make up for it as much as time permits. It is autumn here too and there is much to do, especially for me as my thoughts are already in the New World. Maybe there have been even more demands made on you during the last few weeks and you have hardly enough time to read, let alone answer.*

*What did you think when I wrote you from the Catholic Day in Munich? You should have been there. Those were days of pure spiritual joy. You really belonged there, and probably would have thought: How does it help a person if he wins the whole world but loses his own soul, instead of sending me sermons by the litre and pound? But don't take me seriously. I am only making fun and in fact I am happy when you in Christian love bring this or that to my attention.*

*If we were only so close together in distance as we are spiritually. We would be good guardian angels for each other, but not seriously. We can be very satisfied with the guardian angels we have, at least I am with mine. He is still very energetic and I like him very much because then I am never alone even if the whole world deserts me. Now, you understand how I can be so carefree about leaving my homeland. I have nobody who looks after my handkerchiefs or underwear and I am still darning my own socks as I did when I was a schoolboy. Poor Franz, what must you still experience before you die. Think of death and you will always have joy because then you cannot sin anymore. As long as I live, however, I will strive with all the honest means at my disposal to get ahead so that the evil world will see that goodness can succeed. May God give me his blessing and mercy so that I will accomplish something substantial!*

*But what do these pious ambitions help? Every day one must pull oneself together to fight his passions. Happy is the one who makes out of all these little successes a final victory.*

*You see I can almost preach as well as you. But what does it help if one knows everything but doesn't do anything? So I am going to stop teaching and switch to practising because words only stir one's spirit but an example excites it. You are probably bored with this childish way of writing and so now I am going to answer the subjects from your letter.*

*So, thank you for your card that you apparently wrote in your elegant bedroom.*

*I would really like to see it so I would know what elegant really means and can see what your taste is like. Then, maybe what would happen, is what happened with me and a lady friend in Munich. We wanted to critique the modern home furnishings while taking a walk. But instead we found so much to talk about that we went past all the windows as though we were blind. So we spent two days without actually really noticing anything.*

*I should now thank Victoria for the hay wagon greeting card from Nordendorf. Really, that Father Thin has a false name because he is not thin but fat and then he seems to be always spying on the hanky panky of other people without realising what unhappiness could come out of it. If he doesn't write to me himself, I will invite myself to visit him if I get a chance.*

*Well, your letter of October 22 is full of subtle understatements and unspoken reproaches regarding my not taking over the farm and staying here. I really don't know what more I can say, but I am listening. What's in it for me if I stay in this hemisphere where God has been dismissed by an entire generation?*

## Aloisia

*What kind of a sister is that Emma? You are always writing about her.*

*Your letter of October 20 is full of loving and tender concern for my hand. It is now completely healed. Yes, who looks after me? You would probably be a good nurse. Wait until I visit you again and I will get sick. For heaven's sake, this almost sounds like an advertisement for marriage. How could I feed a wife and child, me, a poor wanderer in the world? For that, I am at the moment, not courageous enough. Perhaps, before I begin my trip to faraway lands, I will get to Munich and will have a chance to visit your hospitable home and maybe say good bye. I am leaving for sure by next spring, if not even earlier. Only very unusual circumstances could hold me back. If it really becomes impossible for me to see you before my departure, I ask you please not to forget me. And please say an 'Our Father"' for someone whose homeland offered so little. But, I do hope we will get to see each other before I leave.*

*Many hearty greetings,*

*Your friend,*

*Franz*

# The Versailles Treaty

Aloisia put Franz's letter aside. It had been dated on the anniversary of the war's end. The fighting had dragged on, adding a steady flow of names to the casualty lists of many countries. On November 11, 1918, an armistice was finally declared

The peace treaty was signed in the Palace of Versailles a half year later. Two years before, Germany had asked President Woodrow Wilson to arrange a general armistice based on the fourteen points considered necessary for a just peace. But a just peace it was not to be. The German delegation was shocked by the severe terms; it was not the treaty they had expected. The Versailles Treaty turned out to be the beginning of more hardships for German citizens. The assurances given at the time of the armistice had been completely ignored. The odious 'war guilt' clause was the most difficult to accept, but there was no choice.

The terms, simply dictated to the German people, demanded compensation by Germany for all damage done 'by land, sea and from the air' during the war. This could amount to $33,000,000,000. Economists immediately said such a huge sum could not be collected without upsetting international, let alone German, finances. The Allies insisted, however, that Germany pay and the treaty permitted punitive actions to be taken if payments fell behind. The treaty reduced the territory and population of Germany by ten percent.

Secret treaties complicated negotiations. The victors had made promises with Romania, Greece and also to each other even before the war was actually over. Most decisions were made by England, France and the United States

Alsace and Lorraine were returned to France. The Saar Valley was placed under the jurisdiction of the League of Nations. All Germany's overseas colonies, in China and in the Pacific north of the Equator, were given to Japan. In the South Pacific and in East and Southwest Africa, her colonies were given to Britain. Germany's colonies in West Africa, north of the Congo, were given to the French. How could Germany make payments if even their colonies were taken away? It was really impossible.

The reparations, even by many non-Germans, were considered to be unfair – indeed criminal. France's Clemenceau, however, was especially forceful in designing a treaty that would make certain Germany would never have enough strength to wage war again. That included limiting the German army to one hundred thousand, which, to war-weary German families, was a relief. Aloisia could hardly blame Franz for not having the courage, as he wrote, to take on family responsibilities during such times. She and Schmid were in the same situation. And surely she couldn't reproach him for wanting to leave Germany and try pioneer life in Argentina. She, herself, often felt like getting away from all the misery.

The Versailles Treaty came into effect January 10, 1920. Living conditions were getting continually worse. How many rosaries said, how many candles lit, how many masses offered, would be needed to change the terrible events befalling her homeland? Nothing had saved the life of Hans, or the in-laws of many of her married brothers.

When Aloisia's brothers came home to help with the harvest that summer, they also reported from what they read in their local newspapers and the hearsay from their places of employment. There was talk about the threat of a widespread Communist revolution in Germany, similar to the Russian revolution. Many alienated ex-soldiers living in Munich hated the terms of the Versailles treaty, but wanted nothing to do with Communism. Some had formed the German Worker's Party. Newspapers reported that their public meetings usually ended up with a brawl caused by disruptive Communists.

That spring in the Landtag, a large meeting hall in Munich, Hitler, a newcomer to the political scene, had outlined twenty-five points that were to be the party's political platform. Some points, like the rejection of the Treaty of Versailles, were unanimously popular. Other points, such as that all income not earned by work should be confiscated and that there should be a thorough reconstruction of the national education system, seemed logical. That a strong central government for the execution of effective legislation was necessary was also obvious to a hungry, unemployed populace.

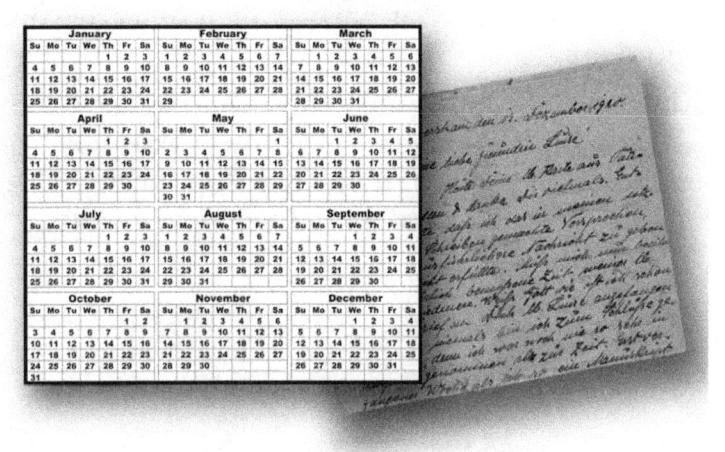

The party adopted an ancient symbol for its flag, a symbol that had been used throughout history by Celts, Buddhists, Greek and Native Americans. It was in the form of a cross with the ends of the arms bent at right angles in a clockwise direction. The Hindus, in the Sanskrit, called it a Swastika. It was to bring good fortune.

The term Nationalist Socialist was added. The party was now officially called the Nationalist Socialist German Workers' Party.

When members of the same family had several different political leanings it was difficult to have a peaceful meal together. Sometimes, even brothers could not sit down at the same table without vigorous arguments ruining a good dinner with one of them getting up and walking out the door. In some cases the sons had to make arrangements to be home at different times to avoid spoiling the meals, meagre as they already were.

## Aloisia

Aloisia's family was unanimously opposed to Communism. Most German citizens agreed that the National Socialists had some good points. That party promised jobs for everyone and the end of starvation. It was said that if you attended their meetings you could get a good bowl of soup. Where did that party get the ingredients? Where did they get the money to rent their meeting places? Even though the mark was so devalued, halls still cost money. The National Socialists seemed to manage well. The Vatican seemed to be closing their eyes to any problems. After all that party was an effective opposition to Communism.

Most in the Schropp family, however, weren't looking for any drastic political changes. Somehow, some way, the happy situation existing in Germany before the war would return, if everybody just worked hard and stayed levelheaded.

# Unsettled Times

*Eggersham,
December 13, 1920*

*My dear friend Luise!*

*Today your dear card arrived from Tannhausen and I thank you very much. Please excuse me for not writing in more detail as I promised in the last note I sent you. Now I must rush and dedicate some of my limited time to you, my dear friend. Only God knows how many times I've started a letter to you, dear Luise, but I never could finish it as I have never had so many demands made of me as at the present time.*

*Only last week when I was halfway through one of those letters, I received mail from someone which, among other things, said a devoted admirer is taking a lot of your time and then I thought 'one shouldn't disturb lovers or try to influence them in any way.' I did that once before with the best intentions. I think that people who are anxious to marry usually feel themselves above good or bad. But I believe you, my friend, are an exception to this. I thought, Luise is smart enough and it is better for the time being if I don't write at all. I will remain quiet about her happiness because I had recently the following experience with another lady friend, which embarrassed me very much.*

*Miss M. sent regards to me through her brother and invited me to visit her as soon as possible, as she wanted to speak with me before she married Mr. N, a man whom I knew. I realised for the first time how close we had become and was very shocked. But I took hold of myself and said to myself: "Let them be happy together. Our Lord certainly knows what is best. Go and celebrate with her and don't be envious." But what an experience I had when I arrived! The girl was completely changed. All of a sudden she couldn't stand her boyfriend anymore, didn't want to think of marriage anymore, wanted to have only me without really having come to any decision and all this eight days before the wedding day. I don't want to say anymore. You can imagine that one takes something like this to heart. Excuse me if I have been too open with you. It is my most interesting experience since my last correspondence with you.*

*Now to come back to your questions, I have only good news. I am not mad at you, as you seem to think. On the contrary, I would be delighted if I could meet you and talk with you again. Maybe it would work out one time when you go to Munich. It is really such a shame that we live so far apart from each other. You could certainly come to our area and visit us. My mother sends her hearty greetings and said I should invite you to come to our place one day. She thinks very highly of you and enjoys reading your letters.*

*Much has altered since I have come back to my family home. We are still in the middle of the heaviest work with rebuilding and preparations. Next year we are building across the road a massive building 15 m long and 8 m wide and about 7 m high. It will consist of three rooms, work place, big drying oven, storage for wood, machine shed, livestock and farm wagon scales and above all else, two big grain silos for future business in seed grain. Granite and building bricks, lumber, roof tiles and also some sand are already here. I could really use you here. Every day I could use your advice and instruction. In 1922 we will build stalls for pigs, chickens, geese, sheep, a cellar for potatoes and a toilet in the house. The kitchen for butchering pigs is already complete. We are now working on the bathroom, laundry as well as paddocks, and enclosures for livestock. Hoof and Mouth disease was widespread but we got through without any loss of livestock. We are all healthy and doing well.*

*Since our last time together I have changed a lot; I have lost weight, but have gained enormously in strength.*

## The Making of a Frontier Woman

*To answer your question, I never was a bad sailor or had reason to regret my actions. The rumour is going around that I had deafening vocal chords. I have to admit that is true, but one sometimes needs a loud voice to call out into the wasteland. Nowadays one needs a little spunk.*

*That is all for today and you must be content with my bad writing and should also write to me quickly, touch on several points and share with me how everything is going with you.*

*Meanwhile I'm asking you again not to write so carefully, just write quickly from the heart and give a long answer.*

*I greet you heartily in sincere friendship,*

*Franz Baumgartner*

*Please leave out your abbreviations. I have no time to figure them out.*

## 1921

*Eggersham,*
*January 14, 1921*

*My dear friend Luise!*

*My sincere thanks for you dear letter of 7.1.21. I took your advice, which I think was well-meant, and have also written a letter to Victoria. Unfortunately my mother does not want to send anything by mail and I must, considering the unsettled times, agree with her. She really wishes that the food be picked up personally. I can promise that in three weeks you could have 15 pounds flour, 55 eggs, 2 pounds lard and 5 pounds dried prunes. I have given your sister the most reasonable prices. This would actually be a good opportunity for you to see my home and give us a chance to talk together. I have also written Victoria that you should both come together. So, what did Victoria tell you about me after she was here at Christmas? Please write me honestly.*

*I was very surprised when I read your letter in what high regard you hold me, certainly much higher than I am worth. I have also been thinking of you a lot, but what good is it when I can't even think of marrying for at least four years. Until then many things can change and to me it seems irresponsible if I would tie someone down and actually be an obstacle to their future happiness. So I have a long time to improve myself in order to make a loving, virtuous, and capable woman truly happy.*

*The words of my sister, who is two years younger, come to mind just now. Last week she said the following to me: "The woman who has to take you one day is certainly not to be envied. She doesn't need any money, but she should first keep house for you a little while so she can see if she could stand you." The evaluation of this sisterly criticism I must leave to you. I must add, however, that there may well be some truth in what she says. My sister also coined these significant words: "Love does not exist. All is pretence, appearance and exploitation."*

*It really hurts me when I hear such words because I love the whole world and would love my wife even more. And then someone tells me that there is no such thing as love. But, unfortunately, I cannot undertake such a responsibility for four years and until then I will really have to work very hard and become a good and virtuous human being. Oh, we poor earth dwellers often convince ourselves that we understand things and often do not even have the grace of recognising our own deficiencies.*

---

*Dear Luise, you ask me if I am in such intimate correspondence with the other girl. I do not know if you mean that certain act. I can assure you that I have never, even as a sailor, touched a girl without permission, not to mention that final act which I would be ashamed of if there was a woman somewhere, whom I didn't even know yet, that I might marry one day.*

*Dear Luise, why are you so interested in these confessions of mine? No girl has ever asked me about such things. But you do not have to be embarrassed about it. Ask me anything that comes to your mind. Perhaps we will get to see each other again and have a good talk. Perhaps you will come for a visit. Please reply as soon as possible. Best wishes from my mother and also from me to your mother.*

*In friendship, Franz Baumgartner*

---

*Eggersham,
February 10, 1921*

*My dear friend Luise!*

*My letter and postcard dated Monday will probably already be in your dear hands. When your sister, Victoria, comes home on Saturday she will report in more detail if and how she liked my home. I wish so much that I could be with you on those first few days. But we are all so overburdened with work that I dare not even think of escaping from here. Perhaps in the fall it will once again be possible to visit you when I am doing a retreat. If Victoria tells me when that retreat is in advance, as she promised, this arrangement can be made. I am already very curious about your next letter and think about it all the time. I am especially happy that you are going to come to visit and I ardently desire a candid discussion with you. Victoria will certainly tell you much about me and she might especially allude to my silence. I cannot actually think of any time when such a depressed state of mind overcame me as during her visit. The big fires caused by arson in the surrounding region and my overindulgence in cigarettes are probably partly to blame. It was as though a great change had taken over my feelings and thoughts. Your sister was good enough to try to influence me and I am also curious to know how well I have got into her good favour.*

*Victoria borrowed a book from me entitled, 'The Ideal Married Life'. It is very well written and the church would agree with it. I saw it by chance in Kleister, by Passau and bought it because I had always wanted to own such a book recommended by ecclesiastical authors. The thoughts expressed in it are very nice and full of information. But nevertheless such a lecture is never without danger and I think one should only read it in the state of grace and it should be regarded as a healing counterbalance to the sufferings of Christ or one could easily fall into serious, most dangerous temptations. If Victoria reads this she will probably say once again, "That Franz writes like a Capuchin Father." But you will just have to believe me because about such things I am a great fighter, but a small victor. It is a thousand times better if people do not read such things at all unless they are serious and not only doing so out of curiosity or lust. Therefore, dear Aloisia, I pray with all my heart that you take my advice.*

*That's all for today. When Victoria comes back home she will solve some of the most difficult questions about me that you have been puzzling about. The solution of these conundrums with other noteworthy garnishes I await with a calm heart.*

*With many hearty greetings from your sincere, true friend,*

*Franz Baumgartner*

*Many greetings to your dear mother and Victoria.*

## The Making of a Frontier Woman

*Eggersham,*
*March 7, 1921*

*Dear Friends Aloisia and Victoria*

Vielen Dank fuer Euer Brieflein,
*Many thanks for your short letter*

Das ich juengst erhalten hab
*Which I just received.*

Aber ach, es grub der Hoffnung
*But alas, it dug without pity*

Schonungslos ein fruehes Grab.
*An early grave for my hopes.*

Frauelein Luise bleibt wohl ferne
*Miss Luise remains far away*

Trotzdem sie's Wort gegeben hat
*Even though she gave her word.*

Und ich sah sie hier so gerne,
*And I wanted her here so dearly,*

Wuenschte ihren guten Rat.
*Wished from her some good advice.*

Moechte gar ihr Herz ergrunden
*Would indeed like to explore her heart*

An sie stellen manche Frag
*Ask of her many questions.*

Ich ahn, sie wuerde sicher finden
*I believe she would find a solution*

Den Weg durch manche Lebenslag.
*For all life throws at us.*

An Keiner haengt bis jetzt mein Herze
*My heart 'til now is not attached*

Mit Liebe, die sich brauetlich nennt.
*With love that could be called committed.*

## Aloisia

Wie will der Mensch auch gleiches finden,
*How can anyone find a match*

Wenn er sich noch nicht selber kennt?
*When he doesn't know himself?*

Freund und Freundin braucht ein jedes
*Everybody needs someone*

Das fuehrerlos verlassen blieb
*To give guidance and company*

Es bebt und seufzt manch junge Seele
*Many a young person's soul beats and sighs*

O hilf mir doch und hab mein Lieb.
*Oh help me and take my love.*

Auch ich ging einst wie ein Verstossner
*Once I also, like one rejected*

Recht und Wahrheit suchend fort.
*To search for justice and truth,*

Lernt mit Fleiss und Gottvertrauen
*Learned with diligence and trust in God*

Gutes an manch fremden Ort
*Good things in faraway places.*

Fand ich dann bescheidne Tugend
*When I found modest virtue*

Die nur weist der Weisheit Bahn
*Which only wisdom can procure.*

Fing ich ohne lang Bedenken
*Without much premeditation*

Harmlos ein Geplauder an.
*I started an innocent conversation.*

Forschte dann in fremden Augen
*Then I searched in stranger's eyes*

Ob mich niemand denn versteht
*Doesn't anyone grasp what I mean?*

## The Making of a Frontier Woman

Selten fand ich mich verstanden,
*Seldom was I understood.*

Niemand dem es schlechter geht.
*Nothing could be worse for anyone.*


Koennt ihr halb und halb verstehen
*Can you understand even half way*

Was sich in meinem Innern regt
*What moves me deep inside?*

Es glaettet sich die Kummerfalte
*The worried lines on my brow will*

Wenn Euch dieser Vers bewegt.
*Disappear if this poem moves you.*


Nun ja ich kam auf grosse Umweg
*Well, I came with a great detour*

Wieder in mein Vaterhaus
*Once again to my father's house*

Auch Viktoria hats gesehen
*Victoria has seen it too*

Was wird alles werden draus?
*What will become of it all?*


Frei und sonnig, schoen gelegen
*A good location, open and sunny*

Ungestoert vom Weltenlauf
*Undisturbed by the world's turmoil,*

Wird hier mit des Hoechsten Segen
*Here everything is with God's blessings*

Alles huebsch und nett und traut.
*Beautiful, sweet and secure.*


Nach dem Land voll Milch und Honig
*Once I searched afar for the land*

Sah ich frueher fragend aus
*Full of milk and honey.*

## Aloisia

Und heute sagen die Autoren
*And today the Luise and Dori say*

"Es ist ja doch dein Vaterhaus."
*"Afterall it is your parents home."*

Getreide liefert hoechste Ernten
*Corn produces highest yield*

Viel Obst gedeiht in milder Luft.
*Fruit flourishes in warm breezes*

Vom Vieh gibts hier die besten Herden,
*Animals here are from the best herds.*

Die Bien schwelgt in Bluetenduft.
*Bees revel in the fragrant air.*

Und wonnig, gottesnah und traut
*And blissfully, trusting in God's presence*

Klingt auch der lieben Voegel Laut.
*Sounds the lovely chirping of birds*

Jedes Maueslein hat sein Nest,
*Every little mouse has its nest*

Ich sorgt fuer Hoehren allerbest.
*I pray for heaven's best blessing.*

Damit man nah zum Himmel hat,
*And so we can be close to heaven*

So ist der Kirchweg weit.
*So is the way to church long.*

Es hat schon oft mein Muarterl gsagt,
*My mother often said to me,*

"Gelt, Franz, dos is recht gscheit."
*"Franz, isn't that as it should be?"*

So wie Ihr recht ists nicht gefehlt
*What suits her can't be wrong.*

Wenn d' Luise einmal kommt
*If Luise comes one day*

## The Making of a Frontier Woman

Und selber sieht wies hier bestellt
*And sees the situation here for herself*

Wer weiss wozu es frommt.
*Who knows how that would help?*

Wenn ich die Bedenken wuesst
*If I knew the concern*

Welche Luise fernhelt
*That keeps Luise far away*

Wurde sie in Reihenfolge
*I would list a whole row of reasons*

Klar und deutlich aufgezaehlt.
*Evident and clear.*

Wars das Zoegern meines Schreibens?
*Was it the delay in my writing?*

Wars das Schweigen meiner Zunge?
*Was it the silence of my tongue?*

Trennen Sprache oder Grenzen?
*Is it speech or boundaries that separate?*

Bin wohl noch ein dummer Junge.
*Am really still a dumb boy.*

Kann wohl nicht das Glueck ergreifen?
*Can't I seize happiness*

Ob es wohl ein solches ist?
*But is there such a thing?*

Wenn der Mensch eh es gereifet
*Can a person, still not mature*

Jugendfreiheit schon vergisst.
*Give up the freedom of youth?*

Bin wohl so ein ernster Streber,
*Am I such a sincere seeker*

Nur nach Gottes Wort und Reich?
*Only after God's Word and Kingdom?*

## Aloisia

Will nicht teilen unsere Felder
*Do not wish to share our fields*

Und Ihr meint es war so leicht!
*And you think it should be easy!*

Kann nicht in Eurer Naehe Weilen
*Cannot linger in your presence*

Wie es meine Sehnsucht ist,
*As would be my heart's desire.*

Will mich auch nicht sehr beeilen
*Do not wish to be hasty either*

Ich stoert Euch ja im Paradies.
*And disturb you in paradise.*

Es wird bei uns auch mal nett
*One day it will be good here too.*

Man nennt es jetzt schon Nazareth
*People already call it Nazareth*

Doch Gott weiss wann vom Krankenbett
*But God only knows when happiness*

Glueck und Frieden aufersteht.
*And peace will arise from its sickbed.*

Zum Glueck, ich mag wetten drauf
*With luck, I'd like to wager*

Frisst Unfriede sich selber auf
*That discord devours itself.*

Dann kommt wohl suesse Friedenszeit
*Then certainly sweet peace will come*

Und schenkt mir Jugendseeligkeit.
*And gives me youthful happiness.*

~ Fz. Baumg

# The Making of a Frontier Woman

*Eggersham,*
*March 14, 1921*

*My dear friend!*

*A week of hard work has passed until I could find time to close this letter and give you a summary. Forgive me the length of this letter, which I give you in a different form this time. I would like to ask you to use merciful standards of criticism when reflecting and judging what I have written. It is bitter truth mixed with humour and a little irony. But I would like to hear your judgement.*

*Today I went to confession. Will try to mail this letter as soon as possible. Hoping to see you again,*

*Your Franz Baumgartner*

*My sister Kathie is feeling better but is not going to Munich,*

*We have 14 live piglets. Tomorrow there is a big market here for livestock breeders.*

---

*Munich,*
*March 26, 1922*

*My dear friend!*

*My sincere thanks for your letter. I was worried that you didn't think favourably of me anymore. Why have you been silent for so long? Was that Victoria's idea or were you sick? Why do you regret that you didn't creep into a cloister? Is it so difficult to have an admirer? Actually, I don't think one should have a long engagement. This view was previously put forward in Moedishofen. What do your relatives think today? Aloisia, I don't think you suit the cloistered life. You will just have to worry and work as I have*

## Aloisia

*to. With a good man you will certainly be happy. If we could see each other again and could talk, I would be very happy. Every day, I wish you were with me at school. Here we get to know about the whole turn of world events and learn to judge it from the Christian point of view. Among both the female and male students there is often much to quarrel about. I believe that we two would be united and support each other. I have used all my savings and sold some of my belongings so I could attend this college but have never been sorry for it. It is a blessing to one's heart when you can look behind previously concealed mysteries.*

*I learn all about world affairs and I can judge human life much differently and come closer to my God. Not only for body and soul but also for practical life, one can learn so much that the expenses incurred are repaid many times over. I made good use of Mardi Gras by studying. From my collected insights, my verdict is that the essential information and principal truths are all in the catechism. That, you still certainly know by heart. If you have any doubts you can present them to your trusted friend. I probably don't know you as well as your admirer but you can still give me your full confidence. Just write me. I have been offered my family's farm again. I am supposed to take it over in three and one half years but I can't make up my mind to go back into slavery again. School is over in June. I will then travel again doing jobs here and there to get experience and support myself or I might go to South America. I am not so sad about you anymore as I think you just can't express yourself very well. Please write me again soon. If there is anything that isn't clear then please just write me.*

*Now I really should answer your questions. If we don't see each other this time then I hope it is God's will that we will meet another time. I still cannot believe that we don't see each other more often. If you have as much patience with me as I have to have with you, we will surely understand each other better.*

*Am I right in thinking that you are not fluctuating*

*so much anymore about whether or not you should get married? I also see so much that is bad, false, heartless and unpleasant in most of womankind. That does not deter me from continuing to strive to acquire something better.*

*I know that our God loves us and hope and trust that everything will turn out for the best. Don't you think so, dearest Luise? You are still praying for me, aren't you? I am also doing the same for you. I always think you are inconsolable and forsaken and misunderstood by everybody. I like you and don't want my letters to burden you. Look, I am a human being, just like you are, and have nobody. I believe that if we had a chance to really talk this out we would have understood each other long time ago. That takes more than just a couple of hours, as my mother seems to think. The longer we have to wait to see each other again, the warmer and lovelier it will be outside in nature. I am organising my things more and more and this gives me more courage and joy. At the same time my savings are growing.*

*You should also take some advice and not work so hard. All the zest for life and courage of your best years will slip by. I don't believe your brothers do as much as you do or they would not have strength left to criticize you.*

*Dear Luise! Hold on to your freedom and your rights. I do not like it when you called me strict and righteous. One has to be like that or one goes under and that would be the last straw. I didn't use to be like that. As it was when I went to agricultural college, my family isn't paying anything for tuition. If I spend over 8 marks a day I will not make it through. The week after next all of us students are going on a retreat.*

*Many greetings from Franz Baumgartner*

# Mangels

Aloisia was alternately dumping mangels into the hopper and cranking the handle. The words in Franz's last letter monopolised her thoughts 'zest for life', 'your best years', 'zest for life', 'your best years' repeated themselves in her mind as she turned the crank around and around and watched the slices fall onto the pile of wheat chaff on the floor. What did 'zest for life' mean? She was too exhausted to even imagine it.

Finally, she stopped cranking and reached for a shovel. She started mixing the sliced mangels back and forth with the wheat chaff to make fodder for the cows. Back and forth, back and forth, 'cloistered life', 'hold on to your rights'. What rights? Back and forth, 'cloistered life', back and forth, back and forth.

This was the last of the winter mangels; they usually lasted to this time, the end of March. No more hauling them in from the storage pile on the field. During the war, when there was a shortage of men, she herself had to fork them on to the wagon. That was back breaking work. Now Oscar, her nephew, did it or one of her brothers gave a hand when he came home to help.

Every year Aloisia wished that something would happen in the coming year so she would never have to do this job again. After all, she was twenty-six years old. But every year, there she was, cranking the handle again.

She shovelled the fodder into two pails, lifted the handles and made the first trip of the evening to the feeding troughs. The cows had already eaten their hay and were starting to chew their cuds but when she threw this mixture into their troughs, they slurped it up with their long tongues almost as quickly as it was dumped. This was the best part of their evening meal.

How lucky the ox and cows were. They weren't even aware that these mangels were the last of the year. Cows didn't experience joy or anxiety. She scratched the haunches of

## The Making of a Frontier Woman

Goldie, her favourite cow. What a peaceful life she had. If only her own life could be so simple, so uncomplicated. If only Schmid could find a way to start their lives together.

Sometimes, however, she envied the nuns. They didn't seem to have any worries. They were cared for all their life. No waistbands to take in or let out, nice loose clothing. No worry about where to place a broach so it would not make a hole. Yes, that must be a wonderful life – regardless of what Franz wrote.

She would write Franz and send some gingerbread made with her own honey. That would be a nourishing snack for any student. And some dried apples and prunes still left from winter. He was obviously just scraping by with his money, but how lucky he was to arrange to study in Munich!

She could not imagine herself ever being able to do that. Even though Franz had so little money, somehow, he was free. Of course, he was a man.

*Cows drinking in the stream, Kuebach, where Aloisia often washed her feet*

# A Long Liaison

*May 17, 1922*

*My dear Friend!*

*I could only answer your caring letter today because of all the studying. Thank you for all your news and nourishing treats. I am happy that you are healthy and that generally everything is going well. That a long liaison must be terrible, especially for a girl, I readily understand. I certainly couldn't bear it myself and that is why I will not take such a step unless I could count on a marriage in the near future. In God's name, I hope everything will turn out right for you. I will pray for you at Holy Communion, but please also pray for me sometime.*

*Everything is going well with me and I am satisfied. I am now used to the frugal living. In fact, it makes me feel very good and I have resolved to stay frugal even later when times are better as it is healthy for ones body and soul. School is over on the 24th of June and I am very pleased with what I have learned. I could easily get employment but don't want to so I can remain a free man and be independent. The very last thing that I want is a government job.*

*Our seaside retreat at Kochel was very useful to me. Now I have finally stopped smoking. I cannot, unfortunately, share the facts of the gossip you referred to concerning Scheufeles. At the time there was so much said by everybody about everybody that even today I still have my head full without knowing who had the least blame. Be glad that you don't know everything that was said. I still believe you the most, though you were painted quite black once by somebody. But let us put all that aside.*

## The Making of a Frontier Woman

*At the end of June I will make myself ready to travel to Buenos Aires where I will try to make myself self-supporting in agriculture.*

*I wish you a very happy future and I send you in friendship the heartiest greetings,*

*Franz Baumgartner*

*I have received a loan of 15,000 marks from home for travelling.*

# Being Practical

Schmid pressed down on the latch and pushed open the back door. He could smell the aroma of coffee or, to be more exact, chicory. Coffee was not available these days. He heard the sound of voices as he approached the kitchen.

"... he's coming. Sh, just...."

It was time to start the evening chores and it was a little late for the family to be sitting around the built-in corner table but there they were: his father and mother, his older brother with his wife and child, his sister.

"Aha! You're here!" It was his father's standard greeting, as though he was surprised to see him, or as if he had been hiding somewhere. Today he added, "Thought maybe a wild boar got you. Ha, ha." (Sometimes the greeting was, "You are here," as if it were a wonder that Schmid could spare some time for his family.) "We were just talking about you."

His sister coughed.

"Really?" Schmid said, giving nods to everyone and looking around the room. The cough was his sister's signal that something needing a careful reaction was in the air.

"We were just saying...," His father's voice trailed off, "Sit down. Sit down, son."

Schmid pulled a chair up to the table. His mother reached for the coffeepot and filled the empty cup that was waiting for him. She passed him the jug of milk and set what was left of the prune cake in front of him. The eyes of his family were all focused on Schmid.

His father cleared his throat. "Well, son, have you ever really thought seriously about your future?"

Schmid looked around at the concerned faces. "Is this supposed to be some kind of joke? I think about it all the time. Just this afternoon, when Luise and I...."

"Well, well, don't get excited," his father interjected, "You can't just think, you have to take action, you know, action that is down to earth for a...."

His mother put her hand to her mouth and coughed. She reached across the table to pick a few crumbs off the table.

"And if one plan doesn't seem to work you have to try another. You know you're thirty-one. Right? Before you know it, you'll be forty. When I was your age, your mother and I were long married and had a few children."

Schmid felt a lump in his throat. First of all, he was still thirty. Secondly, he worked on the farm day in and day out in a very sensible, down to earth way. When his father was young the economy was booming, not like these days. He opened his mouth to reply but noticed his mother give a barely perceptible shake of the head and her eyes had an anxious look.

His father continued. "You know the Meyers. They're getting old and finding it difficult to manage their farm."

Schmid nodded. The Meyers lived a few minutes away, not far from the back of the community hall.

"Well...," His father paused.

"Well?" Schmid looked around for a clue from some member of his family but each one only smiled, nodded or turned towards his father.

"Well, you know their daughter Sophie? She's a good girl, woman, I should say. She works hard at home but there's only so much a woman can do by herself. You know Mr. Meyers has rheumatism so bad now he can hardly bend over sometime, let alone pick things up. What they need on that farm is a strong, young man around the place."

Schmid had never paid much attention to Sophie. Of course, he saw her at church and Sunday night dances at the inn. And yes, he remembered how Luise and he had sort of nudged each other once when they noticed how short she wore her skirt. You could almost see her ankles. It might be excused if she was working in the field or watering the cows but it had been a Sunday.

Maybe she didn't know better, maybe the dress really belonged to her older sister, maybe.... Yes, Schmid had seen Sophie here and there. Their families were never close or anything like Aloisia's mother was to his mother. She wasn't in the choir like Aloisia. But of course he knew Sophie.

His father shifted in his chair. "You know, whoever marries Sophie Meyers will be a lucky man, a very lucky man. He'll get the Meyers farm. Their eldest son is still missing in Russia, God rest his soul and Mrs. Meyer has made very pointed comments to your mother of how happy she would be to have such an intelligent and strong man like you for a son-in-law. And when your mother mentioned to Peter, just in passing of course, what a great help it would be if you ever married onto the Meyer's farm, Peter seemed very enthusiastic about the idea. He didn't mention that there was any commitment between you and Luise."

"What?" Schmid's mouth dropped open, "Peter didn't say anything?"

"That's right. Peter didn't say a word. Luise's name didn't even come up. Obviously she's not all that serious about you or Peter would have made some comment."

"Father, you know Luise and I are going together. Everybody knows that. We just spent the whole afternoon together."

"Well, anyway, there doesn't seem to be any obstacle as far as Peter is concerned. What a stroke of luck and in these miserable times! And just think! You'd be right next door. You and Sophie are both old enough. That's for sure, so...," his father paused. "What do you think?"

Schmid pushed back his chair and got up. "And what about Luise? We've been going together for ages. This, this Sophie and I, we haven't a thing in common. Anyway, Luise and I have an understanding. Peter just wants Luise to help on his farm and not get married. He would be glad if I were out of the picture."

"Mmm, but you've never asked Luise to marry you? In so many words, I mean?"

"How could I in these times?" Schmid's voice was getting

louder. "Where would we live? What could we live off?"

"Just calm down," his father interjected, "We know all your problems and they could be solved."

"But Luise and I have an understanding."

"That Luise is a wonderful woman, a good worker, from a great family. But what future is there in your relationship? It's been limping along forever, but there's nowhere for it to go. Luise is the youngest of a big family. She'll be lucky if they can scrape a dowry together for herself."

Schmid looked at his mother. "Luise has already bought herself a sewing machine, top of the line, from money she's saved from teaching needlework, and..."

"Yes," his mother nodded, "It's a beauty, a portable Excella. I've seen it."

"That's very nice," Schmid's father interrupted, "The Schropps are all hard workers and frugal too, no doubt about it. But a farm she'll never get. Peter has it and even if he can't have children there are ten other Schropps waiting in line. Unless, of course, if he adopts. You can see I've thought of everything. Your mother and I have talked all about it." He raised his hand with his palm towards the others in the room. It was a familiar gesture meaning he wouldn't accept any more input.

Thoughts raced through Schmid's mind. When he turned twenty-four the war had just broken out. He had his eye on a girl at the time but then he joined the navy and she moved away.

By sheer luck, Schmid survived the battle of Jutland but his ship was one of the eleven lost. Statistics said there were 1545 men lost on the German side. That didn't count injuries. There were fourteen British vessels sunk, including their flagship, the Hood. The British had lost over 6000 men. Haunting images from sea battles appeared in his dreams, images about reaching his hand out to someone, but the hand disappearing or how he himself was almost rescued, but then the lifeboat coming to get him drifted away into the mist. Even when he was awake the horrors he had witnessed shrouded his mind at the most unusual times, like now. He couldn't help it. He knew he should be grateful for coming back alive, and not crippled in some way.

Next, his meagre savings became worthless with runaway inflation, which was still raging. The war had swallowed up the years when he could have been apprenticing or studying for a career. There were no jobs anyway. His father often said it was impossible to believe how prosperous Bavaria had been during the decades preceding the war. Yes, under these circumstances Schmid was lucky that he could stay at home on the farm where there was always something to eat. Nothing fancy, but one would never starve. Of course, his family needed him. But, nevertheless, he was lucky too. He had to admit it. He wasn't wandering city streets dying of complications from malnutrition like so many of his countrymen. He and Aloisia had an understanding that they would marry some day when times were better.

"These are tough times," his father's voice echoed Schmid's thoughts. "Now, more than ever, when it comes to something as important as marriage, you have to make a very sensible decision. You and Luise sort of drifted together but...." He stood up and gave Schmid a pat on his shoulder, an almost unprecedented familiarity. "Think about it. You know, son, we all have our fantasies," his father continued, "But I don't have to tell you again, these are difficult times, unusual times. You have to be smart and," he added with a wink, "You have to be lucky."

Schmid looked around the room and wiped his mouth with the back of his hand. It was pointless to say more. His family looked like strangers to him, even worse. They were obviously all in agreement, just smiling and commenting on his good prospects. Of course, it would be great for them. But what should he tell Aloisia? He got up, looked out the window and then sulked off towards the door.

"Where are you going?" his father called.

Schmid glanced over his shoulder "It's time to milk the cows. Is that practical enough?" The door banged loudly behind him and you could hear the sound of his wooden clogs walking through the implement storage area to the barn.

## The Making of a Frontier Woman

As Aloisia strode swiftly up the moonlit incline and crossed the road to the community hall, she heard the sound of a polka. Schmid saw her immediately as she entered the door and walked over to her. With his usual little bow and outstretched hand, he asked her to dance. He clasped his hands around her waist and she rested her hands lightly on his shoulders. Around the floor they danced finding spaces here and there among the other couples. Regardless of the troubles in the world or in their lives, Sunday night was for relaxing. Those who were not dancing gave approving nods, tapping their feet to the music. A schuhplattler in his leather shorts was crouching around the hem of a girl's circling dirndl.

Some onlookers, it is true, wore black and were dreaming of the sweetheart or husband in whose arms they too once circled around the room. Mourning was as intrinsic a part of their lives as laughing had once been. A neighbour, trying to be kind, had coaxed them by telling them it wasn't good to always stay home in their four walls.

*View from choir loft of richly ornamented main altar. All the Schropp children were baptised and received first communion in this church known as the "Pfarrkirche Ried"*

## Aloisia

The accordion player started to play a Straus waltz. Aloisia and Schmid swung in wide loops around the floor. Aloisia was in heaven. She loved dancing, and dancing with Schmid was best of all. He was a great dancer. Spirits were high; some young man, with an edelweiss insert on his leather suspenders, was trying his yodel. Schmid's shoulders seemed a little tense, however, and he didn't smile and nod at the people around the room as he usually did.

Finally, the musicians took a break. The piano player stacked up his music and the accordion player slipped out of his harness. The trumpeter, who had taken the place of the one that didn't come back from France, was waving to a young girl. There was only one drummer now. All four were glad for the rest and a jug of beer.

Schmid squeezed Aloisia's hand and, with his head gestured towards the door, a mannerism Aloisia loved. As usual, she followed him outside. They stepped out into the cool night air and walked directly to the bench they sat on so many times before, where the moonlight filtered through the surrounding foliage. The moon was shining in an almost cloudless sky. They saw a shooting star.

He took both of her hands in his. "Luise, you can never guess what happened when I got home from our walk today. My family all were waiting in the living room. They want me to get married."

"Oh, Schmid," Aloisia lowered her eyes and felt the blood rushing to her face.

He cupped her face in his the palms of his hands and looked deep into her eyes, "But not to you, dearest, not to you, Luise."

She smiled, not fathoming the seriousness of the situation. She knew his mother and father liked her. "What are you saying?"

"It's just that, well times are just impossible and…well, there's a family who is interested in having me marry their daughter. Her mother made it very clear, told my mother straight out."

"Is this some sort of joke?" Aloisia frowned. "What family? What girl?"

## *The Making of a Frontier Woman*

"You know them, right in this village," Schmid shook his head as though he couldn't believe it himself, "Sophie, the Meyers girl."

Aloisia laughed softly in disbelief. "Her? The one we know? Remember what we said?"

"Yes, yes. I know she's...there's no comparison."

"And...and what did you say?"

"Well, I didn't know what to say."

"What?" Aloisia said, "What did you say, Schmid?" she repeated touching his arm.

"No, no. I didn't mean it like that. I said we were very serious, you and I."

Aloisia relaxed a little.

"Of course," Schmid continued, "They knew all that, but they said you and I have no future. You know, we've talked about it. How we'd make a living, the farm business and all, practical reality."

Aloisia shook her head in disbelief.

He shrugged his shoulders. "What can I do? I would be close to my parents and be able to help them."

Aloisia always prided herself in not chasing men like some of the village girls, flaunting themselves. Flirting. She had seen many a young man caught only to be miserable and then make his wife miserable too. In fact, that's what Franz had said he had first noticed about her. She was dignified. She liked that about herself too.

Schmid looked intently into her face. "What should I do?" he repeated.

Her body stiffened. "Do what is right, do what is sensible," the words popped out of her mouth before she realised it. Aloisia had said these same words before, when people had confided in her. This advice seemed to help them make the choice that was best for the situation, at least she always thought it had helped. The words seemed wise for almost any situation. Now, however, the words left a hollow feeling in her chest. They were unsatisfying, so hypocritical. She bit her lip.

## Aloisia

Her throat was tight. "God's will is my will," she said.

Schmid sighed, "You don't seem to mind all that much. Has that Baumgartner fellow maybe asked you to marry him?"

"No, it's nothing like that. He's just a friend who writes about his beekeeping and his travels and experiences, as I told you. I've nobody else. But what can I say? I don't have a farm for you to take over, never will have, even if I should work day and night for a hundred years." Aloisia was determined not to beg or cry. "I really don't know what to say. It's your decision. You have to figure that out for yourself. Only you can weigh all the pros and cons. I won't hold you back." She was strong. She was used to being strong and practical. "So you would get her farm one day?"

"Yes. Yes, it seems so. That seems to be guaranteed."

Aloisia felt a pain in her heart as though a sharp stone had suddenly been placed there. Her eyes welled up with tears but they didn't roll down her cheek. She wished she could find somebody with a farm, but she would never marry someone just for a farm, no matter what. Rather stay single. But, if Schmid was so weak, if he can't find another way out.... "It's up to you," she said again, wishing in her heart that he would take her in his arms and say it was some kind of joke.

They could start a new life somewhere. People were emigrating to South America, Australia, America, many places. Nobody had ever left Ried, but she heard that people were leaving from other villages. Why couldn't she and Schmid? They were smart. They were still young.

Schmid put his arms around her shoulders and pulled her towards him, "Luise, you know I love you."

She nodded and rested her head on his shoulder. They held each other breathing in each other's presence as the muffled rhythms from the dance floor changed again and again.

Aloisia and Schmid didn't feel like dancing any more, nor did they want to be around when everybody came out. Slowly, they walked home and kissed good night. Tomorrow maybe everything would be clearer.

# A Long Shadow

Aloisia didn't see Schmid all week. Usually he dropped in a few times just to say hello, share some news or give her a quick embrace.

Now it was Sunday. They were in the choir loft singing the Kyrie. As always, the atmosphere in church was both comforting and overwhelming: the high vaulted ceilings; the hand carved altars with white linen cloths stitched and crocheted by nuns at a nearby cloister; the tasteful arrangement of flowers and greenery; the priest chanting Latin phrases with the altar boys responding. Incense was wafting through the congregation. Aloisia looked over to the tenor section and caught Schmid's eye. He nodded slightly, but somehow looked withdrawn. His smile was hesitant. He didn't give his usual wink.

When she received communion he wasn't near her, nor was he behind her as she ascended the steps to the choir loft again.

The priest turned to the congregation and lifted his arms in a blessing, "Go in peace."

The organist pulled out all the stops and the choir sang jubilantly.

"Holy God we praise Thy Name. All in heaven above adore Thee. Infinite, Thy vast domain. Holy, holy is Thy Name." The churchgoers slid out from their pews and walked out the aisles.

When Aloisia looked up after putting her music away, Schmid was no longer in the choir loft. When she came down to the foyer and out into the churchyard, she scanned the villagers visiting grave sites, grave sites they had decorated with flowers the day before. She looked at the clusters of neighbours socialising with each other. Schmid was nowhere to be seen. Aloisia went home.

After the evening chores, she got herself ready for the weekly dance. In the past, she and Schmid had often walked to the dance together or became a pair as soon as they arrived in the hall, but tonight Schmid was nowhere to be seen. He came late and seemed preoccupied when he did come. Finally, however, he strode across the floor to where Aloisia was sitting. With outstretched hand and his usual little bow, he asked her for a dance. They waltzed around the floor as they had done so many times before. Villagers nodded and whispered to each other as the pair circled in and out between the other couples. They danced together so well. Schmid slowed the tempo. "So, you don't care?" he whispered in her ear,

"What?" Aloisia said. "I didn't say that. I never said that," she added with even more urgency in her voice. "You know how I feel. I never thought…you're the one who brought the whole thing up." She stopped talking as a couple they both knew brushed by them on the dance floor. Schmid danced with Aloisia over to a quieter corner of the dance floor. "Anyway," Aloisia said looking straight into Schmid's eyes to see his reaction, "I should tell you that Sophie's mother came by to see me yesterday."

Schmid leaned closer, "What did she say?"

"She asked if I had anything against you calling on her daughter. I said, 'No. It was your own business.'"

"Really? That's what you told Mrs. Meyers?"

Aloisia nodded, "What should I have said?"

"It sounds like you don't care," he said once again, "You could have, you could have…." He didn't know how to complete the sentence.

Aloisia said nothing.

Schmid left soon after. They had company at home, he said. He had to go. Aloisia noticed that Sophie was no longer in the room either.

Another week passed. Aloisia was sweeping the dirt road in front of their farm with a birch broom, one that was still left over from when her father was alive. During the winter months, he used to bring bundles of birch branches into the kitchen and bind them together to form brooms. His grown up children in the city appreciated them too. They were quaint but strong.

## The Making of a Frontier Woman

As Aloisia swept the yard, one of her last chores in preparation for Sunday, she noticed a long shadow joining hers on the ground. Aloisia turned around. Schmid stood a few steps away from her. Aloisia leaned on her broom and looked at him.

"What can I do?" He raised his shoulders and arms helplessly. "Everyone is for my marriage to...these are...hard times. You're still young." He held his throat as though the broken sentences were choking him. "Good-bye, Luise," he whispered hoarsely. He turned away and walked towards his home.

Aloisia wanted to say something, but he was gone. Gradually, the reality of the situation was dawning on her. Through her mind flashed stories she had heard of arranged marriages and of women who never married. Was this happening to her? She continued sweeping.

A few days later Schmid's sister confided to Aloisia that Schmid was marrying Sophie. Did Aloisia know? It was definite now. Aloisia was too proud to admit her surprise; the news shocked her. Now, all her chores were done in a dream, a bad dream over which she had no control. It must be the will of God. That is all she could think.

The following Sunday, when the priest climbed the carved wooden stairs up to the lectern, Aloisia held her breath. After the reading of a passage from the Bible and the sermon, Schmid's marriage bans were announced. She looked straight ahead. As she opened her hymn book and smoothed the spine with the palm of her hand, she cast Schmid a glance. Their eyes connected. He gave a shrug and started to sing.

The bans were repeated on the following two Sundays. The date of the wedding was announced. Finally the day came when the bells rang from the church tower for Schmid's wedding. Neighbours kept looking at Aloisia to see how she taking it all.

That evening Aloisia quietly unlatched her bedroom window and pushed it open. As a child she often stood in her nightgown as the laughter and music rippling through the moonlit air came right to her windowsill. Of course, then she lived in the big house and the sounds were closer. Now, though the sounds were farther away, they felt like broken glass piercing her heart. A cold empty feeling seized her as she remembered how Schmid used to hold both of her hands when they sat under their favourite tree. She pressed the back of her hand against her mouth and looked up into the sky.

Was that a shooting star? If it was, she didn't care.

Already the next morning a neighbour brought Aloisia the gossip that was going round the village. Schmid was miserable at the wedding and didn't seem to care to hide the fact.

"But there had been so much laughter," Aloisia said.

"The laughter was not Schmid's. He didn't even want to dance with Sophie but then he gave in. And Luise? Did you know that Sophie is pregnant?"

"Pregnant?" Aloisia said in disbelief.

"That's what they say."

"She's pregnant?" Aloisia repeated.

"That's what Schmid's sister told me."

"Is...," Aloisia could barely choke the words out, "Is Schmid the father?"

"Yes. Who else?"

Dark thoughts flickered through Aloisia's mind. She dared not complete them. If only the war had not come.

## Letter From Argentina

During the days and weeks that followed, Aloisia tried to keep her head up high as she passed other villagers on her daily rounds. Whenever possible, however, she tried to avoid eye contact. She couldn't think of a time when she felt more alone in the world.

One day Oscar handed her a letter. It had strange, foreign stamps on the envelope, but her address was written in a very familiar handwriting. Franz had received her last letter after all. He was alive.

> *Esperanza,*
> *November 27, 1922*
> *My dear friend Luise!*
>
> *I am sure you have been waiting a long time to hear from me, but this is the first day I have had time to write. How are things going with you and your future groom? You could not wish to be independent any more than I do. For me it will still be quite awhile. In three or four years, if I stay healthy, I will have a place of about one hundred tagwerk from my own efforts which is debt free and which I can call my own.*
>
> *I will probably settle in Misiones. It is beautiful, healthy and fertile there, but still covered with tropical forest. Many Germans are there and almost all trades are represented. There are good churches and schools too. Transportation is mostly by boat on the Parana River. German clergymen who have missions up there advise me to go because a family can, with 5 hectares land, do extremely well.*
>
> *One can acquire so much in a short time so what does one need more for one's life? Grain, corn, tobacco, coffee, bananas and oranges as well as all tropical*

*fruit grow up there. Clover is cut as many as nine times a year and marketing the produce is supposed to be easy. A train is soon going to be built all the way through to Misiones. If I buy eight to ten hectares it costs seventy pesos a hectare but if you get twenty-five hectares or more it is only twenty-five pesos a hectare. The small pieces of land are very close to stream transportation.*

*Everything is going well. The trip on the ocean was wonderful and I attended mass every day exactly as when I was in the navy. Those were easy going days on the ocean. In Buenos Aires I lived free for fourteen days in an immigration house. Even if you have a lot of money, every immigrant has a free trip, with all his belongings, to his first workplace or settlement.*

*First, I worked as a welder, then for a church organisation and finally in the harvest. I became ill but have already fully recovered. The insurance paid for the hospital stay as well as giving me about two pesos daily as sickness pay. $ = sign for a peso. 1$ = 100 Centaros. 1$ has in peacetime the value of about 1.78 Marks. Now it has the value of two to three thousand marks if not more. I paid back my travel money to my parents long ago and have sent home 16000 Marks on top of it. Have still about 80$ saved here. Hired men earn 30-60$ a month and are given free room and board; Cooks, baby sitters and housekeepers are much sought after, earning 40-80$. They are often given clothes to wear for their jobs. Foodstuffs are cheap. Bread is 30 centaros, meat 40 centaros, sugar is 60 centaros a kilo. Linens and household goods cost approximately one and a half times as much as they cost in peacetime Germany. The milk production of the cows is high. The horses are gentle. Both are cheap at 30-60$ a head. Cattle stay outside the whole year. There are no barns and milking is done out in the open.*

*When wheat is harvested, machines cut off the tops and they are threshed at the same time. Workers only* *have to gather up the sacks. All the rest is like over there. If one is healthy and strong and doesn't mind doing heavy work, one can save 1000$ in one year.*

*However, if someone doesn't have a strong character, he had better stay home. There he might be successful, but here in Argentina, he would go under. Here one has to be healthy or he can't take it, especially for the first while when he doesn't understand the language. He has to overcome enormous difficulties, especially if he has nobody here to help him. If the immigrant is capable he can get ahead quickly, that is if he doesn't go into the pubs. The strong wines rob men of their strength and willpower. But he who manages his affairs and saves will get ahead quickly. The most important thing, according to my opinion and experience, is that one is good. For he who does not acknowledge the will of God has in difficult hours, which without doubt comes over every immigrant, no consolation. And in the temptations of the soul, which are very great here, he has nothing to hold on to. I have met geniuses on the road who, because of this deficiency, went under.*

*In answer to your question, about homesickness, yes, I have experienced it. But one cannot thank God enough that we have the one true religion, the Catholic Church, which is international. So my Lord is in the altar wherever there is a Catholic Church and it is like being back home again.*

*You can use what I have written for any of your friends. I know many have thoughts of emigration. For today, I must close. I am looking forward to your answer and would gladly give more news again. Best wishes to your bridegroom.*

*From far away I send best wishes as an old friend,*

*Your Franz Baumgartner*

# Threshing

Aloisia answered Franz's letter immediately. She had, just as when he had been in the navy, asked about many of the things he mentioned in his letter to her. She complimented him on being very resourceful and even knowing how to weld. She knew that he had a strong character and would succeed. She wrote him how wonderful it must be for the entire process of harvesting wheat to be done all at the same time. What did they do with the straw and chaff?

But that was a long time ago and Franz had not answered her letter though he must have received it or it would have been returned. The address must have been correct and the postage sufficient. But maybe the ship that her letter was on sunk in a storm or was hijacked by pirates. No, pirates were out of the question.

Aloisia finally looked up the Parana River in an old school atlas. It was the second longest river in South America, second only to the mighty Amazon about which she had heard so many stories: naked or almost naked natives, alligators with gaping jaws, strange large birds flying through dripping jungles, swamps that sucked under the unsuspecting traveller. It was definitely not a friendly place to live. The Parana River must have been named after those little fish with razor sharp teeth that live in the lakes and rivers all the way from Saratoga to the Panama Canal. In just minutes they could devour any unlucky victim that fell into the water right down to the bone. How could anyone survive there?

Lately she heard that the British were giving a bounty for the scalps of Indians down there. Some 'hunters' were even being paid for the scalps of unborn foetuses. Who knew if that was true? Probably not or at least not any more.

There were many positive points about Argentina. With fields of clover that could be harvested all year, it was no

## The Making of a Frontier Woman

wonder cows gave so much milk. It seemed there were coffee plantations. She hadn't tasted real coffee since she had sipped from her brother's cups before the war. They had added extra milk and sugar for her. Banana and oranges were only names she remembered from school alphabet books and later, geography texts showing the produce of different countries in the world.

Aloisia waited. Franz may have received her letter but, on the way to Misiones, was pushed overboard by someone wanting his money. Maybe the piranhas ate him before he had a chance to answer.

Aloisia finally decided to write Franz's mother a letter, a carefully crafted letter, not too long, not too short. How was she? Did she have a good Christmas? How was Mr. Baumgartner? She didn't say that her life had fallen apart, that there was no bridegroom. She just mentioned that she was not getting married after all. Aloisia sent best wishes to all in the family and asked if she had heard how Franz was doing. Certainly, if Franz had died, his mother would be notified somehow.

But no mail came from Pocking. And no mail came from Argentina either.

In Ried, the grain had been harvested long ago but not as in Argentina with threshing machines. The stalks were cut close to the ground, in long swaths. Then the wheat was bundled into sheaves and at the same time stooked so that, if it rained, the water could run off and breezes would again dry the sheaves. One day, the sheaves were hoisted onto a wagon and brought to the part of the barn where the threshing would finally be done. Aloisia gleaned the harvested fields with some visiting relatives, picking up the broken stems of wheat too short to tie together. Like the other gleaners, she put the ears of wheat into her apron before transferring them to burlap sacks.

Living in the nearby forest was an old charcoal burner who came with her grandchildren to do the final gleaning of the year.

It was now winter. When a few people could be spared, a part of the barn floor was swept clean and the threshing began.

Only grains such as barley, oats and wheat were flailed now, though on the wall was an old, specially designed flail that was once used for separating peas from their pods. Now it wasn't necessary; dried peas could be purchased so reasonably.

The sheaves of wheat were brought in and laid out on the floor. Each person in turn would swing the flail in a rhythmic beat until all the wheat had been separated from the straw. You could always tell when farmers got together for this job by the drum-like beating that emanated from their barn. The straw was forked aside and stored for animal bedding; the chaff was swept off the threshing floor and saved for mixing into animal fodder. The precious grain was carefully collected and scooped into sisal bags. These were eventually brought to a local miller to be ground into flour.

"Give us this day our daily bread" was not a small request.

# CHAPTER THREE: 1923-1926

### SPOILED IN ONE DAY

# A Quiet Sunday Afternoon

Aloisia's father had purchased a small forest. A farmer in a neighbouring village had gone into bankruptcy and it could be purchased at a reasonable price.

In this gold mine – that's what everyone in the family called it – were stands of fir, birch and pine. Not only did the Schropp family obtain lumber, firewood and kindling from these trees, but also hazelnuts and blackberries which grew at the edges. In certain sun-dappled places wild mushrooms and fragrant lily-of-the-valley could be found. These were to be picked and sold to the markets in Munich. There was a marshy area where each spring long swamp grass grew and this was harvested for binding sheaves together later in the year. Nothing was wasted.

Managing a forest properly required knowledge and hard work through-out the year. In late autumn, trees were felled right after the last garden and field crops were safely stored away in cellars and barns or under mounds of earth.

When winter came and other young women were sitting next to their warm stoves, knitting or doing needlework, Aloisia was often working in the forest, a hot baked potato tucked into one of her pockets for a snack. Even when frost and snow numbed her hands, she helped one or two of her brothers felling trees. They were cut as flat to the ground as possible to give extra length to the lumber and also make the forest floor even.

The branches were chopped into firewood and kindling, and stacked in neat rows. Yoked oxen pulled the logs to the local sawmill in exchange for either cash or lumber, whichever was needed most at the time. Some stumps were removed. Aloisia helped dig around them and attach the chain and tackle so the oxen could pull them out of the ground. Though very tough, they were eventually split into firewood. Aloisia had become

## The Making of a Frontier Woman

used to such outside jobs and often even preferred them to housework.

In early spring, before the first seeding, she hitched up the ox and hauled firewood back to the farm where it would be piled once again and dried for the next season. Any remaining branches and twigs on the forest floor were picked up, bundled and taken away too. The forest was now ready to be planted with new seedlings purchased from the local forestry. These were set out in long straight rows to make it easier for future generations to harvest. Straight rows were also easier to count when totalling your forest assets.

This park-like forest had become one of Aloisia's favourite places. The thin rays of sunshine coaxed new vegetation to once again transform the forest into a golden green haven, a haven in which Aloisia knew every tree and gentle rise of land.

One Sunday, Aloisia decided to admire the results of her past week's work in the forest and get away from people who wondered how she was making out since Schmid's marriage. Rays of amber sunlight streamed onto the forest floor. There was still no sign of the lily-of-the-valley, always so late in appearing. Not even the leaves were peaking out from the ground.

Through the forest came the haunting call of a cuckoo. It didn't repeat. She must have been mistaken because it was actually too early in the year to hear its mating call.

Aloisia sat down on a stump and took out the brown sock she was working on. She concentrated on knitting four seed stitches on each side of the heel she was turning to form a pattern which was both elegant and strong. At the same time, she enjoyed the sounds of the forest around her: the birds calling each other; a twig dropping to the ground. Suddenly, she realized that a quiet, rhythmic sound had joined the other sounds of the forest. Footsteps were approaching. She looked up. Through the shadows cast by the rows of budding birches, a male figure was approaching. It was Schmid.

"Hello," he said in a low voice, stretching out his hand.

"How did you know I was here?" Aloisia stood up but didn't take his hand.

"I saw you going up this way along the edge of the meadow." He put his hand in his pocket. "I thought you might have come to this spot. How are you doing?"

"I'm fine, I guess. How's your marriage?" She felt mean as soon as the words were spoken. His paleness and sadness around the eyes confirmed the rumours she had heard. She already knew the answer. In church she had noticed that his wife didn't look much better. Of course, she was pregnant.

"Oh, Luise," he groaned. "It's all been a terrible mistake. How could I have ever been talked into it all? Will you forgive me? I...." His voice trailed off.

Aloisia looked into his eyes. "I don't know why this should happen to us, I really don't understand."

Schmid took a deep breath. "I still love you. It hurts me every time I see you in the choir or going up the lane. Even when I don't see you, I can't forget you."

Aloisia nodded. She felt the same.

Suddenly he let out a sigh and pulled her into his arms. "I still love you. Don't you miss me?" he sobbed. "Have you forgotten all about me?"

The warmth of his body comforted her. He held her face in his hands. His lips caressed her face. "My darling, do you know how I'm suffering?"

Aloisia embraced him "My Schmid, my Schmid, I miss you too," she said touching his forehead and stroking his eyebrows as she often used to do. "But, but at least you have someone. I...I have nobody."

"It's not the same. Don't you miss me?" he asked again, his bright blue eyes looking intently into hers.

Aloisia sighed. "It was your decision. You made the choice." Aloisia heard a twig snap and, quickly looking around, realised their compromising situation. Nobody seemed to be coming, but if some passer-by saw the two of them together in this spot it would be great fuel for gossip. She looked at Schmid and pushed him away, gently, but firmly. "You can't stay here. You'd better go. It isn't right for us to be together. You're a married man."

Schmid glanced around. Of course she was right. Life was already hard enough. He knew Sophie would be giving birth much sooner than the respectable nine months after marriage. He didn't need more scandal. He stepped away. "What are you going to do, my Luise?"

"I feel like going to Africa, like Maria did...and die there too. But there is so much work here. Peter needs help. Father is gone. Now my mother's not at all well. I couldn't leave now. But, I can tell you it's not been easy for me since.... " She bit her lip and her eyes glistened. "I am just so tired of putting on a brave face."

Schmid moved closer again.

Aloisia shook her head and looked up into a birch tree. A newly arrived finch was quickly followed by another. Yes, signs of spring were everywhere, but not in her heart. She wiped her eyes. If anyone were coming she wouldn't even notice. After all she had not seen Schmid coming even when she hadn't been crying. "What would your wife say if she saw us together?"

"She's resting," he responded curtly.

"But somebody else could come along."

"Luise, it's breaking my heart. We used to have such wonderful talks." He lifted his arms to embrace her again but this time she stepped back.

"I guess it is God's will, Schmid. I hope you'll be happy soon."

He stood quietly, looking completely forlorn.

Somehow she wanted to comfort him. "Maybe when your child is born...."

"Ah, Luise, it's pointless trying to explain. Life for men is so hard."

"You know, Schmid, women are also human beings. We have feelings."

"Yes, of course. I know, I know. What are you going to do?"

"Don't worry. I'll survive. We Schropps somehow always land on our feet." She shrugged her shoulders as though she wasn't that sure. "And don't forget, you will get your own farm to run now. You would never have had that with me."

Schmid didn't smile. "Maybe, we could meet here again next Sunday. If I could only see you once a week, only to talk."

"No!" Aloisia said hoarsely. "Please Schmid, no. You know that's not a good idea."

Schmid looked at her intently. "I need to talk to you. I have to have somebody to talk to."

Aloisia shook her head. "You have someone. She's the one you married. You have obligations now." She repeated the axiom she had heard since childhood about being responsible. "If you say A you have to say B." If you start a job you must finish it, finish the alphabet. "If you say A you must say B," she said again trying to convince herself as well. She felt a drop on her forehead. She looked around. A fine rain was beginning to fall.

Schmid nodded, cleared his throat. "Good-bye then," he said in a whisper. He turned and walked away between the rows of birches, the same way he had come.

Aloisia followed him with her eyes.

He turned to see if she was looking and gave a little wave. Then he disappeared beyond a rise in the forest.

Aloisia felt drained and totally exhausted. Was it all a dream? Where was her knitting? It was lying on the moss where she had hastily put it down when Schmid appeared. She picked up the unfinished sock, thrust it back into her side pocket and looked around.

Of course there wouldn't be any local woodcutters or road workers around. It was Sunday. She looked around again and hastily took a pathway leading to the home of a sick friend, a pathway that lay in the opposite direction to which Schmid had walked. She wished the lily-of the-valley were already blooming. Then she could have brought her friend a bouquet and that would be her alibi, in case anybody had seen something.

Two young boys she didn't recognise were searching in the bushes. As she approached they looked at her. "Good afternoon," they said in unison.

## *The Making of a Frontier Woman*

"Good afternoon," Aloisia responded. "Looking for something?"

"Sticks. We're making bows and arrows," said the smaller of the two.

"We're playing Indians," said the other boy. "I'm Winnetou!"

Aloisia smiled. The boys had obviously been reading Karl May's books. When she had gone a little past them, she heard them laughing. Why did they laugh? Had they seen Schmid and her together?

It started to sprinkle a little more and she didn't have an umbrella. Aloisia walked more quickly until she came to the edge of the marsh. She picked a bouquet of blue violets. They were always blooming there at this time every year. Her friend would like them.

She came out to the main road. No one was passing by. A fox slunk into some bushes. Maybe it was the same fox that lived behind the blackthorn bushes growing near her home. It braved coming into their yard each spring (just about the time the blackthorn was covered with white blossoms), to steal one of their chickens for his growing family.

Aloisia thought of how her mother always said, 'A good reputation takes a lifetime to build, but can be spoiled in one day.' Aloisia hoped her reputation was not lost this Sunday afternoon. She would arrange to go to confession next time, when she was in Munich.

By the time Aloisia got home the sun was shining again. She went into the kitchen. Dori reached behind the bread box and pulled out an envelope. She waved it around like someone would with an old bone before throwing it to a dog.

"I forgot to give it to you," she shrugged. "It came yesterday."

Aloisia recognised Franz's handwriting immediately.

"Here, you silly ninny!" Dori said, holding up the letter. "Seems your friend is back from the jungle."

Aloisia took it and walked up to her room.

# A Returned Friend

## 1925

*Eggersham,
January 18, 1925*

*My dear friend Luise!*

*I received your letter in the jungle and thank you for your encouragement and anxious concern. I had such a heavy burden to carry and was so sad, that I only wrote to my family.*

*In order to make my getting out of the jungle easier, I sold many of my things and burned all letters I received in America. Because your letters were also a prey of the flames I could not answer your last one. Dear Luise, please don't be angry with me because of this. For me it was a hard blow. It was a test of patience and also a blessed time. For us Catholics every day lived in the grace of God is a good day, even though it may bring loss of time. So our faith is our consolation, our greatest benefactor of peace and blessings.*

## The Making of a Frontier Woman

*Dear Luise, how are things going with you? From the letter you sent my mother I gather the marriage you planned might not be going through. In these questions one has to strongly consider that marriage is permanent. Marriage is a crossroad full of sacrifices and renunciation. Marriage is a sacrifice and a way of the cross full of resignation. If the spouses do not love each other very deeply and do not have exactly the same goal, then it is better to live alone. That's what I think. I would be glad to hear your views or to help you with your doubts.*

*I am supposed to apologise for my mother that she didn't answer your last letter. She waited for my arrival back home. I have been at home since December 4, 1924. This week I finally have time to write because I have been overburdened with work and on Sunday with visiting.*

*This fall I wanted to go to Argentina again as there is much more of a future in that country than in Germany. But my parents will not permit it, so I will stay in this country. In the meantime I have to help at home. There is so much to put in order and straighten out. While I was away my parents built two buildings. The interiors are almost complete. If you like, I can tell you more next time.*

*I have to let many people know that I am back. It would be so nice if you would write again soon.*

*Sincere greetings from your returned friend,*

*Franz Baumgartner*

# Aloisia

*Eggersham,
July 18, 1925*

*My dear friend Luise!*

*My sincere thanks for your letter. I was anxiously waiting for it and the mailman just brought it today. I was beginning to think you didn't care for me anymore. Of course I couldn't know why, but you could have had the misfortune of changing your mind and then we couldn't understand each other any more. I would have, dear Luise, written you again anyway, because I can never forget in my life such a good Christian and thrifty friend of my youth. Your mother's death has touched your heart with a deep sorrow and you are right when you say in your letter that I can hardly measure your deep grief. Therefore your request for forgiveness for your long silence is very understandable.*

*19.VII*

*Yesterday my writing was interrupted. We went to the evening recitation of the rosary in the village church for a girl who was only sixteen years old. Death just makes no exceptions. It should not bring us Christians sadness or alarm. Instead we should thank the will of God that he accepts us as atonement for our sins, that we in submission suffer in His Holy Will. If human beings had not sinned we would not have to die. Who wants to stay on this poor damned earth for other people's sake? When one looks at the unending perfection of God and the joy of heaven in the light of our faith, then a longing overcomes one for a good death and a new resolution for a persistent, strong spirited battle for God. May his kingdom come through every death! Thy Kingdom Come! God helps with his mercy. God loves us greatly, and also your dear mother. She has left the turmoil of the world and gone, as we hope, into eternal peace. There we will all see each other again, if we do God's will.*

*I was just outside. It is a wonderful Sunday morning. Everything is so fresh and green and festive. The linden tree is half finished blooming but still smells as sweetly as the previous week. In it sing little birds. People walk and drive by it on their way to church. I am leaving right away too. A Sunday on earth! Who wouldn't want to live here forever?*

*Oh, nobody who with the wings of the spirit penetrates the heavens and imagines a Sunday there. It is eternal Sunday there, the eternal day of our Lord. When in the jungle, I saw the tropical sun reflecting off glistening rocks and saw how all the rays of sparkling lights enchanted my eye, I thought, "How beautiful my God must be when my mortal eye is so overjoyed by created things." You asked me to tell you about Argentina, isn't that so? But that is impossible to do by letter. For that we must certainly have the luck one time to share our experience in person. Did nothing come of your planned trip to Altoetting? Or will we still have a chance to see each other again? I would really be happy if we could. I think you are my best friend.*

*I just came home from church and there was a wonderful sermon about the virtues a good Christian should have in order to emulate our Redeemer. For that I would really have to pull myself together. What I need most is patience. My main concern for many years now is the establishment of a family. Despite all resignation to God's will or maybe really because of my ideal conception of marriage, I have not achieved my goal. Just as you, in your letter before last, expressed the wish for a good man, so too do I long for a helpmate so we can make each other happy in this world and in the next.*

*Sunday evening: Dear Luise, Celebrate with me! This afternoon I arranged a workplace for my youngest and most promising brother, with this valley's most Christian, diligent and economically successful farmer.*

*Hans, as well as that family, are really celebrating. I have seldom been so happy as this afternoon when I observed how they took a liking to each other and both were striving for the highest ideals. Children as well as hired help, belong to either the women's or men's organisation and go to the sacraments monthly. It is too bad that you are so far away. I would like to show you this model household. In our home we would have to climb many steps to even come close to their way of thinking.*

*The evening of the twentieth: Right now there were disagreements in the family again. Then the parents demand us to be quiet and submit so false-hood, sloppiness and disorder do not lose supremacy in the house. At our place it is hard to obey the fourth commandment. A child needs special blessings if he doesn't become a good-for-nothing or a criminal. Not all children have parents over whose death they could cry.*

*26. VII*
*Dear Luise, I must finally finish this letter. We have a heavy week of harvesting behind us. I have already prayed for you. Please also pray for me. You think I am impatient? You are right. When one gets older one wants to spend their time with someone and for someone with whom one is spiritually united. I therefore will soon look for someone whom I can marry even if we have to live very modestly. Otherwise, I will perish from yearning. Sometimes I think I will get our home, but one cannot rely on my parents.*

*And regarding you wanting to go into a cloister, which cloister would you like to go into? I could not advise you to go to Argentina. The most important thing you need in order to go into a cloister is not talent, but a calling.*

## The Making of a Frontier Woman

*You ask about my parents. They and the rest of the family are not particularly bad. You ask me what are my interests. Well, what does Victoria think of me? How are you dividing your inheritance? I am happy that you have a little niece. I am very fond of children. You really should continue singing in church for the glory of God, even if you don't enjoy it anymore.*

*That even the president's family couldn't imagine itself in our situation, I believe. Anyway, it is best if you have friends from your own class. Well, now I have written you a lot. If you think, as you stated in your last letter, that I am not interested in women's talk, you are mistaken about me. That is why you should write a long letter like I have, even if it takes several days. Then just leave it as it is and send it, okay? I return your 1000 sincere greetings sincerely. I would really like to send a little kiss along with them, but that I do not dare.*

*Your friend, Franz*

*Dear Luise! Do you perhaps have a picture of yourself when you were younger? I would really like to ask you for one.*

*Eggersham,*
*August 15, 1925*

*My dear Luise!*

*Yesterday I received your dear, long letter. It gave me much pleasure, especially your intention to finally come to Altoetting and then perhaps travel on to my home. Then we will finally be able to see each other again and speak freely. Before I tell you anything surprising about me, I would like to express my great sorrow that you had such a bad accident. But I am happy that you are expecting a quick and complete recovery.*

*While I was hoping with longing for news from you*

## Aloisia

*I had again another annoyance because my father considers it unnecessary and excessive that I wanted to get my Sunday pants cleaned once again after half a year. Then there was a quarrel and I became very depressed and experienced a nervous heart condition as a result of the continual injustice.*

*The doctor was of the opinion, "Now finally get away to other surroundings."*

*But go where? What should I start? I gathered up my last courage and strength and visited a good friend in Upper Bavaria who also has a bad time with her parents and is completely forsaken. But when I saw that things were going better with her I was comforted. Then sadness over my own misery gripped me in such a way that I was startled. But my friend did not only have experiences about how heartless parents can be, she could also comfort me and did it with sincerity and love. Oh, how happy I was, how I was comforted. If possible we will soon marry and live and sacrifice for each other.*

*Because you are my dear, good friend and already know much about our family life, I have written you candidly and in detail. Now, I have hope that my heart and also my mood will improve. I admit that we do not know how we are going to start out. For the first year we could live in my parent's house and find work and food there. Then we will probably buy something agricultural, but our entire fortune together is only about 4000 Marks. Maybe we will buy something small or a business or a shop. We like each other very much and the parents on both sides now like us more too. Oh, it must get better or I will die while I am still young. Dear Luise, what do you think? You wouldn't have any advice for us, would you? Please tell me!*

*Now, Luise, wasn't that exciting news? Now I will answer more of your letter. Yes, I worked long and hard in the harvest. Why do you think that I can let off steam there? For that a heavily tested man has no more need. I never was light spirited. For that I had too difficult a time as a child. How is your sister Victoria? Though I have asked about her several times you never write anything about her. I am not angry at her nor at anybody else.*

*You write that your new suitor, a wagon maker, is a very capable man. Don't you love him or is the reason you don't want to get married because he is not good? You didn't tell me the reason.*

*You make me very curious about what your former suitor did that was so terrible and why he is so unhappily married. You don't tell me even though you mention him in almost every letter. Now I wish to close and am hoping for a reply and an opportune meeting.*

*Your sincere friend,*

*Franz.*

*I almost forgot to answer your question about the condition of my dear mother. She is doing quite well, but is very overworked. She always says that you and your sister have it very good to have your own home. My mother also says that you don't write clearly or simply enough. That's what she sometimes says when she reads your letters. What do you mean when you write, "Can I perhaps speak on your behalf to your mother when I come to your place?"*

*Yes, I received your pressed flower and it is beautiful. It makes me very happy. My heartiest thanks.*

*To end now, I send also hearty greetings to Victoria.*

*Your friend,*

*Franz*

# Letters After Aloisia Visits Franz

*Eggersham,*
*October 18, 1925*

*My dear Luise!*

*Your letter written on October 12 arrived here on October 15. We were all very happy you were satisfied with our simple get together at our home. We also have already had two letters from Munich, the latter of which asked about clarified butter, nuts and apples. Unfortunately I have already sold the clarified butter and apples. Nuts are so scarce this year that we don't have any to sell. Next year it may be a better year for fruit and nuts and then, dear Luise, you are invited to come in October once again.*

*You can, if you like, bring along from Munich a tin pail that holds about 20 or 30 pounds. I could send apples and nuts to Munich if you wish.*

*Thank you with all my heart for the beautiful picture of the Blessed Virgin and of the area where you grew up. May God bless you for it! I will place these two remembrance pictures in my Sunday missal and I will never forget that they are from my dear friend, Luise.*

*We are all well, except father. Father has had to stay in bed for eight days because he has a sore foot. Every day I hope that Father will be able to get up. Today he got up for the first time.*

*On the 16th of October we were finished with the potato harvest. I helped too and Kathi cooked. And a hearty blessing for your prayer in Altoetting for us and for your communion offering for me. I will also often think of you in my prayers. I think of you every day and am already looking forward to our meeting again* next year. I would not advise separating from your dear sister, Victoria. Oh, how wonderful it is to have peace in the home! Perhaps Victoria will still become more bearable. I will pray for Victoria so that you will again have better days. If you come to visit us again next year, we will learn some songs.

For my dear friend Aloisia during our annual fair commemorating the dedication of our church:

Finally, I come to write on the Monday evening after the celebration of our annual parish fair. Yesterday I was interrupted from writing by the visit of a friend who wants to go to Argentina soon and I gave him some advice. Then we drove to vespers in Pocking. After, when I went into an inn, I saw a girl who looked just like you and I thought, "If only Luise was not so far away." Yes, in the first days after your visit I had a longing for you and since then more often. And today again, as I was shovelling together the grain, I wished you were here once more.

I also wrote to Scheufeles. You were here for too short a time. You are just too far away. It pleases me, though, that you liked your stay with us. If you come to Munich again you are really not so far away and I do have a longing for you and to speak with you. I was happy that my mother invited you to visit us again. Then it will certainly be nicer and more orderly here. Probably the rooms in the new building will be finished by then. If you give me the pleasure of visiting again then you should be here a little longer and not wear black as if you cannot believe that now your mother has it better in heaven than here with us.

I close with very friendly greetings in friendship.

Franz

# Aloisia

*Eggersham,*
*October 20, 1925*

*Dearest Friend Luise!*

*I have just finished writing my mother and here I am writing you again but, I honestly confess, not with the enthusiasm I would have expected from myself. Nevertheless I feel I must answer dear Luise. There is so much work that I shouldn't even be writing now. I haven't written anybody since you were here, except yesterday a card to you, which my sister again forgot to mail. If I wouldn't be afraid that you would worry about my silence, I would probably wait even longer until most of the work is over. Many thanks for your little letter. I also received the picture of the Blessed Virgin. Why it doesn't please me, I even ask myself. I don't know.*

*You write dear Franzle! How wonderful it would be if I could write dear Luiserl with all the feeling of my heart. Look, dear friend, it also affects my spirits that I have had to live through two disappointments and the oppressed situation in my home also has an influence and I have been through some hard times. Just shortly before you came, I had an upset stomach. On the day that you were here I was healthy. I think it is from that kiss and yes, I mean that seriously. Anyway, I would like to joke together with you one day, joke like children. You know as a child I was never supposed to joke and now I have nobody to do it with.*

*So, when you come again, you should wear pretty house dresses which suit you well (please, no more black) and then you should, as far as I am concerned, stay longer, even if the people talk about hearing wedding bells again and bet like last time, that I will marry.*

*To continue: For days after you left I had a longing to see my dear friend Luise. Maybe you won't believe it. My mother doesn't believe it either. But that's the way it is. You made a very good impression on all of my sisters and brothers and also on my parents. Please Luise, what is it about me that makes you love me so much? Your statement that I am stern, but fair, pleased me, because you figured me out. It is true. But do I know you? You were somewhat reserved. That might have been because I told you what Victoria wrote about you in her letter. So, another time you will be different and I will not be mad at you for that reason. On the contrary, how happy it made me when we were sitting together in my room and you took my hand and drew it around your hips. I know that during those days you were unwell and I was not able to get excited, especially since you anxiously avoided trying to seduce me. It wasn't meant to be this time. Why not, God must know best himself.*

*He also looks after the small flowers and gives them at the right time a fine scent and splendid colours. Then they sway back and forth in the gentle breeze in order to invite insects for a visit. A little bee comes, is happy and refreshes herself and the little flower is dusted and there have been fertilised seeds for thousands of years as God planned it.*

*Dear Luise! Do you understand your friend? I think it is good when one can see from external things what one is called to do. You should also for several days before you come get plenty of rest. So, now you know that I am a good and truthful friend. In compensation I now observe with my inner eye your beautiful eyes, though unfortunately I only looked into them deeply once in real life.*

*Everything that you didn't dare to ask or forgot to ask when you were here you should do by letter. You asked what weighed on my heart at the railroad station. I can't honestly remember anymore.*

*Your friend Franz greets you very heartily.*

# Aloisia

*Eggersham,*
*October 19, 1925*

*Dearest Friend!*

*Every day I would like to answer your letter but I have had to put it off due to all the work. Have a little patience and look forward to a long letter. I send you many hearty greetings and hope to see you again.*

*In true friendship, Baumgartner*

---

*Eggersham,*
*November 4, 1925*

*Luise!*

*I answered your sincere little letter long ago. How are things going with you? Have you not answered because you are sick or didn't you receive my letter? Or for what reason are you angry with me or don't you trust me? If that is the case please write me the reason. Are you worried about me or about Victoria? You certainly should feel free to confide your sorrows. I also have been open with you about my sorrows and have not been ashamed even though I am a man. You know I am definitely sincere and would say the truth even though it would hurt both you and me. You know how open I have been with you. If you didn't get my answer I am very sorry.*

*The contents of my letter were approximately the following: Why I was sad as we departed I don't recall any more. I still think much about you. That you love me more than ever, does not surprise me. I also like you now more as then. It was probably God's will that both of us were not in the mood back then*

*I expressed the wish to see you again, remembered your beautiful eyes and expressed my joy when you held my hand as I wanted to embrace you. I regretted that you gave so little concern about making an impression on me. You were too exhausted from work and appeared in black. On top of it you were not feeling well. If I weren't such a good, sincere friend I wouldn't have written to you like this. I also took an example from nature in order to show that the whole creation is equipped with attractions for the fulfilment of God's will. And all that you have to say or forgot to ask you should do by letter.*

*I am awaiting your answer and I greet you heartily.*

*Your friend,*

*Franz*

---

*Eggersham,*
*November 8, 1925*

*Dear friend Luise!*

*I was so very happy to get your answer and especially because I was sick in bed from emotional turmoil caused by another setback with my father. Then the postman brought your letter addressed to the Baumgartner family. You, my girlfriend did not address it to me. I'm sure you meant well but then you wrote something in a sort of shorthand I could not make out. I really made an effort but it just couldn't be read. I am distressed and out of sorts because there was another time in the past when I had difficulty reading something you had written in short hand.*

*Recently I almost fainted and was deathly ill. Dear Luise! When in the face of death no friendship helps except the friendship with God. That is what I have experienced. I am therefore no longer disconsolate if I should follow my parent's example and cut off friendships. I have not yet been to Munich to visit my lady friends.*

*Luise, you wrote many flattering things in your letter. As my circumstances and mood are today, however, your hopes would be in vain if you are looking for a home here with us. Indeed, the two of you have a beautiful home together. If any two of us would have as much as you two, how happy my family would be! When one gets to that age when one would like to be a mother and father oneself, one no longer wants direction from parents and childlike dependence. We have to prepare ourselves to stand on our own one day, just as our parents had to. And on top of it they had many worries with us, isn't that right?*

*I see our friendship gradually falling apart. Certainly, we will think of each other in later life, especially in our prayers and at Holy Communion. That is the most important duty of friendship. Should you wish further deep, helpful friendship, which I assume, there are first and foremost the priests with whom you can talk things out in the holy confession and be comforted. Then our best friend comes to us in Holy Communion. This is the best friendship for helping when nobody else can.*

*If in the future we write each other less often and our letters are shorter and we finally go our separate ways, then we have the consolation that one day we can say that we meant the best for each other. Let us not be sorrowful over transient things but strive joyfully towards what is eternal. Then we will with transfigured bodies join hands and be unspeakably happy in the eternal friendship of God. If we shouldn't see each other on earth anymore, I would like to thank you in this letter for all the material and spiritual good which I have received from you.*

*To conclude, I greet you very heartily with best wishes and sincere friendship, Franz Baumgartner*

*My mother sends her best wishes and will remember you in her prayers. I wanted to send the enclosed letter when your letter arrived.*

# The Making of a Frontier Woman

*Eggersham,
December 11, 1925*

*My dear friend Luise!*

*I thank you sincerely for your letter with my saint's day card for November 29, 1925. You certainly could not have guessed that I would write so soon. Just happen to have the fancy right now and love to do it because I thought it would make you happy to get mail from me at Christmas. And so I don't forget to do so at the end, I wish you a merciful Christmas and a blessed New Year. Actually I should conclude now and go to sleep but I am not very tired and by tomorrow my eagerness may be gone. So I had to go out of the family room and now I am writing in my cold bedroom.*

*Too bad you cannot write how much you like me! Oh, please do. It pleases me so much. I am really amazed that you wrote you still do not regret the trip to see me, even though on the second evening you said to me, "If I knew that, I would not have come." At that moment you were even sorry for your expense in writing paper and postage stamps. You probably did not mean it and I forgive you gladly as you request. You are so very good, wishing I were with you. Yes, I wish that I could be with you sometimes too. Even forever?*

*No, it is better to be your true friend than to pretend love in order to be looked after. I have thought how would it be, if we could meet again. How motherly you cared for me when you were here! For that I would like to reach my hands out to you in spirit and also help you.*

*Yes, we were together for too short a time, I agree. You do not believe it and think I am happy when you are away. I know you still wanted to tell me so many things. You could empty your heart as to no other person. How pleased I would have been with such trust given in friendship. But no, of more benefit would be consultation with your spiritual advisor.*

*Recently a lady friend from Munich and I went to Muhldorf. Such a visit alone and unobserved is so much more pleasant than at home. It was wonderful. Nevertheless there is for the future no other prospect than to remain alone. It is too bad that you are so far away. I would really like to see you again.*

*I greet you very heartily,*

*Your sincere friend, Franz Baumgartner*

*I would have almost forgotten. Since your being here I have been praying for you.*

# 1926

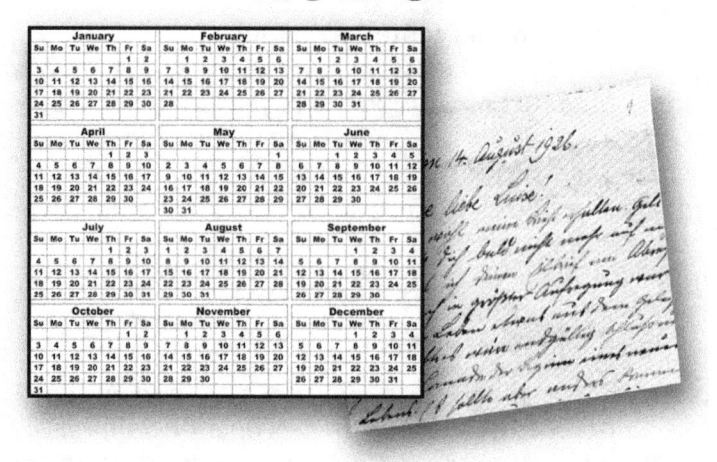

*Eggersham,
January 17, 1926*

*My very dearest girlfriend!*

*I have answered your dear letter and am already eagerly your answer. How are you? What do you think about our future? I am already looking forward so much to our meeting again. Since I feel more drawn to you and I have written this to you, several girls have crossed my path but I wish to think only of you until*

## The Making of a Frontier Woman

we meet again. Then we might discuss if we couldn't make each other happy and be able to help each other to heaven. Only if after a mutual exchange of views, we should find out that it is not God's will and not our fortune to marry, only then will I look around for another girl. We should pray for one another that we sincerely reveal our thoughts and feelings. You should write me any questions about which you are concerned and also how you think and what distresses you.

Especially when we meet again, I think we should be open books to each other. Isn't that so? You must have confidence in me and I will also say everything even if I risk you loving me less or even that you don't wish to hear from me anymore. And in the meantime you will also tell me of your weaknesses and struggles and we will have an understanding heart for each other, console each other, pray for each other and help each other upwards. If we will become one according to God's will, we must in all things strive for his will. But I think it would be tiresome for you if I repeat what you have already often read. So, let's change the subject.

How are things going with you and Victoria? Things are going terrible with my sister Kathi, too. She also thinks she is right and I am wrong exactly as it is with you and Victoria. The whole week she was sick in bed but today she is out for the whole day and is freezing in the cold church.

I have a lot of mending to do and you are cutting firewood in the forest! I would really like to trade with you. I certainly could chop as much firewood as you but in mending and darning you are certainly far better than I am. Since about one month my health is much better. I don't get so worked up. If I just weren't lonely and dependent for much longer.

You know my whole troublesome life and have had an insight into our "order" and family life. For a long time now I have wished things were different, then things would have been better and finer for me. Instead of being able to get an example from my own family I had to find out for myself how it should be at

## Aloisia

*home and in the management of affairs. It makes it even more difficult for me that my good opinions are misunderstood and suppressed.*

*I have now rested for a quarter of an hour. In one month, if there are warm days some birds will already be starting to sing, Finches, chickadees, larks and also yellow hammers. How merry and carefree they will build their nests and search for sustenance for themselves and their young ones among the flowers and blossoms!*

*Now I am thinking that you, dear Luise, have never talked or written about children. Before I get your inclination and views about this subject I will immediately write my opinion. I hold all these little hearts unspeakably dear. Yes all, not only those which are especially pretty and well cared for. Often I have purposely been with poor people so that I could joke and flatter and look into their innocent trusting eyes. If I get a little kiss, then I cannot hold myself back and like to give them back two, hold them to me fervently and wish I were myself a happy father. Such hours are dearer to me than the theatre or the movies.*

*In the Argentina jungle everyone thought I should be a teacher. I had to decline because I could not teach music, as I don't understand that subject myself. And a school without singing seems very sad to me.*

*In that way I am completely different from my father. He never liked it when I wanted to be happy. I only want to emulate my parents in what is good, otherwise woe is me.*

*Now I will look forward to your answer that will probably come tomorrow. Then on Sunday I will write again.*

*I greet you most heartily until we meet again in sincere, honest sentiments,*

*Franz*

## The Making of a Frontier Woman

*Eggersham,*
*January 18, 1926*

*Dearest sweetheart!*

*I am just mailing the letter I wrote yesterday, today. Perhaps I will get news from you tomorrow. I wish you were here so you could see how disorderly everything is and you could understand why I am so anxious to get away from here. I could not feel less happy than at this time.*

*Therefore I wish to see you as soon as possible so I can plan my future or know if I should take on something else. I must get a faithful, orderly and understanding being close to me for whom I can also live with all my soul. Otherwise I will not survive. If it is possible, I ask you, dear Luise, to invite me very soon. I would also gladly come to Ried. I received some printed material with an invitation to Kochel. I don't know if I should go there. It would really be the nicest if I could be together with you! Please write me very soon and be heartily greeted.*

*If God wishes,*

*I am your Franz*

# A Shot Is Fired

It was an evening, an evening just before Palm Sunday. Aloisia and Dori were at church practising the Easter mass for the following week. Peter and his nephew, Oscar, were sitting in the front room. They heard a tap on the window. When they looked up, a well built young gentleman with black hair was standing there.

Peter sent Oscar to open the door. The stranger introduced himself as Baumgartner, Franz Baumgartner. Oscar immediately recognised the name as the sender of the letters over which Dori often fought for possession. Oscar had also heard the name during some lively family discussions.

He led Franz into the living room and the two men formally introduced themselves to each other. Peter knew that Baumgartner had corresponded with Aloisia since they met at a beekeeping course during the middle of the war. Sometimes, Baumgartner was not heard from for long periods of time and Peter thought the relationship had ended. But then there was talk of another letter, not only in the family, but among the villagers as well. What could this all mean? Aloisia must be writing back or he would have given up. Since Aloisia visited his family farm in Eggersham last October, there had been many letters, more than ever before.

Peter and all the other siblings were against losing Aloisia from the farm. Peter had used both ridicule and anger to make it clear that these letters were an embarrassment to the Schropp family. What must people in the village think with all those letters, often from different locations, coming to Aloisia? Baumgartner was obviously back in Aloisia's life again. And now this unexpected visit.

Peter asked Franz what his plans were for the future. Had he the means to support a family? If he hadn't, he had no right to disturb the wonderful life the two sisters shared in the house in the back garden.

Franz knew from Aloisia's letters that the connection between the two sisters was, at best, strained and usually much worse. Nevertheless, he responded politely, that he did not wish to disturb the situation of the two sisters. He felt, however, that Aloisia should make the decision herself.

While the two men were talking, Aloisia and Dori came back from choir practice. As they passed the front window, they saw Franz sitting there with Peter and Oscar. Aloisia tapped on the window. When Dori saw Franz, however, she immediately shouted, "That man is not coming into our house!" Then she turned down the lane to the house she and Aloisia shared. Dori, like most of the other siblings, saw a relationship between Franz and Aloisia as a threat to the whole status quo in Ried.

Aloisia, however, came into the parlour and greeted Franz. They talked together for quite awhile and then Aloisia, Franz, Peter and young Oscar also walked down the slight incline to the house in the back garden.

When they got there they found the front door bolted shut. Dori shouted through the door, "Luise can come in. Baumgartner stays out!"

Peter tried to persuade Dori to be reasonable.

Instead, she opened the window and spat at Franz.

They finally had no other choice but to walk back to Peter's place. By this time it was evening and Peter invited Franz to spend the night. Then Aloisia went home alone.

Already at 6:00 the next morning Dori was at a neighbour's house, the one that had a telephone, trying to reach her brother Ludwig, in Untermeitingen. But no telephone connection could be made so early in the day. Two hours later, when she finally did get through, she told Ludwig that Baumgartner had arrived in Ried and it looked like trouble. Baumgartner had even spent the night at Peter's! He should bicycle over as fast as possible to abort any new developments. She would wait at the village entrance so she could give further details and directions upon his arrival.

Peter saw Dori leaving the house in the garden and going

## *Aloisia*

up the road. He told Oscar to hitch up their old horse and the ox and take some sacks of wheat to the mill where it would be exchanged for flour.

Peter then told Franz that he could visit Aloisia in the house in the garden. Aloisia showed Franz her bedroom....

At about eleven o'clock Oscar was already returning from the mill, having made good time in order not to miss what was happening at home. He had just unloaded the flour and was unhitching the animals when he heard shouting from inside the house in the garden. Then Aloisia and Franz ran past him with Ludwig waving a pistol in hot pursuit.

Ludwig aimed his pistol and fired.

Peter was working behind the barn reinforcing one of the wire rabbit hutches when he heard the shot. He came running, hammer still in hand, and saw what was happening.

"Ludwig, put that pistol down," Peter shouted. "Put that pistol down right now or I'll hit you over the head with this hammer!"

"Enraged, Ludwig waved his pistol. "I'll kill you. I'll kill you all!"

Aloisia and Franz had already fled to the inn across the road. Peter and Oscar ran into the main house and bolted the doors behind them.

Ludwig, despite his long ride from Untermeitungen shouted again, pounding several times against Peter's heavy front door. Then he went around to bang at the back door.

Nobody came out. Even Dori had disappeared.

Ludwig had time to cool down. He shouldn't have let Dori get him all worked up. Why should he be the one to stick out his neck? Had he not enough to do on his own farm? If Aloisia wants to throw away a free home, a home many families would be so glad to have, that was her business.

On the other hand, maybe he had scared off that Baumgartner for good. Finally, Ludwig got on his bike again and started the long trip back to Untermeitungen.

When Aloisia and Franz saw Ludwig riding back towards his farm and were certain that he was really gone, they said

## The Making of a Frontier Woman

goodbye to each other. Franz went on foot to the Moedishofen train station.

Aloisia looked for Peter and found him in the harness room. "What were you talking about with Baumgartner," Aloisia asked hesitantly, "before we came back from choir practice?"

"Ach, he was just fishing around trying to find out if you were really available and he wanted to know what kind of a dowry you might have. I told him your dowry was to stay on the farm and live in the back house."

Aloisia looked at Peter in bewilderment. "You said that?"

"Sure," Peter nodded, "something like that anyway. And, by the way, I found out that man's in no financial shape to be looking for a wife. Who does he think he is, anyway? And did you know he's a political activist?"

Aloisia cringed at Peter's words. "What do you mean, a political activist?"

"He was in Munich when the National Socialists were starting to have their meetings at the Landtag. Even back then he was shouting Hitler down. He said Hitler glared at him and so did some of his right-hand men."

Aloisia's shook her head. "Well, he's not a Communist, if that's what you think. He told me he wasn't."

"You don't have to be a Communist to be against Hitler. Anyway," Peter added, "Baumgartner actually had to flee across the Swiss border. He was afraid to go directly home in case they followed him. He had to wait in Switzerland to let things cool down before going back to his farm. You know that people can go missing if they're too outspoken? That was one of the reasons your Baumgartner went to Argentina."

Aloisia stood quietly, listening to his every word.

"You don't have to look at me with such disbelieving looks, Luise. That's exactly what he said. Luise," he continued with a pleading voice, "you're getting yourself mixed up with a man who doesn't even know enough to keep his mouth shut. He should stay home and work instead of sticking his nose in here and there and everywhere."

## Aloisia

Aloisia knew from Franz's letters that he had a loud voice that certainly could be a disruptive force in a public meeting. But maybe if people spoke out more it would make a better world....

"And Luise," Peter's voice broke into his thoughts, "when you associate yourself with questionable people you draw suspicion on yourself. You know what mother always said. "Tell me who your friends are and I'll tell you who you are.""

"Don't mention what mother would think about him. She read some of his letters and said he seemed like a very good man and very intelligent too. If she were still alive, what do you think mother would say about chasing a visitor away with a gun? And what do you think she would say about the spitting? Maybe you don't think much of Franz, but what must he think of us? I always tried in my letters to give him the impression that I came from a respectable family." Aloisia put her hands on her hips. "Dori spitting at Franz was the last straw. You can force me to live under the same roof as her but you can't force me to talk to her. And I won't!"

With those words, Aloisia turned and walked away. Franz had invited her to visit him on his farm again. Maybe she would. But perhaps her family was really trying to protect her. She would send a letter to him with her kisses anyway. Or did that look too anxious? But she would have to write and apologise for the shotgun incident. That was certain.

# The Letters Say It All

*Pocking,
Palm Sunday, 1926*

*My dear Luise!*

*Today when your letter came I was in a very sad mood. Outside it was springtime but my heart was cold and empty. I thank you for your reply. Right away I saw who had written. First I read the closing and, full of longing and joy, inhaled your kisses and greetings. I read your letter over and over again. And then I was left as sad as before. How is it with you? Can't you or don't you wish to imagine yourself in my place?*

*Right now I am resting awhile in order to find heart again to continue my writing. How hard you make the hours for me! I wish I had it as good as you have it, that I also had so little longing for you as you have for me. So you think we should wait until May until we see each other again? Now it seems your choir practices are more important. If you have so little enthusiasm for us to see each other again or even have fear that it may lead to marriage, it is better we discontinue our acquaintance. What do beautiful, loving speeches and closings in letters help if it is only words? I no longer notice hardly any of the courage you once expressed. Being timid is a very bad substitute.*

*Don't hang your thoughts on me if you only love me half ways or are pretending. We are still both free people. Let a meeting decide! Until now, nobody has a claim on me nor do the two of us have a claim on each other. I would just as easily wish happiness with another, if you would rather. I find that I am not understood. But one day my luck will come even if it is not in this life. Should I be cheered by your invitation, I will visit you.*

*If I could live like it says in Hessenabach's book about the ideal marriage and my wife would agree, I would do it. But the more I think about it now, the more I must admit that I probably could not. For me marriage is not only for the reason of reproduction but must also have the purpose that I don't go insane from the suppression of the mightiest of all urges.*

*Dear Aloisia, you must wonder what has taken hold of Franz? Or after all, can you understand what a struggle I have with my life? Only if you have to suffer like me can you feel what I am writing. You will ask yourself, what does Franz do in his suffering? Well, it all takes its natural course without me touching a woman but sometimes it lasts weeks and months and then it is terrible. Certainly I would be considerate of my wife but the ideal as given in the marriage manual I will not achieve.*

*At this point I must write you again what I have expressed before. When we meet again you should try to dress a little more seductively. Again it was your family which frustrated and hindered everything. We were there like captured criminals. We who, have known each other for ten years as few others could look back on! I wish I had not let Peter take me on that excursion, as you wished at the time. Instead, you could then have changed out of your work clothes into something pretty and we would have gone on our way, just the two of us, unobserved. I would have been overjoyed about my Aloisia. You could have joked a little with me and teased me. It would have been wonderful and we probably would have understood each other very well. But what could we have really started at that time? It wasn't meant to be. Yet we were happy as far as it went. You, my good Luiserl, I think almost only of you every day and every hour and there....*

## The Making of a Frontier Woman

*Dearest Luise!*

*While I was writing you, I received a visit from my friend, Joe Pizweger, who also is always talking about immigrating to Argentina. He brought me a brand new pamphlet about Canada put out by the St. Raphael Organisation in Hamburg. This charitable organisation highly commends this land for farmer's sons and daughters. Taking everything into consideration, I consider it better than Argentina and will immediately ask for more detailed information and prospects. I will then send them to you or we can study them together.*

*I can hardly believe that we cannot see each other in the near future. Maybe we will emigrate together. That would be wonderful. I am just saying this, who knows? Since I was with you I love you even much more. As far as I can tell from the aforementioned pamphlet, we could easily start something there if we put our fortunes together. The climate is the same as in Germany. Religion is Catholic. The selling of the produce is well organised. Mixed farming is the same as here. Yearly salary 300 dollars. The cost of cultivated land is about $60 a hectare minimum. A cow costs $50, a horse $80—$100, a pig $10. At this moment it seems outstanding. What do you think?*

*Write me very soon how you are doing and how you are making out with Victoria. Even if we almost have no hope for being together after all that has happened, I am still writing this to you because of our long friendship.*

*Hearty greetings,*

*Franz*

## Aloisia

*Eggersham,
Easter Monday 1926*

*My dear Luise!*

*You asked me how I got home after Ludwig tried to shoot me. I arrived safely at Moedishofen train station even though I had no protection or weapons. In the evening I took the train for Munich. I wanted to talk to the mayor in Ried and to the constabulary but nobody was at home. Before I got to Moedishofen I met a policeman and told him about the incident and how your brother shot at me. He left it up to me if I should make an official complaint against your brother for him threatening me and against your sister for insulting me. I think I will let the matter rest.*

*In Munich I spent three nights in a journeymen's lodging house because I am a member of that association. I visited several of my former friends from school. The immigration office was closed and I couldn't get into the Argentina consulate either.*

*I also visited Eva whom you saw on the little portrait. My warning to this poor girl regarding her having too much self-confidence was in vain. She should have followed my advice more, her best friend. She trusted her own strength too much and that is why she fell into misfortune at only 28 years of age. "I had absolutely nothing except the pure physical and then afterwards the terrible pangs of conscience," she said to me. She is still like a desperate person, almost inconsolable. I visited her again two more times trying to encourage her. May God give her peace of soul again like that of the contrite Magdalene under the cross.*

*Dear Luise, you can easily appreciate how thankful I am that I have never brought a girl into such a sad situation. You also are fighting the good struggle, isn't that right? With God's grace we want to strive always for what is good and furthermore pray that the fallen will again, full of hope, trust only in God. "Without* me you can do nothing" spoke Christ. That is why we should strengthen ourselves very often with Holy Communion. Without Jesus I would have despaired long ago. He also is a better friend for you than I could be.

Yesterday I got home. Today I shaved off my moustache and it doesn't look bad. I went to Holy Communion again. That's enough about me.

And how is it going with you? What else is new? It is unfortunate that we are so far apart. Otherwise we would often be together, wouldn't we? It is too bad that the time was so short. Thank God we used it well. In spite of everything, I am happy that I was with you. Your dear picture looks on as I am writing. It is sad that your sisters and brothers hold you back so much. I don't think the two of us would be unhappy even if we were poor. What are they saying about our liaison? What will happen?

I think:

Be fruitful said the spirit of the world,

Otherwise longing will consume you.

Let love make you so rich

That you can do without many unnecessary things

Because marriage is the purpose of life.

Rather than giving up spiritual convictions,

It is preferable to live a single life in my honour

Instead of procreating.

Die with your convictions intact.


I wish for a quick, sincere reply.

In spite of everything be very heartily and sympathetically greeted

from your sincere Franz.

## Aloisia

*Pocking,*
*Easter Tuesday, 1926*

*Dear Luise!*

*Yesterday, I wrote hurriedly about my immigration intentions to Canada. Today I inquired more closely from two gentlemen and their information seems so negative that I don't even want to wait for the information from the St. Raphael Organisation to tell you that for the time being I prefer immigrating to Argentina again. So don't have any unnecessary worries or make any plans.*

*Today we concluded a forty hour long novena. That was, after my Easter disappointment of not being able to visit longer with you, a great delight for the heart.*

*How are you doing? Don't be sad. You are doing your best. I thank you heartily. Everything else you can hand over to God as I do. He knows us and loves us more than people can love us and nobody can withstand his power. We must trust that everything leads to what is best for mankind.*

*How do you think your brothers and sisters are inclined? If I knew that they weren't against me any more, I would rather not look for any replacement for you, dearest. It certainly would not be easy to find somebody to replace you. How good it is that God is still our first and highest aim, otherwise we would be very unhappy. Nobody can keep God from us.*

*I love you mostly because you were a good helper in my struggle and have had such feelings of understanding on this earthly plane. Beauty and riches are vain. However beautiful and rich one may be, one must first possess that virtue which I know that you have.*

*Too often have I already prayed, "Thine will be done" rather than be in despair over yet another disappointment. The hardest for me is that my parents have broken their promise so many times about my taking over the farm.*

## The Making of a Frontier Woman

*Dearest Aloisia, we will pray for one another that both of us will be happy. I have already done it. More I cannot do. Each should hope for the other's good fortune. I don't want to grieve alone for a long time, even if I don't know yet whom I will marry. If you or I should marry someone else soon, we will still, I believe, remain good friends.*

*Be therefore very heartily greeted from your sincere Franz.*

*Eggersham,
April 12, 1926*

*My very dearest sweetheart, my Luise!*

*What should I write first? I would like to be with you. I was out overnight visiting my cousin. I just came home. Oh, how your letter gave me pleasure! When the longing of a 30 year old is unsatisfied it is almost dangerous. For a few hours now I have been completely out of self control, even at night. Never would I have believed that love sickness could be so terribly powerful.*

*Yes, I am just like you, rather poor than lonely. With what irresistible might are man and woman drawn together! We should see how we can soon become one body and one soul. How many women have I known and yet it is as though there is only one Aloisia in the whole world. You also say that there is nobody like me. Certainly, each of us, you and I, will have faults and shortcomings but we will help each other adjust, right dearest heart? When and where will we meet again? I believe it would be eternal shame if we couldn't marry. There is no doubt that I will marry one day before the desire for a woman destroys me. But, according to my opinion, I will never again find another Luise.*

*I believe you too, my dearest, when you say that I*

am your everything despite my weak points, which you forgive and wish to help me improve. Isn't that so dearest Luise? I am very happy that some of your more sensitive relatives, sisters and brothers are encouraging us to marry. I will now make every effort to find something for us. Considering my bad experiences and worries recently, my desire to emigrate is getting less and less. Another hindrance is that we don't have enough of our wealth in cash.

This year we can celebrate our tenth anniversary of friendship, right? We certainly were good angels. Perhaps it is not God's will that we will in the future lead and help each other. Oh, but what wonderful hours we were decreed in spite of everything! Were you satisfied with me my dearest? I am still happy even today.

Regarding your question, I did not leave home because of a fight, but in a fight. I was threatened that I would not get my marriage portion because I refused to work in an oppressive situation. Today they are saying again that they will do their best. The uncertainty and months of longing for you drives me to you. A decision should be made. You are right, I wish to get a home very soon. Poverty does not hurt me but we never would be poor. What hurts me is being misunderstood and being lonely on top of it. After all, I was not roaming around aimlessly but went expressly into a wild country to find a home. When I was alone in the jungle I did not have to pay attention to my wrong notes and often sang, "The home of the soul is up there in the light."

A foretaste of pure joy was given to us eight days ago. We were unified spiritually and embraced each other intimately, kissing each other softly. Those were blissful moments, even minutes. Yes, we love each other and support one another. That is all that we are allowed to give each other.

Yes, I must have told my family of my experience with the shooting because they were very sorry that such things come to pass between brothers and sisters.

*You don't have to be embarrassed or ashamed. It is not your fault.*

*When I came back home everything was very orderly. It made me so happy. Marie had whitewashed the living area and kitchen. My room (I live in the new building) was also cleaned. With my father I have to summon up all my strength. He is so completely without love, false hearted and deceitful, that I would rather not even look at him but that is difficult. With my mother I get along fairly well.*

*Today it was nice and warm. All afternoon I went barefoot while I was raking the straw. Last evening I was asked to give a three hours long talk about Argentina and it was midnight before I got to bed. Today it will probably be in bed by nine o'clock as I'm tired already and will go right to sleep. May you slumber very peacefully. Good night dear heart! Dream of forgiveness, a beautiful future (and dear children I almost wrote). May our dear guardian angels give us holy convictions, devotion and the spirit of sacrifice with heavenly strength!*

*Beloved! Greetings, embraces and kisses from your Franz. Don't have too many hopes. Disappointment hurts so much. I have very little faith in reconciliation with Victoria, especially since she even spat at me.*

*P.S. If this letter causes you pain then I recommend you find comfort in the school catechism.*

---

*Eggersham,*
*April 28, 1926*

*Dear Luise!*

*Today I already wrote you three times but couldn't mail the letters. I am very despondent and in low spirits. You suffer a great deal from my letters, don't*

## Aloisia

*you? It is all because of your sisters and brothers. In haste I made a mistake and accused you of deception. Please don't think I said this with the intention of getting rid of you, otherwise I wouldn't write anymore. I would like to comfort you personally and beg for your forgiveness but I dare not come. I think now all of you are even more angry with me.*

*Perhaps, despite all absence of prospects everything will turn out right. Please write me again and don't be angry with me. My life is hard enough. My mother does not understand your statement but sends her greetings. If we marry she extends a friendly invitation. I am also afraid of your family and with our money we can't go far. In these bad times emigrating is the only thing*

*I would like to give you many greetings and all allowable caresses as compensation.*

*Franz*

*Eggersham,*

*May 10, 1926*

*Dear Luise!*

*I just got home. I have to answer your card in a hurry as I still have so much to put in order. I am leaving on the fifteenth. That you, despite my letter, still want to talk to me convinces me that you do understand my candid, well-meaning character. Yes, I have always meant well and will always in the future hold to good principles. Your confiding that you came to Munich to see me and waited for nothing, I will never forget. I feel sorry for you and because I think it would be a little easier for you if you at least had me as a friend, I have decided to write you when I get to Canada.*

*What might be your goal? Let us be honest with each*

## The Making of a Frontier Woman

*other and have strong self discipline. Then the truth will be a joy to us and death will be easy.*

*Here everything is a struggle. Beyond, there is blissful peace.*

*May God bless you!*

*With greetings from a friend, Franz.*

---

*Passau,*
*May 15, 1926*

*Dear Luise!*

*For the time being I can give no other address, as I am homeless until I once again have a permanent address in America. I received your express letter at noon today and in the afternoon I departed. Tomorrow noon I will be in Hamburg. I recognised your writing from far away and I gladly paid the 45 cents postage due, despite everything. Yours is the only letter I am bringing with me to America. I burned all your other letters yesterday and also those of other friends.*

*I have ordered things at home, so that all my worldly possessions can be forwarded to my new address in America because I no longer have any intention of coming back to Germany. With the value of my things left behind I will still be getting 1913 marks. I have over 400 pounds of luggage with me. What I can do without, I will sell. I will be able to deposit about 500 marks into the bank over there right away. Then I will immediately get work in the middle of Canada where there are many German Catholics. That is my plan.*

*Now to your letter. It pleases me as it shows your trust in me. In the last hours of our bitter farewell the letter did not impress me so much as it would have in earlier times. But let us leave everything to providence. It is beautiful everywhere, where one loves God. How*

## Aloisia

*could I be angry because you love me? I can, however, at this time give you no hope though my heart is still free. Lately I have been very sad. I have experienced too much bad from my family and also from strangers since my return to Germany. Now, because I know I am leaving, I have courage again.*

*Regarding your question of how you should resolve your troubles with Victoria, I cannot answer because I have too little insight into the circumstances. You still did not write about how much cash you could scrape together so how can I make plans? Turn all your possessions into cash, even your furniture. Pack your linens and sewing machine up, send them as freight to Hamburg, travel to Canada and look around to see how you like it. You could always go back, if you can't get used to it but I think you would stay there.*

*Of course you shouldn't rush too much. I have to tell you first how everything looks over there. Now I am writing this all as a friend, not with the purpose of trying to lure you to come over. I stand in completely new circumstances and can't make new plans for myself let alone give anybody else any hopes. I only see that in Germany the future is very hopeless. Over there I hope for something better. Now my train is leaving very soon. I close and greet you as your well-meaning and sincere friend.*

*Franz Baumgartner*

# Keeping the Connection

Overshadowing Aloisia's personal loss, another threat was looming ever closer to reality. The Schropp farm was slipping into strange hands. Strange hands, those were the words used whenever her older brothers and sisters got together and Peter was not around to hear.

Peter, as the eldest Schropp male, was running the farm. He and Mina could not have children. Recently the couple had arranged for a young niece to move in with them. She was not from the Schropp side of the family; she was from Mina's side of the family. Her name was Ottiel.

Though not legally adopted, Peter made it more and more clear that legal adoption may be a possibility. Ottiel was already treated as if she were Peter's and Mina's own child.

If Ottiel were ever legally adopted, she would inherit the

*Aloisia and her nephew, Oscar, harvesting potatoes*

*Aloisia*

farm. Being so pretty and capable, Ottiel would surely marry one day. If she married and had children, any claims of the Schropp side of the family would be fruitless. The Schropp family farm would slip into strange hands.

If only Ottiel would marry someone from the Schropp side of the family! Then the crisis could be averted. Perhaps Oscar, Franz's son, would be most suitable. Peter had brought him to live on the farm right after his mother's death in 1922. He was only eleven years old at the time but was developing into a strong young man. He was already as tall as Ottiel. He was six years younger than she was. But how important is age anyway when keeping the family farm in Schropp hands was at stake?

However, Oscar was still too young and the Schropp clan concurred that Aloisia's presence made an important bridge with those brothers who had moved away from the farm and appreciated the odd box of apples or pound of butter, or head of lettuce. Dori, being eight years older than Aloisia, might get married and leave. One way or another, Aloisia, being the youngest, must remain on the farm for keeping the connection.

And Peter had always been generous, even to Emma's husband, Christian. At first Aloisia and Emma had helped him twirl the soft fragrant leaves into firm cigars. Aloisia liked their smell and even tried one once, but only once. It was amazing how many people found money for cigars, cigarettes and tobacco when there was not enough money for food. Sales were so good that soon Christian could buy all the cigars and cigarettes he needed.

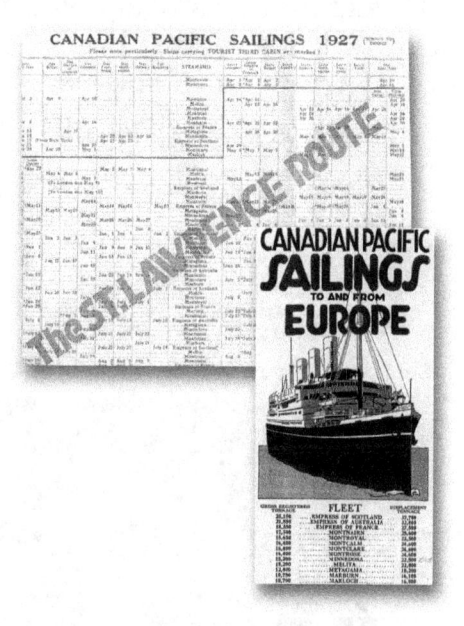

*CPR Schedule of "The St. Lawrence Route" 1927 and description of fleet*

## The Making of a Frontier Woman

But even the wealthiest people had difficulty getting food since the enforcement of the Versailles Treaty and collapse of the economy. Sunny rose gardens were turned into vegetable gardens to supply fresh produce. Flower boxes were planted with basil, chives and parsley. Aloisia often took the train from Moedishoven to Munich, bringing fresh milk and fruit in season. Eggs were individually wrapped in newspaper, carefully packed into a suitcase for safe delivery. Clothing and cigars came back in the same suitcases. It was a win, win situation.

Yes, Aloisia's presence on the farm was a guarantee that this arrangement would continue. Emma had worked hard, not only helping with farm work, but also looking after the twelve younger siblings before she finally left to be a nanny for a wealthy family in Munich. Of course Emma reasoned, as did the other siblings, that something was owed back for her part in not allowing the payments on the farm to fall in arrears.

In summer, haying season began. The yoked oxen pulled load after load to the barn where, by means of cables, pulleys and a levered fork the hay was raised into the loft left bare from the previous winter's feeding. Their shirts stained with perspiration, one or two of the Schropp boys, Aloisia and Oscar, pitched the hay and spread it layer upon layer across the hay mow, pushing as much as possible in the space under the eaves.

Showers often delayed this process as the hay had to be thoroughly dry before loading onto the wagon and storing it. Damp hay would generate heat that could create instantaneous combustion. Then hay, the barn, even animals could all be lost, proving that someone had not tested the hay carefully enough for dryness before bringing it off the field.

Sheaves of wheat, barley and oats were tied together in bundles using the long pliable sea grass, collected earlier in certain well-known areas in the forest. This strong grass was cut earlier in the year and stored ready for women to tuck into the tops of their aprons when the time came for harvesting.

In the fall, stacks of huge, hand woven potato baskets were brought out to the fields. With her long canvas apron tied around her waist, Aloisia crawled along the ploughed-up rows of potatoes. The small and damaged potatoes would be sorted out later; they were good for making gruel for the pigs. The filled baskets were then hoisted onto stone boats, hauled back to the farm and the potatoes were rolled into wooden storage bins. The empty baskets were needed again out on the field.

Aloisia had seen a copy of a painting somewhere in which women were crawling across a field, scratching out potatoes from the brown earth. What a miserable scene! To think that people could want such a backbreaking picture in their home was beyond her.

After the first frost whitened the fields, mangels and sugar beets had to be hacked out of the ground and forked onto an oxcart which was driven to where they could be dumped into piles. Then earth was shovelled over the piles to keep the roots firm and in good condition until they were fed to the cows as winter fodder. Naturally, the mangels had to be sliced in that old grinder mounted on the barn wall. The cattle couldn't eat them whole.

Pigs ate the corn in their entirety, stalks and cobs. When the potato, corn and mangels harvest season was over, it took weeks for Aloisia's hands to get back to their usual state which wasn't that good at the best of times.

The day the butcher came to slaughter the pig was a major event. It took several people to get the animal hoisted up with pulleys into the right position so that when its throat was cut, the blood would run into the waiting buckets. The organs were removed, the intestines carefully washed and rinsed so that they could be used for making sausage casings. The fat was set aside for rendering or making soap. Aloisia knew what had to be done. It was a happy day for their dog, Butsi, and the farm cats.

As before, when both sisters lived in the family home, Dori always had the lighter chores like feeding the chickens and geese, collecting the eggs and cooking their small meals. Or Dori was in the city giving a hand to a relative with a new baby.

All the heavy chores belonged to Aloisia. Yes, she had the muscles; she wasn't frail like Dori. So, on washdays, it was Aloisia and Oscar who pumped the water from the well, carried the pails into the kitchen and filled the galvanised tubs on the stove.

"You're so lucky," her older brothers said when they came to the farm. "In our day the pump wasn't installed and we had to crank each pail up from the bottom of the well. That was a hell of a lot harder."

Aloisia and Mina, with the help of a visiting sister-in-law, made the soap. It was made from potash obtained from the ashes of burning their own hardwood such as oak or beech and stored in a barrel until ready to use. To this was added lard from the pigs as well as the fat from other animals killed on the farm.

Some pieces of clothing and linen were too large and unwieldy for the wash board. These articles were spread on a table, the top of which was well whitened by years of use, and scrubbed with already reddened hands.

Wash had to be pegged on lines properly; there was a right way to hang each type of laundry. What would the neighbours think if it weren't done properly? Most importantly, Aloisia's mother had impressed upon her long ago that, whenever possible pieces should be given a shake or two before hanging. It saved on the ironing.

Of course the whites had to be white. Laying linen with bloodstains out in the sunny back yard and keeping them wet with a watering can did wonders. Bloodstained bandages, bloodstained menstrual pads and the belts which held them, bloodstained sheets when the red flannel protection cover had slipped during the night or when, due to heavy work, a menses came early.

Aloisia's hands flew over the work of folding, ironing and putting away the wash. By the weekend it was all done except for the mending. Bedding, shirts and socks that needed special attention were put aside for a rainy day.

The linen cupboard, shelves edged with lace, was the pride of every well managed home and the Schropp home certainly was well managed. Opening its doors always released the sensuous, sweet aroma of properly folded duvets, sheets and pillowcases.

## Aloisia

There were many little skills required to achieve this result, details which were attended to as a matter of course. The whiteness was from boiling and also exposing the wet linen to the strong rays of the morning sun. It was also important to use enough soap that the wash water was slippery, but not so much soap that there would be difficulty getting all the soap thoroughly rinsed out.

The fresh aroma came from drying the linen on a day with a stiff breeze. If clothes were hung on the line when snow was in the air, so much the better. Ironing was a skill all of its own. How and when to dampen the clothes, how not to scorch the linen, how to fold. Of course everything had to be completely dry before being put away. Otherwise a musty smell might develop and that was definitely not the smell you wanted. Finally, the cupboard had to shut tightly to seal in the freshness.

Aloisia used much of her energy for the Schropp farm and that meant also for the extended family. It didn't seem to be in God's plan for her to have a life of her own or to get away from Ried.

She was, however, still luckier than many people. She had learned to teach sewing and needlework of all kinds. This gave her an opportunity to gradually build up a little bank account. Yes, she was luckier than many people.

A scene often haunted her. She had been on her way by train to a cloister where the nuns were giving courses on how to spin wool. When Aloisia got hungry she started eating a sandwich she had prepared for the trip. A lady next to her asked if she couldn't have a piece. Aloisia gave her a sandwich

Another traveller cried out, "oh, if only I had been sitting next to that lady I could have had a piece of bread for my daughter and me. If only I had been sitting there!" The same words could be read in the eyes of the other travellers too. Now, almost ten years after the war's end, it seemed there would always be hardship in Germany. No relief was in sight.

# He Loves Me, He Loves Me Not

More than ever before, Aloisia's life seemed to be on an endless treadmill. Her few joys had now became unpleasant. Choir practices, which had been one of the activities she had always looked forward to with such enthusiasm, were now unbearable. Schmid was there. She even talked to the choirmaster about withdrawing. He was sympathetic, but firm; she must stay. Aloisia was his best alto. She should offer her discomfort up to God as a sacrifice for the sins of the world. And Aloisia remembered the words of her mother. "If you cannot carry your cross, drag it." She realised that the idea of leaving the choir was really impossible anyway. It would just cause more gossip.

Aloisia also felt uneasy attending Sunday night dances, though once they used to be her happiest hours in the week. Schmid did not attend anymore. It was better that way. But Aloisia was tired of being asked to dance by men whose sympathetic girlfriends and wives nudged them on.

Aloisia didn't perspire when she did physical work, but whenever she thought of that last letter she sent by express post to catch Franz before he left, she flushed with embarrassment. She told him she loved him and offered to join him maybe even by November. Now it was the end of summer and except for that one quick answer written on May 15, no letter had come from him. She felt a little knot in her stomach when she started to think of what she had written. What a fool she had made of herself, writing that she would join him and love him even in poor circumstances! If her family knew she had written those words they would think she had lost her mind. Why hadn't Franz written again?

There were always stories. One emigrant who boarded a ship in Hamburg had died during the crossing. He was buried at sea. The captain had to write his mother and father. Perhaps that is what happened to Franz. He was wrapped in a shroud

– with her letter still buttoned into his breast pocket.

Another emigrant, who apparently landed safely enough, because his family received a letter postmarked from Quebec, was never heard from again. Did some American gangsters get him, some gangsters from Chicago? Surely it couldn't be Indians. People she had questioned said that was hardly likely. According to what she had heard indirectly from Karl May's books, it was usually the Indians who were getting killed.

Aloisia also heard of a case where a son came home broke and sick after thinking he would get rich in California. And Aloisia remembered seeing an etching of a shipwreck right off the coast of America.

But perhaps Franz wasn't dead. Perhaps he had decided to discontinue a friendship that had lasted ten years, but which, she too had to admit, had recently become painful. Why prolong it longer? All the doors seemed to slam in their faces.

Franz may have found somebody else in Canada. That was a definite possibility for someone so handsome. Maybe he found a woman who didn't have red hair – and the freckles that went with them. That, however, had really never have seemed to concern Franz. In fact, he loved her eyes and stroked her hair saying it was the colour of cloves.

That's what he said when Dori was out on the road waiting for Ludwig and she and Franz were alone in her bedroom. They had some magical moments together, talking about subjects she had never ever discussed with Schmid, even though she used to see him almost every day, for years. They embraced and kissed. He asked if she liked the smell of his skin.

"Yes," she nodded.

Franz had answered that that was good. That was very important.

And Franz had asked her a question, which now on reflecting, seemed unbelievable. But at the time, the way he asked her made it seem very normal. If he weren't so religious she would never have consented, but the way he asked to see that part of her body which might nourish their children some day, well there just didn't seem to be anything wrong about it. She unbuttoned her blouse, slowly and deliberately. His gentle touch thrilled her. Then Franz carefully buttoned up her blouse again. They kissed again.

Down deep Aloisia didn't regret those moments. He loved her as she loved him. At least the feeling was mutual at the time. She was certain. That is when Ludwig appeared on the scene.

After the gunshot incident, word got around that Aloisia might be thinking of marrying Franz and immigrating to Canada. Relatives arranged a meeting with the two of them. Only when everyone was together did it become clear to Aloisia and Franz that the meeting was simply to abort any such plan. Why should the two of them suffer hardships just because the Canadian Pacific had ads everywhere calling themselves 'the world's greatest travel system' and 'Canadian Pacific all the way'. One of the Schropp sons had found out that the Canadian Pacific had taken over immigration from the Canadian government and that is why even people from former enemy countries were now welcome to come to Canada. Naturally, that would make the company more money.

As Germans were known as hard workers, Canada would not be the first country to invite them with open arms. Their skills and know-how came in very handy for opening up any country.

And anyway, Baumgartner – he was always referred to this way – should go to Canada first and check out the situation. Maybe he would return, disappointed, just like he did from Argentina. Her family did not want to understand that things were going well for Franz in Argentina but his father called him home.

And going across Canada by train, another brother interjected, was very dangerous. Canada was going through a depression too and there were hobos jumping trains and reaching into windows and stealing handbags. Why should Aloisia exchange a furnished home with all the comforts for who knows what?

Franz had to admit when questioned directly that he really didn't have much to offer. Actually, by the time he paid his fair, there would be not much money left at all. But he intended to sell some personal belongings, some tools. He was strong and intended to get work in Canada right away. Aloisia's relatives looked at each other and then at Franz. It was all wishful thinking. Aloisia finally nodded reluctantly. The relatives had won Aloisia over. Franz was left with no allies in the argument.

The relatives, now realizing that they were at an advantage, got a little more forceful. Franz should stop bothering Aloisia. If he wanted to roam around the world, that was fine for him but he should realize, once and for all, that the idea of marrying Aloisia was simply ridiculous, fruitless. The matter appeared to be settled once and for all.

Franz told them he would put all his affairs in order and immigrate to Canada – alone. He solemnly said good-bye. Aloisia could still remember his dignity and erect bearing when he departed.

On the days and weeks after Franz left the meeting, however, Aloisia felt more and more lonely. She tried to be sensible and concentrate on her work but her sense of balance seemed to be gone. Her home was just a house. The meals were tasteless. She realised that life without Franz was really not worth living.

Even though it was the month of May and lambs were frolicking on the daisy-covered meadow, her heart was breaking! She plucked the petals of several daisies to see if they had the answer.

> "*He loves me.*
> *He loves me not.*
> *He loves me.*
> *He loves me not.*

He loves me," whispered the daisy petals one after another.

Finally, on the day she knew Franz was leaving his home, she could bear it no longer. Aloisia hurriedly wrote him a letter. She loved Franz, even if they didn't have much money. She trusted him. She would wait for him.

She jumped on her bicycle and rode to Moedishofen. There the post would be picked up sooner. When she ran into the office and up to the wicket, Aloisia, with a little embarrassment, asked when her letter would arrive at its destination.

## *The Making of a Frontier Woman*

The clerk looked at the address. She raised her eyebrows and peered at the wall clock.

"The fifteenth."

"Oh, that's too late. He's already leaving on the fifteenth."

Then you'll have to mail it by express. It will make it on the fourteenth. That will cost a little more."

Aloisia didn't have enough money.

" Well, you could send it anyway," the clerk smiled, "and the receiver might pay for it. But if he doesn't, your letter will come back. Somebody has to pay. If you want it to get there at all, you have to send it express and just hope he'll pay the extra."

"Send it," Aloisia said firmly.

Franz received her letter just as he was leaving home for the last time. He paid the amount due. He wrote back but made it clear that there was no chance for them to get married now. Certainly not after that meeting when she sided with her relatives against him. Anyway, he did not know how things would develop in Canada. He did, however, feel sorry for her. He should at least remain her friend. She needed somebody with whom to communicate.

That was all months ago, three months ago to be exact. What kind of a friend was one who didn't write for over three months? Of course, if he were dead....

Other scenarios also tumbled through her brain. Maybe some gangsters killed him, stole his money. Many people just disappeared there. America was a gangster country. That's what the newspapers said. That's what people said. Maybe he's dead, maybe he's dead," went around in her mind like a refrain of music repeating over and over again when a needle caught in a deep scratch on an old "His Master's Voice" gramophone record.

Aloisia hoped Dori wasn't hiding a letter from Franz like she used to when she insist on reading Aloisia's letters first. No, that had changed. Peter had sided with Aloisia saying that even though Dori, as an older sister, was only trying to protect

Aloisia from a foolish liaison, the letters were addressed to Aloisia and she should be the one to open them.

After that, Dori started taunting Aloisia with their probable contents. Aloisia didn't plead for them anymore. She had learned that within a day of a letter's arrival Dori would fling it at her with some comment such as, "Here then, you silly little fool, have your gypsy letter." No, there had been no letter from Franz.

Besides living with such a jealous sister, Aloisia was in the awkward position of having her former boyfriend openly displaying his unhappiness with his arranged marriage. At first, she was somehow comforted by his misery. But his aloofness to his wife was painful for Aloisia to see. She wished he would accept his role with dignity. After all, he had gotten a farm of his own out of the deal.

Schmid's sister-in-law told Aloisia that Schmid had made a terrible mistake. He was making his wife miserable and even Sophie's mother, who had prayed a novena so her daughter would get Schmid, felt bewildered by her daughter's unhappiness. The Meyers farm had the help it needed, but it was not a happy situation. They all shared the same house and could hear the quarrelling, she told Aloisia.

Well, Schmid had to make the best of it. One had to accept things the way they were. If he could not carry his cross, he would have to drag it. That was a common expression in the village, the rule, you might say. And Aloisia would have to drag hers too. What else could be done? Annulment was out of the question. There was no doubt the marriage had been consummated, even a little early for that matter, and divorce was out of the question. That procedure was only for those unfortunate souls, the Protestants, who read the Bible for themselves, not seeming to trust their clergy to interpret the Holy Book properly as the Catholics did. Yes, in Catholic villages marriages were until death. If you can't carry your cross, drag it.

# Bee Class in Ried

It was July. The Bavarian government had made arrangements with village mayors to conduct beekeeping classes in certain villages. Honey production should be increased as much as possible as sugar was still scarce. Ried was selected as one of these locations. Some people came from nearby places such as Osterkuebach and Dinkelscherben, but others came from Untermeitingen, Biberbach and Zusmarshausen. The instructor was coming all the way from Donauwoerth, a distance well over 100 kilometres.

When Aloisia had attended her last apiary class in Freising, Blumental had said there were always innovations and ideas to share with fellow apiarists. That was ten years ago, when she met Franz. He certainly was a new idea. Now Franz had emigrated to Canada. She had lost him, just as she had lost Schmid.

Most of the thirty-three who attended this class were men. Of this number only three were women, including Aloisia. There were eight children of varying ages, all of whom had hair the colour of dressed flax except for one boy. He had brown hair. Some of the younger boys (there was also one little girl), had fathers who were beekeepers but never came back from the war.

The instructor was an older, well-built man with a full white beard, something like Saint Nicholas. Only St. Nicholas was dressed all in red and the instructor was all in white. He welcomed each of them and was, like Nicholas, especially pleased to see so many children.

On display was a new design of wax foundation reinforced with crimped wires, which prevented the wax from slipping off the wooden frames. He brought beekeeping catalogues showing where these new foundations could be purchased. If one could afford it, they were certainly worth it. The instructor also brought a tray of his own design for carrying honey frames to the separator, and of course, for carrying empty frames back to the hives again. He welcomed participants to copy his innovation.

He gave many tips to increase fruit yield in orchards. He looked at the children. "Bees find it much easier to collect pollen and nectar from dandelions than from the blossoms of fruit trees. Even though bees are hard workers, where do you think they would go first, the cherry blossoms or the dandelions?"

"The dandelions!" shouted the children all in unison.

"Very good!" he smiled. "So should you let dandelions grow in orchards?"

"No!" The children shouted again.

"My, my," the instructor laughed, stroking his beard. "You are all going to be very good apiarists! Yes, if you want the bees to pollinate your fruit trees, you must remove the dandelions, or at least keep the flowers cut. And," he smiled and lifted his index finger, "that rule goes for areas around blueberries, raspberries and gooseberries too."

Aloisia's mind wandered to Franz. He would have enjoyed these children. The way his letters sounded, he also had a good way with them. But he was now, if his plan was working out, somewhere in the middle of Canada. Franz said that he would keep in touch, just as a friend. But that was months ago.

The instructor told them that the entrance of hives must be oriented towards the east so the bees can warm themselves by the morning sun. He explained how a gentleman had approached him at the last town he had lectured in and complained of never getting much honey from his bees. After some questioning, the instructor found that the man had planted a hedge around his hives to protect them from the wind. Of course that was good. Bees must be protected from wind, especially cold winter wind. But the hedge also blocked out the morning sun. So the bees slept in and had a very short working day. It was a wonder the bees hadn't swarmed and moved to a better location already. They like to be busy, but require sunlight and warmth to wake them up. It's not always easy to find the right location to make bees happy.

"If you have trouble with mice," he continued, "put wire mesh over the openings. And don't put your hives anywhere near where you're threshing because where there's grain, there's mice. You can't trust mice. They can gnaw into anything if they're in the mood. They can become a real nuisance."

He talked about how to know when honey is ready for harvesting. At least three-quarters of each side of the frame should be capped. Another way to tell if it's ripe is to turn the frame horizontal to the ground. If the honey starts dripping out, it's not ripe. Aloisia knew that.

"Bees not only need pollen and nectar, they need a watering hole of some kind. The water should be lukewarm—but fresh. A nearby water trough is fine." He looked at the children. "Have you ever seen bees on the sides of a watering trough taking a drink?"

*Beekeeping class in Ried, 1926.*
*Aloisia is second from right, second seated row from front*

The children nodded and put up their hands.

"Yes, it's not only cows and horses and oxen and geese that drink water. Bees need it too. Even a sponge in a pan of fresh water will do."

There were many questions and answers. Finally, one little boy with brown hair put up his hand and asked if hives weren't made out of woven baskets when the instructor was a little boy.

"That's a good question," the instructor smiled enthusiastically. "But I'm not quite that old," he said, stroking his beard again. "That was long before my time. Yes, hives used to be made like a large upside down basket put on a round, wooden board. They were called skeps. In the fall, beekeepers chased the bees away with smoke or even killed them." He explained how the apiarist tilted the hive and scraped out the honey with a long curved knife made especially for that job. "But that was long before my time," he repeated. "In some countries, like in Africa, they still use clay pots and hollow logs." Then he turned to the adults. "As far as we know, Luis Mendez de Torres was the first man to make bee hives using boards. That was way back in the sixteenth century in Spain."

Now the adults nodded and smiled as though they already knew about Luis Mendez de Torres of Spain.

"And," the instructor continued, "it was only after the invention of square wooden hives that people gradually began to understand what goes on inside a hive. Virgil, a Roman writer, called the ruler of the hive the king instead of the queen. Even up until a couple of hundred years ago, people assumed the same.

"And we're still learning about bees," the instructor continued. "For some time it had been suspected that bees prefer the colour blue. A university professor and I have been keeping exact honey production charts and there seemed no doubt bees find their hives more quickly if painted light blue. They seem to be attracted to that colour. And if they don't have to waste time looking for their home that increases the number of trips they can make to the flowers. In other words, there is a direct correlation between painting a hive blue and

## The Making of a Frontier Woman

increased honey production. "Try it yourself," he said. "See if you don't think it makes a difference."

The boy with brown hair put up his hand again. "What about painting a hive red or yellow?" he asked excitedly.

"Those are wonderful happy colours but," the instructor shook his head, "For some reason bees don't seem to like that colour for a home. Maybe someday you could do a study and see if that isn't true. What do you think?"

The brown-haired boy now became a little shy and shrugged.

"By the way," the instructor asked, turning to the women, "Did you know, that a mixture of turpentine and bees wax makes a wonderful polish for wood floors?"

The women looked at each other. They knew that, but nodded appreciatively. They clasped their hands on their laps and smiled.

"You apply it on the floor with a bristle brush and then polish with an old rag," he continued, "Like you polish the shoes for your family."

Finally, the instructor brought out a camera; it was time to take a picture. Part of the background was to be the honey shed. Maybe some of its interior would show up if the door were left open. The children grouped towards the front. Beekeeping paraphernalia such as smokers and frames were distributed around to make the picture more interesting.

A few weeks later, when the photograph arrived in the mail, Aloisia was disappointed. Her hands were clasped together in a dignified way. That was good. She was looking directly at the camera and that was good. Her teeth weren't showing, so her smile was just right. A broad smile would not be considered acceptable.

She had tried to put on a brave face, as she was often doing these days, but she looked too serious. She looked old and tired. The part in her hair showed too much. Aloisia had not taken time to use her curling iron. She always had trouble with her fine hair. Of course, Franz wasn't in the photograph this time. He was gone. Gone to America.

## *Aloisia*

Aloisia sometimes kept her portable sewing machine at her sister-in-law's place. Since Hans hadn't come back from the war, Aloisia often did her work there keeping his widow and four little girls company.

Schmid, unhappy with his marriage, often came walking across the backfields to visit. When he came, the children were taken out to play. No wonder Aloisia looked haggard.

# CHAPTER FOUR: 1926-1927

THE BLUE RIBBON

# A Lark Was Singing

Peter had promised to be at a neighbour's place at the break of dawn to do a little bartering; some firewood for the pick of a sow's litter. But when the roosters in the village started to crow, he and Aloisia were already up helping a cow that was calving. They had been alerted by the unusual mooing sounds coming through the barn wall. This was one of those many farm jobs that often required not only two strong hands, but also two people. Aloisia had to help, so now she was behind schedule. She had planned to stook hay but now Peter asked her to look after his sheep. Hopefully the weather would hold so the hay would stay dry.

Aloisia's eyes were on the dusty road, her bare feet following the ruts made on previous trips. Now, having milked the cows and done all the other related morning chores, she was late bringing the milk to the dairy. Ahead, some ducks and geese were waddling to the side of the road as the mailman bicycled to the house that served as the local post office.

"Miss Schropp!" He stopped and got off the bike. "Miss Schropp, you're always running. Slow down! You're going to kill yourself one day."

Aloisia glanced up. She laughed off his comment and kept going. Then out of the corner of her eye she saw him reaching into his leather mailbag.

"You might slow down if you knew I had a letter from Canada for you!" He pulled out an envelope. "That Baumgartner sure gets around."

Aloisia stopped, lowering the cart handles as quickly as she could without bumping off the milk cans. As if in a dream, she reached her hand out to take the envelope. The postage was strange to her, but it was Franz's handwriting. He had arrived safely in Canada!

"Your friend sure gets around. I like his wax seal."

"Thank you." Aloisia smiled, not knowing what other comment to make at the spur of the moment. A neighbour was coming back from the dairy with empty milk containers. She felt the smoothness of the envelope between her fingers before lifting her apron and thrusting it into the warm depths of her skirt pocket. Then she grasped the handles of the milk cart and hurried along the dirt road to the milk depot.

Finches were playing in the wild rose hedgerows. A lark was singing high up in the almost cloudless sky. It was a wonderful day. Franz had not forgotten her. He had not forgotten her, but still had no money. Or had that problem changed? Or did she care?

Aloisia helped hoist the milk cans from the cart onto the weighing platform. While they were being weighed, she quickly replaced them with empty cans. Then, without waiting a moment to chat with anyone, she turned her cart around and started back home.

When she had only gone a short distance, she looked around and stopped. It wouldn't look good for her to be seen standing idle in the middle of the road, reading a letter. She pulled the cart into the shadow of a lilac hedge on which a few faded blossoms clung.

With fingers trembling with excitement, Aloisia took her small sewing scissors from her pocket and cut open the envelope. She disliked breaking the wax seal. The stamp was of King George V and postmarked with a date in August she couldn't quite make out. The letter was dated August 14 from some place in Canada called Windthorst.

# Letter From the Middle of Canada

*Windthorst,
August 14, 1926*

*My dear Luise!*

*You certainly must have received my letter. Pretty soon you don't know what to make of me any more. Yes, since I received your express letter on that turbulent day of my departure, my life has been really off track. I thought it was definitely over between us and here in Canada I would start a new life. But things seem to be turning out differently.*

*It would be all right if you bind me to you. Only it is very hard that we are so far apart, especially for me because I often wonder if I love you enough and I also don't know if you desire me in the physical way a woman should in order to get married. Because of the rejection of your sisters and brothers on my visit, I decided it was useless to talk more. According to your letters, you did not want to get into poor circumstances or wish to emigrate. And without emigrating, there is no hope.*

*On that occasion, you yourself must admit and sense that we did not see eye to eye on this matter. However, I now realise with certainty that you desire me as I desire to be with a woman. Yes, the longing to be finally united with a woman, body and soul, is what drives me crazy.*

*Dear Luise, I write all this very reluctantly, but I have to tell you so you can understand me. I certainly cannot tell you in person. I expect, however, that you let flames consume this letter, which I also ask you to do with the previous letters.*

*Because of my open and direct personality, I have to tell you frankly that I am no longer of the opinion that*

*I could comply with such a holy ideal marriage as is described in the book by Hessenbach. Tormenting doubts could arise that I could not love you enough. But if you only were here, I believe I would like you very much.*

*You, dearest, have supported me and taken me into your heart as no one else. Yes, you are sweet and gentle. Of all, you understand me the best and nobody has ever been so concerned about me. Why should I look for others and scorn your love now that I am so in need of your love? And you pleased me very much when you wrote, 'trust me that I would want to make you happy even in poor circumstances.'*

*You are wondering about my letter, right? Yes, I am sure.*

*I am feeling fine again and am, since yesterday, working in the harvest again. I am quite well. The daily wages are at least $4=16,80 Marks. I realise now that the source of my physical and spiritual illness was caused by unfulfilled love. If it is the same with you, dearest Luise, it would be certainly fine if you come to me in November as you wrote in your last letter. Living quarters are easy to find here and I am sure you could find a little work here soon, if you would like to try dressmaking, but I would prefer it if you wouldn't need to.*

*There are also many opportunities for young couples to find work on farms because there are many unmarried farmers here. The monthly wages are about $50 for both and room and board is free. In most of the places at which I have been, the food is as good here every day as in the annual parish fair at home. I got around a lot when I was whitewashing. Now I have $205 in the bank.*

*I am thinking of getting someone to build me a small, transportable little American house. You can pull that for miles. Even if you were only a friend I would advise you to come as girls as very prized here and earn $35 per month as housekeepers.*

*In the country people rarely get up before six o'clock and people are better equipped as they would be in the old country under the same circumstances. For example, where I am right now with the harvest, some of the farmers have steam or warm air heat. The hired men live in the house and have good beds. I really like it here. Almost every household has a washing machine, often motorised. The food and clothing is very cheap in comparison to the high wages. After all, the country is rich.*

*However the people are not as efficient and frugal as we are, because they don't have to be and see nothing else and are not used to anything different. Some hired men have their own cars. It is possible to buy one with one year's wages. The majority of women wear their hair short but I don't like it. Most of them wear clothes with open necks and short sleeves.*

Inflation was so out of control that money had to be stamped with the new value

*That is all for today. I have to stop now or I won't get supper anymore.*

*Please write when you are coming. Then I will, after consulting with my spiritual advisor who administers the immigration in this area, give further directions.*

*I greet and kiss you from the bottom of my heart.*

*Yours sincerely,*

*Franz*

# The Four Leaf Clover

With crook in hand and Butsi circling along the way, Aloisia brought Peter's sheep to pasture. She was carrying a small tin pail with milk and a cloth bag holding some apples and a hank of bread. Deep in her pocket was Franz's letter.

Soon she was sitting in the shade of the hazelnut trees bordering their forest. Butsi was resting nearby but keeping a watchful eye on the grazing sheep. It was September and their fleece had grown long since spring shearing. They didn't move about more than necessary. The lambs had grown more lethargic too.

Repeatedly, Aloisia put her knitting aside and took up Franz's letter instead. Her eyes paused here and there to absorb the full meaning of each word – and number. She had not made a fool of herself after all.

Her last name would not be Schropp any more. It would be Baumgartner! A new name for a new land, a rich land! The two of them would work hard and succeed. Mixed with the occasional bleating and the click of her steel knitting needles, Aloisia imagined hearing Franz's voice. He was holding out his strong hand calling her, waiting for her.

One of her needles slipped off her apron and when she picked it up she spotted a four leaf clover. Oh, God, how lucky she was! And how lucky that she had saved herself for him.

That Franz didn't agree with Hessenbach's book was no problem. Franz was so smart. If he, such a devout Catholic, had figured something out, she wouldn't question it. It was entitled *An Ideal Marriage and Its Blessing for Mothers and Children*. According to the description on the cover, the book was to be studied by betrothed couples as a preparation for marriage. Aloisia had read it. The main theme, repeated throughout the book, was that sexual intercourse was for procreation only. When the wife was certain she was pregnant, the couple were to abstain from sex not only until the child was born, but until it was weaned – perhaps a year or two later. The purpose of the sex drive was for procreation and for procreation only.

Well, Aloisia thought, Franz is probably right. One doesn't have to believe every single detail the Catholic Church preaches. For instance, it was hard to understand how the Virgin Mary ascended up into the clouds. That was no place to live. Aloisia tried to imagine how it would feel if she herself lifted off the ground, higher than the church steeple even, and then looked down. But Mary wouldn't be frightened. She wouldn't even be concerned about things like falling. Mary's eyes were already focused upward on heaven. Of course, Aloisia would never share such thoughts with a single soul. In fact, it was already a sin just thinking about it.... But a person shouldn't be fanatic.

However, Aloisia couldn't help thinking. A farmer always saw to it that he had a rooster for his flock of chickens. There was no abstinence there. The hens always laid more eggs when a rooster was around. Cows, on the other hand, had to be kept calm. They could not produce much milk if they were busy with the bull all the time, running here and there across the meadows. Actually, the bull was usually stanchioned in a separate part of the barn from where the cows were so his proximity would not disturb them.

When a cow came into heat, she was coaxed into a fenced enclosure behind the barn. Then Peter would snap the end of a strong pole, designed with a clamp on one end, to the bull's nose ring. The bull was then carefully led to the same small fenced field and set free. Aloisia had often looked on, even though it wasn't considered the type of thing a woman should watch.

But human beings were not animals. One couldn't really compare. And really, it wasn't her obligation to think about such things or even her right. The Holy Catholic Church did that for her. It had priests, bishops, archbishops and cardinals who were well educated, read Latin and could determine what was good Christian living and what was sinful.

And that is also why catechisms were written. She had

memorized many parts almost word for word: "If we deliberately violate an important law, if we die in mortal sin, our separation from God is eternal, that is, we are in Hell. We have forfeited our right to the kingdom of light and joy, and our lot is cast with those who dwell in the realm of darkness and eternal pain."

The question was whether breaking Hessenbach's admonition was considered a venial sin. Surely it wouldn't be a mortal sin.

The Pope, however, was infallible. Hessenbach's book did have the imprimatur. It was, therefore, endorsed by the Church.

Well, Aloisia had other things to think about. Thousands of other people were married and seemed to manage.

A shudder passed through Aloisia as she thought of the life that would have been hers if Franz's letter had not arrived. She imagined the rest of her life with neighbours nudging each other, whispering behind their hands as she walked past. She had been discarded. Even though that was not really the case, the end result was just that simple. It was how she herself often felt.

Then there was Schmid. He often accidentally bumped into her as she made her daily chores in and around Ried. Surely, the conductor must have seen how often Schmid looked over at her in the choir loft. Had anyone noticed how often he dropped in to Aloisia's sister-in-law when she was sewing there? Had someone seen them in the forest together?

She gave her head a shake to clear her mind. She felt a little dizzy. What should she do first? She must plan, make lists of things to do, not only in her head, but also on paper. That way she would not forget anything. First, she would write Franz and say yes. Yes, she would come. She would bring her Franz – yes, she could say 'her Franz' now – some special cigars from Scheufele's store.

What else? Her treasured Excella sewing machine, her new undershirts and she would finally make up that good cotton fabric into a summer dress. Franz would like that. There was so much to think about. Now she understood Franz's excitement in that last letter from Passau before he left.

But how would she tell her sister, Dori, Peter and everyone? As Aloisia started the plain knitting below the heel of another sock she prepared for yet another encounter with Dori. How many scenes had she already with her since Franz's letters started coming?

Finally the day came to an end. The sheep were in their enclosure and the barn chores completed. The cows were chewing their cuds. She walked down the lane to the house she shared with Dori.

Even though the evening shadows were lengthening, the walls of the house radiated back the sweltering heat of the day like oven heated bricks taken into bed on winter nights. The white stucco had done little to stop the absorption of the sun's rays by the brick and mortar beneath. And Aloisia knew that what she was now going to tell Dori would make things even hotter. This time, however, Dori's comments would not intimidate her. She wasn't going to be pushed around.

Dori was in the kitchen. Aloisia set the jug of fresh milk down beside the potato salad and dark bread. The sisters bent their heads over their food. Dori's red hair, like Aloisia's was braided and pinned into a tight bun behind her head. That was about all the two seemed to have in common.

Aloisia cleared her throat. "Got news from Franz today," she said, trying to appear casual as she waved a bee away from the salad.

"How could you?" Dori said. Her face went ashen, as ashen as it could go with the freckles she, like Aloisia, had in abundance. "I picked up the mail at the post office myself, and there wasn't anything for you. Or maybe Baumgartner sent it by carrier pigeon?"

"No, he used flag signals."

Dori bit her lip to stop herself from smiling. Her jaw muscles tightened.

Aloisia continued, "The mailman gave it directly to me when I delivered the milk."

## The Making of a Frontier Woman

Dori shrugged, "So you finally got another dream letter. I thought we had heard the last of him finally. What does the wanderer have to say for himself this time?"

"Franz has decided to stay in Canada. Franz says the country has great promise and the wages are good, lots of work and ...."

"Well good for him," Dori snapped. "Hope he stays there and doesn't come back like he did from Argentina. Anyway, he's just words and poetry. You can't do much with that."

Aloisia reached her hand deep down into the pocket of her dress and felt the smoothness of Franz's letter. "Well, things have changed. I'm going to marry him. Things are much better in Canada."

"What?" Dori banged her spoon down on the table. "Have you lost your mind?"

"Say what you like, I've decided to go. Why should I listen to you? You, with your wonderful manners."

"I didn't spit at him! I wasn't even aiming at him, just on the ground. Somebody has to teach him a lesson and make him understand that our family doesn't want him."

Aloisia shook her head. "Well, I guess your spitting didn't work, nor Ludwig firing his pistol. I'm just surprised Franz wants anything to do with me after that. It's so embarrassing. Franz could have complained to the police. He could have laid charges, you know." Aloisia shook her head again. "You're really something else."

Dori shrugged. "And what kind of manners does he have, visiting unannounced? You're not going to take him seriously are you...." She tapped her index finger on her forehead. "Are you crazy? You, you bleary eyed fool? He admitted that he didn't have much money. We've gone all through this before, for heaven's sake. You don't seem to have any clue of what you're getting yourself into."

"Things have changed. I wouldn't go unless I knew what I was doing. Franz has written me every detail."

"And what about the work here? Don't you think of anyone but yourself?"

"Dori! You should be ashamed to talk like that. I was the one who helped mother look after our father when he got stomach cancer. And when mother died last spring, I was here, not visiting here and there in the city."

Aloisia remembered how her father was so thin his body couldn't be seen under the quilt and how the family had asked the doctor if there wasn't anything for his pain and how the doctor gave him an injection and said, "He will sleep tonight." And how a few hours later he died peacefully in his sleep.

She remembered the morning, ten years later, how her sick mother kept asking, 'When will it be noon? When is it noon time?' And just after the clock struck twelve, she stopped breathing. Aloisia gently closed her mother's eyes with her fingertips, just like that neighbour prophesied so many years ago.

Dori shrugged. "We all have our duty."

"Well," Aloisia said, "God knows I was glad to do it. But I'm twenty-nine years old. What should I wait for now, your wedding, I suppose?"

Dori, for once, said nothing.

Aloisia used a crust of rye bread to scoop the last of the potato salad off her plate. She wiped her hands on her apron and pushed her chair away from the table. When almost at the doorway, Aloisia turned and shouted back into the room, "Pity the poor man to marry you!"

Dori jumped up, almost tipping over her chair. "Ha, you've had itchy feet to get away from Ried ever since you turned twenty. It's tiresome. You don't know how lucky you are living in this house. Most women would be happy, but not you, of course. Free food and housing mean nothing to you."

Aloisia gave an almost imperceptible cringe. Franz had once written something very similar in one of his letters. She wondered for a moment if her words were from that letter (she doubted that there was one letter Dori hadn't managed to read – except a couple she had hidden under the false bottom of a box.) Or was Dori just repeating what the rest of the Schropp family were always saying?

"You should talk," Aloisia said, pointing her finger at Dori. "You would take this, what you call a gypsy, in a flash, if he would have you. I'm not blind, you know. You would have taken Schmid too if..."

"Shut up!" Dori's face reddened. "Now you're really going overboard. I didn't call him gypsy, you...."

"Dori, you're beating around the bush. I'm not so stupid to know what you meant when you called him a wanderer. You've called him gypsy lots of times before."

Dori banged her hand on the table and looked up to the ceiling as though some assistance might come from there. "Do I have to put up with this nonsense, I who am the older sister?"

"For heaven's sake, Dori, calm down. How else do you expect Franz to find out where to emigrate if he doesn't look around? He had to go to Argentina to see how things were. Germany is certainly no place to be these days. There's just wiped out bank accounts, people looking at you with circles under their eyes. And no jobs anywhere. They can't even afford to get their shirt collars turned, let alone getting new shirts made up. Some can't even afford having two old shirts made into one."

Dori sighed. "Do you think I'm blind? I'm a seamstress too, you know."

Aloisia ignored Dori's statement. "No, I'm telling you, they can't even afford that. Germany has reparations to pay until the end of time. Maybe you think it's worth staying in this misery. It still haunts me how that woman on the train cried when I gave my sandwich to a lady sitting beside me. And another woman cried out that...."

"Yes, Luise, you've told me that story a hundred times but that's no reason for you to jump from the frying pan into the fire!"

"For heaven's sake, the war has been over almost ten years and there's not a ray of hope in sight. Look at that embroidered tablecloth mother traded for half a pound of butter. We had no butter to spare but mother felt so sorry for her. And we sure didn't need that tablecloth, as nice as it is. What we need is the government to give our money back at its original value, before the inflation. One thousand mark notes stamped over in red with one million! Who would have believed it? Saving all that money for nothing. All that money with absolutely no value!"

"And what value is a pile of letters tied with blue ribbon?"

Aloisia pushed a stray wisp of red hair back into her bun and walked towards the door again. She didn't even bother asking Dori how she knew about the blue ribbon. They had been through that before. "I know Franz and that's what counts," she said firmly.

# Pieces of Kindling

Aloisia walked down her front stairs and turned left up the incline leading to her childhood home. She found Peter sitting in the shade of the house, in his shirt sleeves, smoking his evening pipe and reading the newspaper. Butsi was sprawled out on the grass beside him.

"Good evening, Peter," Aloisia asked, trying to keep her voice calm. "How are things going?"

"So, so," he said, waving off a fly.

Aloisia took a deep breath. "Peter, I've got some news. Franz has asked me to marry him and I'm going to America, to Canada, probably in November." She said it all in one sentence so she would not lose nerve, so she could finish without being interrupted.

Peter looked up and took his pipe out of his mouth. "Now what nonsense. Can't I have some peace, even in my own home?"

Aloisia clasped her hands together. "I'm serious, Peter."

"Serious? It seems not so long ago you were trying to find out all about Argentina. Now it's Canada. What next, China? The family has discussed this before. I thought you said you didn't want to live in poverty. You're not stupid. Use your brains. That Baumgartner name might have a nice sound to it, but he's certainly no Rothschild."

"For heaven's sake, Peter, please...."

"Don't bother me with such nonsense. Talk to me when you have something sensible to say," he turned away from her and continued to read.

Aloisia stood quietly for a moment, looking down at a loose bit of leather on her clogs that she had been meaning to repair. She turned away.

## Aloisia

"Luise," Peter called after her, "Can't you see that Baumgartner is just a troublemaker?"

Aloisia came back, relieved that he was giving her an opening to speak after all.

Peter put the newspaper down and looked up at her. "I told you right from the start, when he dropped in last Easter, that he had no business disturbing your peaceful life. He should stay at home and look after his family's farm instead of wandering all over the place and disrupting other people's lives. Maybe Ludwig should have aimed better."

Aloisia stared past him at the bushes of ripening gooseberries and began to speak, "Franz has invited me to join him". Her words came out slowly, softly. "And I am going to make arrangements." There was an almost imperceptible tremor in her voice. "We're bringing in the last of the hay tomorrow and I wanted you to know that the day after I'm going to Munich to make inquiries about passenger ships going to Canada."

"You can't be serious!"

"And I'm going to tell Emma and Maria," Aloisia continued. "But don't worry, I'll be home for chores."

"Has Baumgartner sent you passage money?"

Aloisia had prepared herself for this question. "Of course not, he's saving his money for the farm he's buying. I have some savings and I can sell a few things." Aloisia took a deep breath. "Maybe I could make you a deal with my part of the forest our parents left. It would be easier for me if I could get paid out now. Then it would be done with."

Peter shook his head. "No, that won't work. I don't have the money to spare. And," he raised his voice, "don't go bothering your sisters and brothers. They have enough problems these days trying to make ends meet." Peter shook his head. "I've been through that scenario with a couple of your brothers already. Anyway, the money might come in very handy at a later date. You never can tell. Don't worry, you'll get your equal share."

Aloisia didn't protest or plead. She realised it was a long shot but she thought she should try. When you want something you have to knock on every door.

## The Making of a Frontier Woman

"Ach, Luise. What can I say? Think about what you're doing. Use your head. Winter is coming. It's no time to travel on water, or on land for that matter. I've heard stories. You should go with somebody, not all by yourself. It's too risky, especially for a woman. You could be robbed, or worse."

"My aunts went to Africa and so did Maria. And she was younger than I am now."

"Luise, don't tell me as though I don't already know. I remember it clearly as though it was yesterday. You were just a babe in arms. And Maria wasn't alone. She travelled with other novices and to a safe place, a cloister. And she got help from that house in Munich."

"You mean the house run by the order called the 'English Ladies'?"

Aloisia was seventeen years younger than Peter and this time found it comforting that she knew something he didn't. Actually, she knew a lot more than just the name of the order. Every time she travelled back and forth to Munich she would smile at some nun and pick up a conversation. It wouldn't be more than a few minutes before Aloisia was talking about her sister, Maria, who became a nun and died in Africa. From these nuns she gradually pieced together information about the 'English Ladies' who were sometimes called the 'Institute of Mary' or 'Loreto Nuns' depending upon the country of their mother-house. Maria Ward, a English woman, founded the order about three hundred years ago. She originally belonged to the Poor Clares but wanted a more active life rather than a simply contemplative one. The main goals were to give girls a good education so they could be self-reliant women and future mothers.

Peter shrugged. "Whatever. Who cares."

Peter's response numbed Aloisia's heart reminding her of a supposedly true story someone had told her. When the goals of Maria Ward's order were explained to some spiritual dignitary he had responded, "Their zeal will soon dwindle. And anyway, women are, all in all, just women!"

"Well, Peter, times have changed and many women travel

alone now. Thousands of women go to Canada by themselves every year from all over the world."

"Who told you that nonsense?"

"The Canadian Pacific told me when I just dropped in at their Munich office once."

"Naturally, they would. They're looking for suckers."

"Peter, can't you look at anything from the bright side? It would be nice if you would give me some support, after all I've done."

"After all you've done? After all you've done?" he repeated. "Haven't we all worked hard? You think you're the only one in the family who has had a tough time? Don't you think Sepp and Paul and Franz and all of us boys had to work from morning 'til night? You and Dori have it much easier than any one of us, I can tell you. Ask any one of your brothers if they got a house virtually given to them."

Aloisia sighed.

"We've built you a house," Peter continued, "What more could you ask for?"

Aloisia put her hands on her hips, something she rarely did. "You seem to forget that I worked night and day hauling bricks, pails of cement and whatever else to help build that house. And if you think Dori is a picnic to live with...."

"Ach, I know, I know," Peter propped his head on his good hand and sighed. "But aren't things going better lately?"

"After what Dori did, phoning Ludwig to come and even spitting at Franz?"

"Ach, you know how she gets carried away. Anyway," Peter shrugged, "You promised to plant the forest this fall. The seedlings are already ordered. This Baumgartner, comes sauntering into our village from halfway across Germany and now he's trying to lure you halfway around the world. And everybody is wondering that he can spare the time away. Doesn't he have any work to do that he has time to write poetry! How come a woman from his own area never married him? That would be interesting to find out."

## The Making of a Frontier Woman

Aloisia crossed her arms. "He could have had lot's of women. He's had lots of chances. He's intelligent and has lots of courage, more courage than most people I know. He even gave up the right to his farm to avoid all the bickering."

Peter took a deep breath. "Ach, Dori told me about that. You call that intelligent? Now if Baumgartner had stayed on his family's farm…. But giving up his right to the farm?"

"There's more to it than that. His father promised to hand the farm over to him if he would come back from Argentina. But when Franz came back, his father never honoured his promise. Anyway, do you see a better husband for me anywhere? One with a farm close by so I could help when you need a hand?" Oh, that didn't come out right, Aloisia thought.

Peter shook his head. "You know many men died in France or are still missing in Russia…." His voice trailed off. "And if it weren't for my hand, I would have been conscripted too."

Aloisia didn't know what to say. Her thoughts were diverted like one of those pieces of kindling that fly from a chopping block. She felt sorry for Peter, as everyone did. Once Peter had everything going for him. He was handsome and strong like all her brothers. Then fate took a twist. He lost those fingers on his left hand. Still, as the eldest son he got the farm, could still get a wife. And he did. Eventually, however, it became clear that for whatever reason, his wife couldn't bear children. The Schropp name would not be carried on in his family.

Peter's voice interrupted her thoughts. "Luise, I know that whole thing with Schmid has hurt you. But it's no sense crying over spilt milk. I know what it means to have one's pride broken. I understand it all too well. Not marrying Schmid and then finding out that Sophie was pregnant. The way that turned out, well…." He shook his head. "Well, believe me, life goes on. Many people have had similar experiences. You just keep on living. You have to. What choice is there?"

"But I do have a choice," Aloisia said, relieved that Peter perhaps understood after all.

"Don't think I'll give you my blessing to marry Baumgartner." Peter said sharply.

The tone of his voice shocked Aloisia back into her reality, her block of wood, her life.

"But how come you didn't want Ludwig to hurt Franz last Easter and you brought Franz over to the house so we could talk and sent Oscar off to exchange grain at the mill so we could be alone?"

"Aloisia, I thought the two of you needed time to talk things out, realise the situation. Sometimes people need to talk things over. You have a good situation right here in Ried. There are thousands of women who would be thrilled to have a house like you and Dori have. You think married life is all bliss? If you leave Ried you'll regret it soon enough and don't say I didn't warn you. Here you have family, friends, your choir, your church. You just take them for granted now. And what will your brothers say? Franz, Paul, Ludwig and all of them?" He pointed the stem of his pipe at the ground. "You're best off right here."

"But they have their own lives. That's all I want for myself."

"What's the use." Peter let out a loud sigh. "Anyway, wasn't there that wheelwright who was interested in you?"

"Him?"

"Yes, him. What's the matter with him? A bird in the hand is worth two in the bush. And as far as I can tell that Baumgartner is definitely in the bush if he's in Canada."

"It didn't work out."

"It didn't work out?" Peter stared at Aloisia. "It didn't work out because you didn't want it to. You have fancy ideas in your head, want something better. Well, I hope you get it. I've done my best. I can't explain anymore. Nobody in this family had better blame me for your decision. I wash my hands of it."

Aloisia realised the futility of the situation. Certainly, some of her friends were sympathetic, but words are just words. Or were they really sneering behind her back? That smart Aloisia, who knows everything, can't even get a man. If all her work on the family farm got so little thanks, staying longer wouldn't be appreciated more.

Obviously, Peter had no clue how difficult it was to live in the same village as Schmid. Schmid had made arrangements with the widow of Hans to meet Aloisia at her home. The house was a little way from the village and Aloisia often did her sewing there. Finally, Aloisia brought those rendezvous to an end.

That was all long ago now, but Schmid still tried to see her and catch her eye with his mournful looks every time he thought nobody was looking. Aloisia didn't dare tell Peter, nor mention that clandestine meeting Schmid had with her in the forest.

If there were any scandal, Aloisia would get the blame. She remembered that poor woman weeping as she slowly walked around the church which the priests did not allow her to enter because she had out of wedlock children. There seemed to be little or no stigma attached to the fathers of those children. It's the women who get the blame.

Aloisia turned into Peter's house where she had spent those innocent days of childhood when nobody knew the meaning of war, when she was surrounded by the culture of peace. "I'm just going up to check the pigeons," she said turning into his doorway and kicking off her clogs. She walked up the first flight of stairs and then, hitching the hem of her dress into the waistband of her apron, she climbed the ladder-like steps into the attic, one of her secret refuges when she was younger. Here she could listen to the cooing and the soft flutter of wings – and dream of the future. Today when she slid open the lock, the heat was stifling. The pigeons weren't on their roosts but outside perching among the leafy branches of the linden tree. She should have known. What was she thinking?

Aloisia came down again and walked out the doorway. Peter was scratching Butsi's neck who was happily wagging her tail from side to side to show appreciation. When Peter saw Aloisia he forcefully exhaled some smoke. Butsi's tail thumped a little more quickly when she saw Aloisia, but she stayed where she was, at Peter's feet.

Slowly, with her lips firmly closed, Aloisia walked away through the longer and paler shadows to the house for which everybody said she should be so grateful. Aloisia did not notice the full moon, the singing crickets or the fireflies dancing

## Aloisia

along the gooseberry hedge as she passed by. She was now as determined to leave home as Franz had been. There must be a better way to live.

When Aloisia arrived back home, Dori was sitting at the kitchen table mending something. She muttered something into her lap but didn't look away from her work. Aloisia went up the stairs to her bedroom and closed the door.

She reached under her mattress and took out a thin booklet. On the front cover were the words: An Ideal Marriage. Hessenbach had it printed in Switzerland. She opened the cover and read the verso which was in Latin:

> *Imprimatur.*
> *Augustae Vindelicorum, die 26. Octobris 1918.*
> *Vicarius generalis*
> *M. Niedermair.*

Aloisia quickly leafed through it and put it back under her mattress again. She sat down at her little table and opened the drawer. From it she drew out a piece of paper and an envelope. She flipped up the pewter lid of the ink-well. Soon all that could be heard in the room was the careful scratching of her pen. Yes, she would come, she was happy to come. The day after tomorrow, she would go to Munich and start making arrangements. She would write him the exact date later.

Aloisia sealed the letter.

She quickly jotted down some lists: things to do, people to talk to, things to buy, even clothes that would wear out and those she would now save for her journey to America. Thank goodness there had been a red sunset. The weather would be sunny. Haying could be finished for the year.

But first she would bring her letter to the post. She could check off the first two things on her list:

1. Write letter to Franz
2. Mail letter to Franz.

# The Last Hayride

Long before the last load, Aloisia felt a dull numbness in her groin and stickiness down her legs; her menses had started. Of course, she couldn't ask to go home in the middle of the day for proper cloth bandages. That would be considered frivolous, a waste of time. Women were expected to keep going, unless they fainted, of course. But that seldom happened. She stooped behind a haystack and quickly knotted together the front and back of her cotton undershirt between her legs. She came back to the hay wagon and continued pitching hay.

Finally, the last forkful of hay was loaded. Aloisia used the small wooden ladder, smoothed by years of use, to swing up to the back of the wagon. She passed the top rung, quickly climbed onto the load and then, leaning on her pitchfork, scanned the bare field. This was the end of the haying season for 1926. This was her last hayride home in Ried.

Where would she be next year? Somewhere in Canada where money was easier to earn and where no depression could wipe away savings. Gone would be Schmid's sighing and Dori's sarcastic comments.

She sank down into the hay. It must have been almost thirty degrees today. Oscar coaxed the horse and ox with giddyup sounds and gently slapped the leather reins. Looking around to check that she was unnoticed, she thrust her hands under her skirt to adjust the double knot of her undershirt. It was secure; it would hold until she got home.

The fragrance of sun dried grasses and the sound of creaking axles combined to make a soothing lullaby to her, a comforting song from the earth. The muffled sounds of the beast's hoofs on the well-trodden road caressed her ears. The aroma of dusty sunshine surrounded her as she reached for a long stem of hay and chewed on its nutty nodule.

As she lay there, she thought how Franz would one day tell her more about how he escaped to Switzerland, how he got to Argentina, about his life there before he came back to his family's farm and then decided to emigrate to Canada. Had he taken along his navy suit and the compass he had shown her when she visited his farm? He had also showed her his navy uniform and its black tie made from his mother's silk scarf.

Aloisia raised her other arm to shade her eyes and watched the white lace ribbons drifting high overhead in the periwinkle blue sky. A breeze from the nearby forest caressed her face leaving her immersed in the rich aroma of the harvest season. A fly buzzed around her head. She shooed it away and pulled he head cloth over her face.

Franz wrote that his wages in Canada were $4.00 a day. Can you imagine? Franz said that is like seventeen marks a day here! Aloisia sighed. By this time next year all her troubles would be left behind.

Moving into the smaller house in the garden had made life easier for Peter and Mina, but not for Aloisia. Dori still liked making sarcastic comments about Schmid's marriage even though that was now some years ago.

"I can never get over how gullible you were considering his child's date of birth. It seems that he was fooling around even before you broke up. If I've told you once, I've told you a hundred times, men just can't be trusted."

But the occasional arrival of a letter from Franz was a great escape, mentally at least. His letters were so interesting! She was so glad she had let Franz persuade her to correspond with him. His letters proved to be a window on the world.

Aloisia reviewed in her mind the history of her husband to be. He had been a signaller on the flagship Frederick the Great, had studied in Munich, had worked on the family farm and lived in Argentina. Then his father wrote him to come home, said he could run things his way. When he got there, his father changed his mind, again. Franz had written her how betrayed he felt.

Aloisia had answered that she could have been able to help make it into a model farm. Certainly, there were difficulties in the family but she could have smoothed them out. The farm was so big.

But the idea of running a farm with Franz had collapsed.

## The Making of a Frontier Woman

He had taken all her arguments into consideration yet finally decided to give up his right to the farm. His father could play games with somebody else. Aloisia didn't really understand all the circumstances. She had to give up coaxing.

In one of his letters Franz tried to distance himself. He said Aloisia was lucky to have such a nice house. She should be content to stay in Ried. He could promise nothing.

If he only knew what she had to put up with every day. She had her own problems too! When she wrote back, she thought ignoring his aloofness would be best. And it was. Franz's reply was cheerful again. He claimed the political unrest had upset him. Communists were gaining power everywhere and then there was that upstart Hitler whom he had shouted at a rally in Munich. She would have to ask him more about all that one day.

Franz wrote he planned returning to Argentina but then changed his mind. He might stay in Germany after all. But finally Canada seemed more promising and that is where he finally decided to emigrate. That is from where he was now writing, asking him to join him. That is where she herself was now emigrating.

Should she bring along his letters, even though at one point Franz had asked her to throw them into the fire? She couldn't do it then and she still couldn't do it. Instead, she organised them according to date, carefully placed them in small white cardboard folders trimmed with pinking shears. She tied the folders together with blue ribbon. With them, she put Hessenbach's book, a little worse for wear.

Now the letters were hidden under her mattress. If she took them along to Canada she would have to somehow keep them hidden. She didn't think Franz would appreciate her having gone against his express wishes, but then again, he might just smile – if he ever found out. She took a deep breath, yawned and fell asleep.

# Even an Ocean

*Broadwater,
January 30, 1927*

*My dear Luise!*

*I am waiting with longing for mail from you. Hopefully I will get news from you tomorrow when the ship comes. How are you? I couldn't earn anything here with my partner. He doesn't understand much about work and with him even the best man could not accomplish much.*

*When he left, Mr. Mackereth, the farmer for which we were working, asked if I wouldn't like to stay on. Now I'm working on his farm but mostly we are pulling telephone poles out of the forest.*

*They are cedars. These evergreen trees symbolise your unwavering love for me and that makes me happy. I hope we will be together very soon.*

*Today I went around the region looking for land as it is very cheap here but so far I haven't seen anything that I liked. So I will only work here for the month of February even though I get $50 a month. Then I will probably go back to Edgewood, which I like more. A few German families live there.*

*I am living here alone in a good house. It is not cold in this area but the stove is crackling while I write. Firewood costs nothing here except work. Yesterday I worked the whole day in the forest without any gloves. The winter climate is very pleasant here. My mother wrote me that she will send my 700 Marks by spring.*

*What should I write? There has been no mail from you for one month. Will your photograph be enclosed? I found a picture of a girl's face in a newspaper. I thought it looked like my Aloisia so I cut it out. Now it*

## The Making of a Frontier Woman

*is hanging on the wall. On one side is a picture of a pair of birds and on the other side a picture of a loving couple dressed in modest clothes.*

*My thoughts are flying over the ocean to you. I am lonesome here and without any news. How much longer? I hope perhaps the springtime will see a happy couple, then it will be better than ever before.*

*I greet you and kiss you ardently.*

*Your faithful Franz*

# The Photo Album

To be honest, Aloisia had stopped her preparations for awhile, being overwhelmed by the enormity of the task. To say the least, her family was not encouraging and she was using every cent of her savings. Should she really go?

Franz's letter gave Aloisia new courage to continue making preparations for the journey. She wrote she was gradually getting things organized.

She arranged for the village cabinetmaker to make two large pine trunks reinforced with strips of black iron and strong handles on each side. There must be a lock on each, of course, and the keys to go with them. The village locksmith could provide that. For smaller bundles, like the ones containing butter and apples she had sent to Franz when he was still in the navy, she would need canvas, rope – and a good pen for marking.

Aloisia bought black patent leather shoes in Moedishofen. They had elegant narrow straps that buttoned on the side and would be perfect for her wedding day. In another shop she bought black leather gloves. She wondered what Franz would be wearing. It certainly wouldn't be his navy uniform though she remembered how handsome he looked in it. She wondered if he even took it with him to Canada. How time and circumstances change everything!

She would surprise Franz with the things she accumulated over the years. An uncle bought her an oak clock with brass trim and legs. It was small and could fit almost anyplace in a home, he said. It wasn't too heavy for packing. It had an elegant oval face and the hours were marked with Roman numerals.

She would not forget practical things like her enamel mixing bowl, apple corer for making dried apples, a meat grinder and button-hole scissors. Of course she would take feather beds

## *The Making of a Frontier Woman*

and quilt covers. Her round sewing basket, always stored on the sewing machine when she wasn't using it, would be well stocked with thread, a new measuring tape, thimbles, dressmaking chalk, a wooden darning egg, her large black scissors for cutting fabric for shirts and dressmaking as well as small ones for embroidery. She packed in spare cloth buttons that could prove useful one day when making more duvet covers.

She needed flannel undershirts for the cold weather even though Franz had written about working in the forest without gloves in the winter. Maybe that was just a mild winter. She had always heard that Canada was a land of snow, so she would buy a pair of work gloves just in case Franz didn't have them already. Anyway, it's better to have a spare pair of sturdy leather gloves.

For some reason she thought of utensils again. She needed a paring knife, of course, but she also needed an all purpose knife for cutting bread, meat and also scraping spaetzle dough into boiling water.

Spaetzle were so easy to make. Just beat three eggs, a little cold water, a pinch of salt together and add enough white flour to make a heavy consistency and you had it!

Consistency? That made her think of mixing cream and icing sugar to make icing for decorating cakes and tortes. She mustn't forget her special icing dispenser with different nozzles for creating miscellaneous shapes such as flowers, stars, ribbons and swirls.

For some reason her mind flew back again to the undershirts, and undershirts made her think of the new red flannel pad she would have to sew to protect the bedding at that certain time of the month. This thought reminded her that she must make up some personal sickness pads from parts of old bedding that were still strong. She had already sewn up several pairs of split bloomers and four of the regular kind for special occasions.

A ceramic statue of Jesus pointing to his bleeding heart, only thirty centimetres tall, could be packed in too. 'Sacred heart of Jesus, I place my trust in Thee,' Aloisia murmured as she thought of it. And of course the leather missal with the brass cross on the cover would go in her purse so she could attend mass on the boat. Yes, there must surely be mass said on the boat. Franz probably attended mass too, if it was the same as on his trip down to Argentina. And she would carry with her the white gold watch so finely engraved with clusters of grapes, the one once belonging to her mother. She didn't even have to think of her rosary, the one Maria had sent from Africa. That was always with her.

Years ago her mother had personally given her the linen tablecloth embroidered with purple clover, the one traded for a pound of butter during the war. And she would finally be able to use those embroidered display towels to hide the regular towels hung behind the kitchen door. Her Canadian neighbours would be impressed.

The two cushions she had sewn from those parts of her grandfather's black wedding suit must come too. At the age of thirteen Aloisia's mother had said she might as well make something out of it rather than just having it lying in a trunk. He had worn it for most of his life and it was worn in many places but she could find some good parts and sew them together. She could embroider large bright green and magenta stars on it to camouflage some of the seams.

The family was not surprised that she was soon teaching courses in mending, sewing and darning. She also taught the complete range of embroidery stitches: lazy daisy, blanket, eyelet, seed, backstitch, all the stitches required to make flower garden scenes or birds on pillowcases and tablecloths. Of course, she also could crochet suitable lace to edge those same articles.

Then there was the large blue enamel pot in which her mother had brewed coffee or a substitute like chicory on Sundays and Holy Days. And also the smaller matching tea and coffee pot which her mother always planned to use when all the children were gone. But that never happened. Only in the months before her mother died did they enjoy drinking tea and coffee poured from these small pots.

Should Aloisia bring spices like nutmeg and summer savoury for seasoning cauliflower and green beans? Franz probably had all these things. After all Canada was a rich country. But a little package of each wouldn't hurt, as well as some bay leaves for making beef broth. She might as well bring some cinnamon for making baked apples (he said in his letter that he was eating an apple), and cinnamon stars for Christmas baking.

For heaven's sake! She almost forgot about the seeds in her seed box. Seeds were important for a new land. She must remember to put aside some vegetable seeds when she planted the garden in spring. And surely she would take some love-in-the-mist, one of her favourite flowers. Why not take the whole seed box with the porcelain enamel knob! The box was very sturdy and would make a perfect protection for the cup and saucer painted with red and pink roses.

Naturally, she would pack in the brown photo album Emma had given her the first Christmas after Aloisia turned twenty-one. There was an engraving on front of a boy holding a rake. With the other hand he was shading his eyes and looking into the distance. The inscription inside said:

> For Christmas 1917
> From your sister
> Emma Scheufele

In Broadwater (what a beautiful name!), she and Franz would turn the pages, looking at her collection of photographs she was now carefully inserting into appropriately sized slots. There was a picture of her grandmother and grandfather taken when they were already quite old; photography wasn't known when they got married. The suit he was wearing was probably the one she had now cut up to make cushions. There was a wedding picture of her parents taken in 1874 when her father was twenty-five and her mother was twenty. Of course the family photograph taken when she was just a baby in her mother's arms was included. Every one of her brothers and sisters had a copy of that one. By the time Aloisia's mother was thirty, like Aloisia was now, her mother already had eight children.

How many photographs there were of relatives and former classmates in military attire! There was a photograph of Hans in his army uniform before he went off to France that last time.

How many pictures of gleaming, granite gravestones flanked by grieving relatives in black crepe!

Many first communions too, of nieces all dressed in white. There were pictures of her aunts who had always been so good to her. One of her favourite photographs was obviously done in a studio. It was of Emma's Maria when she was little. She was holding a doll and standing on a white sheepskin rug.

Then there were the wedding pictures of her handsome brothers and their wives. There were two pictures in which she and Dori were each wearing blouses and skirts sewn from the same pattern and the same fabric. Why not put in the picture of Oscar helping with the potato harvest?

What a different life was in store for her! Sometimes on Sundays, Franz and she would play cards together. So she would bring a new set depicting scenes of different German cities on the back. After playing cards, they would have guests over and eat a torte she had decorated with different patterns of her icing sugar dispenser. What kind of stove would she have? Surely something more up to date than the ancient one bricked into their kitchen that she polished with lard every Saturday.

She must be sure to bring some recipes. She would love to take the cookbook that had belonged to her mother but Dori wouldn't like that. Nevertheless, she had another, smaller one – and some recipes she had copied down over the years. She would surprise Franz by making liver dumpling soup.

She was given to understand that deer were plentiful in Canada, not like in her country where only rich people with titles could afford the expensive hunting licences. In other words, hunting was forbidden to all except privileged classes. Poachers were severely fined. When she got to Canada, she would make those special venison recipes she had always had to pass over. Surely sauerkraut would go well with venison. Wouldn't red cabbage also be delicious, maybe with spaetzle? Her mouth watered just thinking about it.

And she would not only bake bread but also apple streudel, prune cake and steamed dumplings. Those were only some of her favourites. But first she would bake a cherry cake; cherries would be in season when she arrived. She would cover it with streusel made of butter, sugar, and flour. Or maybe she would make the topping with egg yolks, sugar and a touch of flour. And at Christmas she would bake gingerbread cookies! Ah, there was no end to the meals one could make if you had all the ingredients!

She would, of course, bring her mother's hand-tooled prayer book with the brass cross on the cover and the lockable clasp. It still looked as new as when her mother passed away. Her mother would wonder at the long journey her prayer book was now taking. Inside were remembrances of Sister Mary Clotilde (Maria's religious name), who died in South Africa on August 7, 1908, and Johann who was killed in France on June 16, 1916. Aloisia always said a special prayer for their souls on the anniversaries of their deaths.

The small silver and ebony crucifix that once belonged to her sister in Africa would be packed too.

The most valuable (and heaviest), possession she would bring was her sewing machine, her Excella. The stand was of ornamental cast iron. Even the treadle was a work of art. On the horizontal surface of the cabinet, where cloth was fed under the foot for sewing, was inlaid a ruler crafted in marquetry. Fruit and nut woods were inlaid alternately so each centimetre was clearly distinguishable from the next. This served as a handy measuring tool often eliminating the necessity of reaching for her cloth tape.

The ornamental handle was not just for looks or to remove the cover. What was unique about Aloisia's Excella was that the sewing mechanism could be removed from the base and treadle section thus making her sewing machine portable. Aloisia could carry her Excella to other homes to either sew or give classes on mending or dressmaking.

The drawer, underneath the left side, had small compartments for arranging her sewing chalk, crochet hook (so handy when darning ladders in socks and stockings), threads, thimble and measuring tape. There were needles for the sewing machine, for hand sewing, darning and embroidery. A large safety pin held a collection of other smaller safety pins of various sizes, all closed of course. Open safety pins brought bad luck. There was a ball of bee's wax that came in handy when threading a needle.

There was also a key for locking the little side drawer, but Aloisia never bothered. The same key was used for removing the cabinet lid when she came home from using her machine as a portable. She didn't have to use the key to lock the cover as it automatically snapped shut when the lid was pressed down.

The day came when Aloisia completed her last work with her sewing machine. It was a summer dress in a cotton print, the kind she thought Franz would like to see her wear. That's what he hinted at, anyway, in one of his letters. Aloisia's fingertips glided over the smooth varnished oak veneer, the carved ornamental corners and the cast silver handle. Silver? Well if it wasn't silver, it certainly looked like it.

Her sewing machine would next see the light of day in the New World. Would she put it in her bedroom as she had always done in Ried? It was really attractive enough for a living room, perhaps in a spare bedroom. She thought of the deep blue flannel print fabric that she had purchased but didn't want to cut up until she saw the styles in Canada. Then she would impress Franz with how quickly she could sew. But no use thinking about all that now. She could assess the situation when she arrived in Broadwater.

Her irons! She needed them and they were in the warming oven above the stove! Now, she realised that she should only take the small, lighter one for ironing into little corners. Surely Franz would have a large one and her baggage was already heavy enough.

# Last Letter from Broadwater

*Broadwater,*
*March 27, 1927*

*Now I have arranged things in my new house and am settled so comfortably that I can finally sit down to write. So much mail has piled up recently that I have already been writing for hours and now it is 1:30 a.m. But I must surely write you because mail will be picked up today. The anticipation of writing your letter has kept me going and now I have made some good cocoa and I will drink it after I find out why my dog is so restless. Then I can begin.*

*It wasn't really anything. The dog just doesn't want to be on a chain and sleep in his own house. He wants to sleep in my bed as he did with his previous master. But nobody is allowed in my bed but me and oh, I am already looking forward to when you, my dear Luise, will be sleeping there too. Hopefully, you are coming soon. Before going to sleep we will drink cocoa just as*

## Aloisia

*I always do now and then we will love each other as much as we are able. Should I continue or go to bed?*

*Over there the sun is already rising and you might wonder if it is shining warm enough or maybe is even too hot for your Franz. And here I am still sitting and writing you by moonlight. But here I can do what I want. I am both my own boss and my own servant and today I will sleep in as long as I feel like. Then the sun will already be high up over the mountains and the waves of the lake will be sparkling like silver and the neighbour's bees will be humming past my house because it is a little warmer here than at his place.*

*I tell everyone how glad I am*

*Having my own home.*

*I live on a mountainside overlooking a lake.*

*The area is covered with forest.*

*I don't broadcast that I would gladly*

*Exchange it for my homeland.*

*A wife as companion to help in all situations*

*Is the foundation to my future.*

*I am pleased that you wish to be this little wife and I am firmly convinced that it is better and easier here with more opportunities than over there. Right now I am eating a good apple. The neighbour gave me a whole box full today when I went to get my milk. It is too bad that I can't let you have a bite. That would make you strong so that you could show me your strength by lifting me up again.*

*Well, Luiserl, I should answer your dear letter of March 5. It made me very happy. And the picture most of all. You are a sweet girl who understands me so well. Your picture postcard aroused feelings impossible to express. Luise, I love you very much and am happy that you were always so good, otherwise the two of us could never come together.*

*But now I must finally answer your question. I don't*

## The Making of a Frontier Woman

*think you should wait until Mrs. Wimmer leaves. You don't need anybody else in order to travel. If you are lucky, you will find good people on the ship right away and Mrs. Wimmer is as much a stranger to you as any other person. I really don't know her very well but if she has the same outlook as her husband, and this is usually the case, I don't want you in her company. Anyway, it seems very uncertain that she will get her travelling money and immigration permission in time. If you wait for all those who might want to come over if they could, then we will only meet in heaven.*

*You don't have to send me the travel information that you saw in the Jungfrau Newspaper as I think I have it. And anyway, if I had enough time, I could write travel brochures myself. I can only worry about helping your neighbour's twenty-five year old son when I have got things going here for myself. Proof that it is good here is that in 10 months I have earned more than $500 and now own a debt free home. If I stay healthy and don't have any particular misfortune, I guarantee that with work I will become wealthy here and will have a better life with less drudgery and stress as over there.*

*So, to conclude, I hope that you come within the time estimated in the enclosed printed material. I greet you and kiss you hoping to see you again in the near future.*

*Your faithful, loving Franz*

*It is two o'clock in the morning. Good night!*

*Greetings, Franz*

# Cast Iron

It was evening. The lowing from the cowbarn that had signalled milking time had changed to the contented sounds of cows chewing their cuds. Aloisia was sitting on her milk stool, her kerchiefed head firmly pressed against the flank of Goldie, her favourite cow. Aloisia's agile hands gently but firmly stroked Goldie's teats releasing the last few cups of milk from the large udder.

So many thoughts were flying through Aloisia's mind! How this would be the last time she would ever milk cows in the Schropp barn; how Franz's hard work, searching and persistence had resulted in him being able to already buy his own home in Canada; how she would soon be with him. Aloisia's didn't notice Peter standing at the other end of the stalls, behind the calf pens, watching her.

She was thinking about how all the arrangements for her trip were under control. She had booked a ticket, one way, on the Princess of France, a ship with third class accommodation. Only the other day she checked off another important item from her list (once there had been several lists but lately she could consolidate the items onto a single piece of paper), the approval of her certificate of departure with the local constabulary. She felt a slight shudder of excitement and disbelief as she remembered filling out that form—Date: May 21, 1927; Destination: America; Departure: Ried. There was no turning back. Only some sort of catastrophe could prevent her leaving now.

It was impossible for her to fathom that this time tomorrow she, who had never been more than a few miles away from home in her life, would be on her way to America. She always liked to hear about far away places, how the people lived, what they ate, what they did to earn a living. Now she would get some firsthand experience. With Franz at her side, she would succeed financially, too. And there would be time left over to write long letters home, enclosing photographs of her new farm in Canada.

One day, they might even be able to afford to come back for a visit. She would show Franz places where she had spent of her childhood years, places that brought back the memories of laughter as she taught Oscar's little sister, Frieda, folksongs when she came for a visit. She would show Franz where they would sit under the birch trees at the edge of the forest and sing *All the Birds Have Come Again, The Linden Tree, To Wander is a Miller's Joy, My Hat It Has Three Corners, Sleep, Baby Sleep, The Edelweiss* and *The Lorelei.* Oh, those were marvellous days, weaving wild daisies into chains. Then Aloisia would slip the garlands over Frieda's little head so the flower necklace mingled with the blue and red embroidered ones on her white dirndl blouse.

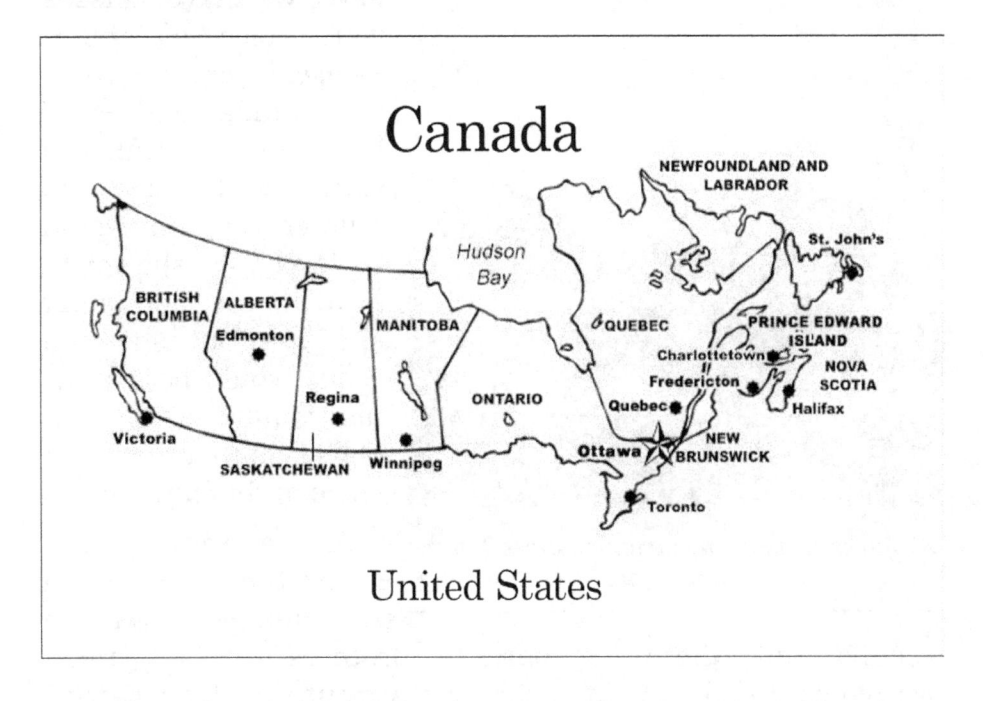

Of course, if she and Franz came for a visit, they would attend mass together right here in Ried. After mass was over, they would join her former neighbours socializing in the churchyard and visit the Schropp family grave on which she had placed a bouquet of fresh flowers the day before. If it were springtime, they would be lilacs. And as she stood there looking at the Gothic letters on the family gravestone, just a few steps from the church wall, she would say, "Hello mother, hello father. Don't you worry, dearest ones. Everything has turned out well in spite of everything."

And if Schmid would come over and look at her she would pretend not to see him. Or then again, she might make it clear that she saw him but would look away and take Franz's arm and stroll through the village nodding and shaking hands with everyone who came to say hello. If Schmid extended his hand? If he wanted to shake her hand? She would not take it. No, he had his chance.

And someone might ask, "Oh why didn't you come up to the choir loft? We have missed your voice so much. Please, please come next Sunday and let us hear your beautiful alto voice." And she would answer, yes, that would be lovely. Or she might have to say how sorry she was but she and Franz would be visiting his family next week. Maybe on their next trip, she could join them.

*'X' marks Aloisia's home when she left in the spring of 1927*

Aloisia would show Franz the little stream she jumped over as a child and where her barefoot brothers reached under overhanging rocks to catch the brown trout they later carried home in sacks hidden under their shirts. And she would lead Franz through the forest to where the old woman lived, if she were still alive, the one who made charcoal by piling the wood just right and letting it burn ever so slowly. That would make an interesting visit and the old lady was always happy to have Aloisia drop in and say hello.

## *The Making of a Frontier Woman*

Near her little hut was where Aloisia always picked mushrooms. Aloisia's mother would say "Hoi, hoi" when she saw Aloisia's apron bulging with them. How they sizzled in the frying pan on the bricked-in kitchen stove and later melted in her mouth! She would show Franz the forest that she had planted and the respected Hielerhoff farm in Moedishofen where her mother grew up and that even had its own weaving loom. Of course, sometime during their visit, she would check the family's bee hives and answer questions that people in the village might ask.

She and Franz would have lunch in the inn, the very inn that she and Franz had to run to when Ludwig went sort of crazy with his pistol. They would laugh. Yes it was all over now. Franz would pay for all the food. For her brothers Otto, Alois, Paul, Sepp, Franz, even Ludwig and of course Peter and all their families and even Dori. When one is rich you can do things like that. Maybe the gathering would be in Munich, close to her Maria. Relatives from Wassertruedingen, and Augsburg could all congregate there. It was central....

She was finished milking. She gave Goldie a final pat on her haunches and brought her pail, almost brimming over with frothy milk, over to the wall. She reached for her stool and set it nearby.

She heard a cough. "Luise...?"

Aloisia looked around and straightened up. "Yes Peter?" She wiped her forehead with her apron.

"Ach," Peter cleared his throat.

Aloisia lifted the pail up and placed its handle over the hook of a scale. It was a habit. She always liked to know how much milk Goldie gave. "Did you want something, Peter?"

"Luise, I just wanted to tell you, to talk to you...." But then he just stood there, his thumbs holding his braces.

Aloisia lifted the pail down from the scale. She looked at Peter. She slipped off her head scarf and held it in her hand. She waited.

"You know," Peter finally began, "I've only wanted what's best for you. I'll not hide the fact that I've opposed Baumgartner

## Aloisia

from the start and that I wish he'd never set foot in Ried. I thought we had all decided that you were better off here and that joining him in his adventure would be a mistake. A big mistake," he repeated.

Aloisia looked at him quietly.

"You know when you transplant a tree, how long it takes to adjust, if it survives at all. I looked at this map of Canada," he said, pulling a small piece of paper out of his pocket, "and can't even find Broadwater on it."

Aloisia glanced at it and shrugged.

Peter stuffed it back in his pocket. "You have everything here, Luise. But...." He breathed out a slow sigh. "I know. There you stand, just looking at me as though I don't know what I'm talking about." He lifted his arms as if for a moment he was imploring some help, but then dropped them. "It's no use. There must be a force, a much stronger force, which draws the two of you together. Even an ocean can't seem to keep you apart. It must be God's will or...." He shrugged. "Or fate. I don't know."

Aloisia unknotted her head scarf and tucked it into her apron pocket. She didn't know what to say. After all, she needed the family cart to bring her to the railroad station, and the way Peter had been acting lately she wasn't sure if he would let her use it. Of course she could probably use the neighbour's, but that would not be a nice way to leave.

"Peter, don't worry. You'll find someone to take my place," she said, hoping Peter would protest and say, "Never! No hired man could ever do all that you did." But he didn't.

"Yes, Luise, life goes on. Not much change here. But at least we know what we have."

Were his words envious or sarcastic? True, Aloisia wanted to get ahead, wanted to succeed, but not at the expense of the rest of the family. She just didn't want her own life to be so hard and more than anything, she just wanted her own life.

Aloisia's remembered the time Peter had sent her to pick up a freshly weaned piglet from a neighbouring village. She was still a little girl and had to carry the frightened, wiggling, little pig over her shoulder in a burlap sack. By the time Aloisia got

## The Making of a Frontier Woman

home her back was covered with urine and, of course, she smelled like a pig. Peter thought it amusing. Much to Aloisia's embarrassment, he added this story to the repertoire of family anecdotes related around the Schropp kitchen table.

Peter cleared his throat again. "I've arranged for Oscar to take you to the Moedishofen train station tomorrow. He's already cleaned the cart this afternoon. Between the two of you, I guess you can handle your trunks and things. He's got two strong hands." With those words Peter turned and walked slowly towards the door leading to where the horse and ox were stabled. As he reached the threshold, he turned around. "Is your sewing machine well crated with lots of padding? Mina said she would have something you could use to stuff around it."

"Thank you, Peter. Thank Mina too, but no, I'm fine. I used the woven floor mats from my bedroom. Anyway the stand is made of cast iron."

"Even iron can break," Peter said in a hoarse whisper.

Aloisia said nothing.

"I guess you have your passport?"

"Yes, everything's in order. The passport office wrote down that my hair is blonde."

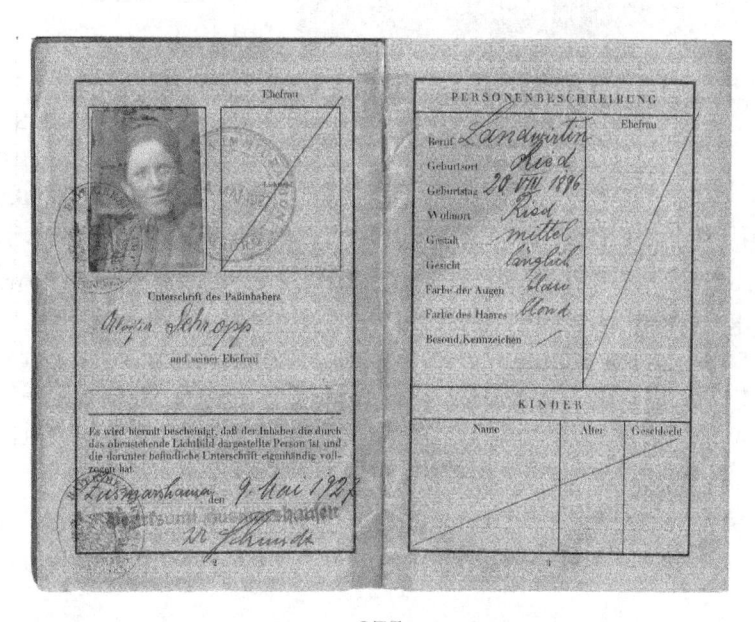

*Aloisia*

"Peter shook his head and gave an almost imperceptible smile.

"I had another, full length picture taken at the same time. I thought you might like it as a remembrance."

Aloisia had been pleased with the way the photograph turned out. The waves in her hair looked natural. She was sitting in an armchair, holding an open book. The stylish, long sleeved plaid blouse, that she herself had made, looked dignified. Her wristwatch just peeked out below one cuff.

"That would be nice, I guess. Just give it to Mina."

Aloisia hesitated. "Peter? Wouldn't you like to drive me to the station? There would still be room for Oscar."

*Photograph used for passport, which was made out in Zusmarshausen, May 9, 1927.*

Peter shook his head, slowly walked into the stable and closed the door. He was gone. Aloisia carried the pail full of Goldie's milk out to the cooling trough.

Oscar began pitching rations of freshly cut clover into the feeding troughs. The aroma was almost intoxicating. Cows liked this green forage best of all. Their metabolism, however, wasn't used to it. Germany was not like Argentina where clover seemed to grow all year long. The cows stomachs would bloat if they were given too much fresh clover.

Aloisia watched the cows eagerly slurping up their ration with their long tongues. Aloisia scratched Goldie's haunches.

## The Making of a Frontier Woman

If only Aloisia's own life could be so simple, so uncomplicated.

She turned around and looked into the barn one last time. She took a deep breath of the pungent blend of ammonia, grain, hay and whitewash. Everything was in order. The cows were placidly chewing their cuds and beginning to lie down on their fresh bed of straw. Tomorrow it would be another voice calling them in from the field with "Ko-boss, Ko-boss, Ko-o-boss."

And her bees? She had added supers just the other day. They would be fine, her little bees. When fall came, a neighbour, also an excellent beekeeper, had promised he would help Peter and Oscar carry the filled frames into the honey room and also help with the separating.

It was hard to believe that the rhythm of chores for every season, with which she was so familiar, would be none of her responsibility any more. Her knowledge about how much land each neighbour had under cultivation and how many cows each family was milking was of no importance to her. Soon she would be helping Franz cut clover on their very own farm in Canada. She would show him that she could swing a scythe as well as most men.

She quickly walked across the barnyard and up the stairs of the home in which she and Dori had now lived for over seven years. She was going to Canada! The Canadian Pacific was still advertising for good farmers. Aloisia was already on her way! She would not be found wanting. Though slim, no other woman could lift heavier loads. She even showed Franz how strong she was the year before when he visited her bedroom and she lifted him off the floor. Franz laughed, surprised at her strength.

Aloisia thought of Franz and how the time in Broadwater was nine hours behind Ried. She knew she was too excited to get much sleep that night.

# The Cookbook

On her wall calendar, Aloisia had long ago marked a circle around May 22, her departure date. That day had now come. Aloisia was ready, with time to spare, to look around.

The snowdrops had wilted long ago, the crocuses too. In the vegetable garden, peas were now beginning to twine up their stakes. The tomato plants had been taken out of the containers where they had been started on deep bedroom windowsills. They were planted in the garden. The kohlrabi had been thinned out.

At the edges of the forest, black elderberries were in full bloom. She wouldn't see them ripen, or the apples in the orchard. The yellow roses on the trellis would bloom even if she were not there to admire them. The pink and purple fuschias would dangle in abundance from the wicker stands her mother once had a local carpenter make especially for them.

Aloisia put on the same travelling suit she had worn when she had gone to Freising so many years ago. It was still like new though perhaps a little tighter. There had been few opportunities to wear it. The stockings she had knit out of two ply wool the previous winter completed her outfit. She looked around her bedroom. There was nothing more to do.

Her Excella was downstairs in a strong crate. Anything left in the room was to stay; the bed, the dresser, the mirror (this morning Aloisia had noticed the fine lines around her eyes), the armoire. She touched the white lace curtains she had once sewn and now was leaving behind. She had some left over yardage she had packed in. When she arrived at her new home she could sew new ones to fit her new windows properly.

The sound of footsteps approached her room. It was Dori. In her hand Aloisia recognized mother's old cookbook.

Dori held it out towards her. "I think you've forgotten this."

"Oh! I thought you wanted to keep it."

"No, no. You should have it. You have used it the most. Anyway, I have another one almost like it."

Aloisia reached for the old recipe book. It opened at once to one of her favourite recipes. "Oh, here's Cream of Tomato Soup, one of mother's favourites. It's tricky but so delicious." She read it out loud – to delay having a conversation with Dori.

> *Simmer 3 cups tomatoes with 2 teaspoons sugar until cooked.*
>
> *Strain to remove skins and seeds. Put aside.*
>
> *Blend ¼ cup flour and ¼ cup butter. Put aside.*
>
> *Scald 1 litre of fresh milk with a slice of onion.*
>
> *Remove onion.*
>
> *Slowly add flour-butter mixture and bring to boil.*
>
> *Cook thoroughly and remove from heat.*
>
> *Stirring constantly, add tomato mixture to hot milk mixture.*
>
> *Heat thoroughly but do not boil.*

Aloisia looked up at Dori. "It sounds so simple, doesn't it?"

Dori gave a little smile and nodded. She made no move to leave. She just stood there.

"Luise," Dori said, shifting her weight from one foot to the other, "I wanted to talk to you about something, if I could. This might be our last chance. I still remember Maria going off to Africa and how she hugged me and now you're going off to America. I just wanted to say I know everyone in the family seems to have doubts that I'm really weak, that I don't pull my weight."

Aloisia looked at Dori incredulously.

Dori continued. "Oh yes, I've overheard comments. And you have had to work so hard. But really I'm not strong and that's the truth. I do the best I can. I'm not built like the rest of you Schropps."

Aloisia didn't know if she could believe her ears. Soon the two would be on separate continents. It probably would be better to leave each other on good terms or at least in a neutral state. Her mother would have wished it.

"And," Dori continued, "About you and Schmid...."

Aloisia clenched her teeth and said nothing.

"You know he paid attention to me first and it hurt me when he started going with you. That's why I was happy about you losing him. You could feel how it is when the shoe is on the other foot."

Aloisia just looked at her but said nothing.

"And about Franz," Dori continued. "I hope everything will turn out alright. Really, I do. I'm sure it will. But," she paused. "I have to say it's no fun being left behind in this house. I have to admit it."

Aloisia reached out and touched her shoulder. "Everything will be alright, Dori. Everything will be alright for both of us."

Tears welled up in Dori's eyes. "There, I've said everything I wanted to say." She turned away.

"Dori," Aloisia called her back, "I'm just thinking. Did you know there's an opening for a priest's housekeeper? It's not here in Ried, but it's not far away. I've been so busy organising everything I didn't really pay attention in which parish, but just ask our priest. You might like that. I'm sure you could manage."

"Really?" Dori looked at Aloisia with surprise. "I...I didn't know. I don't know...."

"The work wouldn't be heavy," Aloisia added when she noticed Dori's hesitation. Like a fly in cold weather is how someone once described Dori.

Dori nodded. "I might look into it. Thank you, Luise. I might ask our priest." Then she turned away again and Aloisia could hear her footsteps getting fainter as they went down the stairs.

Aloisia drew her curtains aside and leaned out the window. Oscar had already harnessed the horse to the cart and hoisted her two trunks and crated sewing machine in place. He was very strong but maybe Peter had given a hand.

White apple blossoms were scattered on the lane winding

between the church and Peter's house. Yesterday the sky had been overcast and it seemed that her departure might be in the rain. This morning, however, the sky was clear and breezes caressed her cheeks like fresh washed linen. Aloisia pulled the window shut and latched it.

She picked up her travelling suitcases and carried them down the stairs. Dori, Peter and Mina looked on as she carefully placed them in front of the load. Aloisia bent down and stroked Butsi's head. She shook hands with Dori and Mina. Few words were exchanged. Oscar was already sitting in the cart, reins in his hands.

Peter came forward. He extended his hand.

Aloisia shook it.

"Best of luck little sister." He quickly turned and walked into the barn. Dori and Mina were biting their lips.

Aloisia climbed into the cart and sat on the seat beside Oscar. A flick of the reins brought the wheels in motion. The cart started up the incline to the lane past the church, leading past the inn and towards the Moedishofen train station. Some villagers waved good-bye. Butsi followed for awhile and then, seeming to sense that something unusual was happening, gave a strange whimper and turned back home.

Aloisia was surrounded by the melodies of finches and twittering swallows. The purple lilacs were in full bloom and permeated the warm air with their fragrance. Or was the scent from a wisteria? Their scent was so much the same

She turned around and looked at the steeple of her village church. Her last choir practice, after which the whole choir had gone to the inn, crossed her mind. That is when they gave her that white and blue porcelain platter as a farewell gift. Schmid had sat alone, engrossed in his jug of beer. She had intended to have some parting words with him in private, before she left, but an appropriate time never seemed to come up. And then time ran out.... Anyway it served him right. Aloisia did not see him standing behind the roadside hazelnut trees. The shadows of their arching branches hid him from view.

The steeple of her village church was no longer visible.

## Aloisia

When Aloisia and Oscar entered the train station, the familiar smell of old varnish and leather suitcases surrounded them. Her baggage was weighed: 1500 pounds, not counting her hand luggage, of course. The train's baggage door slid open; her two trunks, crated sewing machine and suitcase disappeared from sight. They were going straight to Hamburg. Now all she had to carry was her purse, a little suitcase and a canvas bag holding sandwiches, dried apples and prunes. The tin she carried, full of rich fresh milk, would be refilled with water. There was a small suitcase of carefully packed eggs for Emma and Maria Scheufele. She was going to spend a night with them before leaving Bavaria forever.

She turned around. It was a habit her mother had impressed upon her since she was a little girl. Whenever you are leaving a place, turn around to see if someone is waving or trying to catch up, or even calling you to come back for some reason.

There stood Oscar, now fifteen years old. He had grown so tall, his feet apart, as though to steady himself. Aloisia had been like an older sister to him since the day of his mother's funeral when Peter had brought him to Ried. He had been like a younger brother to her. Aloisia thanked him for helping, not only that day but in other ways before. She asked him to send her greetings and thanks back to everyone in Ried. He, in turn, sent greetings for her husband-to-be. "Your Franz will be happy to get those fine cigars. He is a lucky man in more ways than one. And best regards to Auntie Emma and Cousin Maria."

Aloisia bit her lip and nodded. The whistle blew. Aloisia gave Oscar a hug and then, holding up her skirt, climbed the steps to the passenger car.

She found a window seat. There was a hissing sound. Aloisia and Oscar waved to each other until clouds of steam and a curve in the track obliterated the view.

Yes, she had thought of everything, and now she was going to have the biggest adventure of her life. During her months of preparation, thoughts often appeared in her mind like questioning ghosts. What do you think you are doing? Isn't it strange that you are the only one from the entire village – man or woman – to leave the Old Country for the New World? But Aloisia continued spending her evenings stitching nightgowns with ribbons at the neckline.

She had always tried to keep her thoughts in check. She was doing what she had to do. But now, exhausted, her mind ran its own course. She was afraid. She could still change her mind in Munich.

Even though it was now too late to worry, Aloisia was still preoccupied with her packing. Did she have her flannelette nightcap? Yes, it was tucked inside the matching winter nightgown. Sewing thread? Yes. Embroidery classes cancelled? Of course, long ago. Cigarettes and cigars handy? She was told they were the best payment, if she needed help moving her trunks while travelling. Yes, everything was in order. She would buy a lightweight coat in Hamburg. That would complete her wedding ensemble. She was on her way to Canada, to Franz.

But first she would overnight in Munich with her sister Emma and Maria. It was all arranged. Aloisia took in a deep breath and slowly let it out.

She looked around at the other passengers and smiled. Peering out her window, she saw the shadows of white, fluffy clouds on fields already greening with the barley, oats and rye.

A few fields were lying fallow. Perched on a stile, a buzzard was intently looking across a meadow where the blues, yellows and reds of cornflowers, buttercups, daisies and wild poppies shimmered in the morning sun. In a few places, she saw drifts of pink flowers for which she never did find out the real name. The dandelions were already in seed.

In the distance, beyond a flock of birds circling a newly disked field was the young forest that she had planted for Peter last spring. There were over a thousand trees, a living monument that she was now leaving behind.

At the Munich station she walked up to the wicket and checked that her baggage would really be going on to Hamburg, where it would be then transferred to the Empress of France.

"Yes, definitely," the clerk said glancing at Aloisia's receipts.

## Aloisia

She left most of her hand baggage at the station taking along only the carefully wrapped eggs and her overnight case to Emma's. She didn't have time to see the city monuments for the last time, the Marianplatz or the famous Frauenkirche with its twin domes. To be frank, she did not even think about those historic places. Faces that she would not see for a long time –who knows how long – were uppermost on her mind.

Next morning relatives surrounded her at the Munich station. Emma and Maria had promised a camel hair blanket to take along. Now they handed it to her in a cloth bag with handles. "I'm sure it will come in handy."

Other signals of a final farewell were heard. Good advice flowed as heavily as tears.

"You can always come back if you don't like it."

"You don't have to get married right away. Just check everything out."

"When you get to Canada, don't open the train windows. Be careful about the hobos."

"Send us some pictures."

"Tell us if you need something in particular."

Alois and Otto no longer reminded her that she had only

*The Empress of France. Aloisia left Hamburg on this steamship on May 26, 1927. Photo courtesy of Canadian Pacific Archives.*

met Franz on three occasions after her first meeting. However, Aloisia's thought of how Franz was chased away when he visited her in Ried. On that third occasion she and Franz were surrounded by some of the very same relatives who were now seeing her off. Aloisia was doing what they had then said was ridiculous. In spite of everything, she was following Franz to Canada. As Peter said, it must be a stronger force that pulls two people together right across an ocean.

When the conductor waved his flag, there was not a dry eye in the group. "Auf Wiedersehen, Auf Wiedersehen," Aloisia called out the window as fluttering white handkerchiefs disappeared from sight.

A trail of steam swirled past. She was on her way to Hamburg, the next lap of her journey.

# Irish Crusaders

The rhythm of the train started to comfort Aloisia. She was settled with her hand luggage around her. But she didn't feel like taking out her knitting. There would be time on the boat and anyway, right now she had to keep an eye on her baggage.

As her train travelled northwest towards Augsburg, the landscape was quite similar to the gently rolling land around Ried. There were low hills covered with forest, others in varying earth colours. Most homes, their neat vegetable gardens already showing rows of green, were clustered into villages.

Aloisia thought of her home-to-be and wondered how advanced Franz's vegetables would be when she arrived. He had mentioned in one of his letters that the neighbour's bees come to his place because it was warmer there. And when he was working in the bush in winter, he didn't wear gloves. Maybe the tomatoes were already forming on the vines!

When the train pulled in to Augsburg with its beautiful city hall, probably the most valuable civic building in all Germany, she thought of her brother Paul who was a civil servant there. Joseph and Franz both worked for the railroad. They had all received several promotions. She was proud of them and knew they would be thinking of her too.

Many of the places she passed were familiar from conversations with her brothers when they were home visiting. The known names, except for the major cities, gradually changed to unfamiliar place names.

What remained the same was the topic of conversation around her. As in her home village, her fellow travellers shared a deep resentment of the Treaty of Versailles. It took only months after its enforcement in 1920 for inflation to wipe out the entire life's saving of almost every German family. The joke went around that families had to go shopping with a wheelbarrow full of paper money in order to buy a loaf of bread, but it was no joke.

## The Making of a Frontier Woman

It was bitter reality!

When men got their wages, they bought groceries on the way home from work because by the time their wives could go shopping the next morning, their money would often have depreciated again. Before the depression, paper money in denominations of one, five, ten or twenty had real value. It was carefully counted and saved. But by the end of 1922, the printers could not keep up with printing bills of higher and higher denominations. Finally they simply stamped 'One Million Marks' diagonally across one thousand mark notes. Even that soon had no value. The government passed a law that all gold and silver coins were to be exchanged at banks for paper money. Many of the coins, however, were sealed into tight containers which then disappeared above rafters in the attic, into crocks in the cellar or under sacks of grain in the barn.

Some passengers got off the train but more got on. The train was getting more crowded. An elderly gentleman wearing a tweed jacket approached her.

"May I sit here?" he asked Aloisia, pointing to the seat beside her.

Aloisia nodded and moved her belongings to make space.

Her fellow traveller was no sooner comfortably seated then he unbuckled the flap of his old leather briefcase and pulled some papers out with writing on them. Aloisia observed him out of the corner of her eye. He took a monocle out of his breast pocket and soon was making notes on the papers with a pencil. After awhile he shuffled the papers together and put them into the briefcase again.

He stretched a little and then turned to Aloisia. "Travelling far?" he asked.

"Yes," she paused, "Canada." Aloisia could hardly believe her own words as they came out of her mouth. "I'm immigrating to Canada."

"Oh, that's far. What part, if I may ask? It's such a large country."

"Broadwater."

## Aloisia

"Broadwater?"

"Yes. It's in British Columbia, west of Winnipeg. It's in the Rocky Mountains."

"Oh, that is far. You're going to be a frontier's woman!"

"Oh no, my future husband has bought a farm there."

"Really?" He hesitated. "Well, well. That's a long trip but Canada is such a wonderful land and travelling is so interesting."

Aloisia sensed that he didn't want to talk about farming.

"There are people in Canada from virtually all over the world." he continued. "There are French, Ukrainians, British Loyalists from the United States, Germans. Yes, next to French and English, the greatest population there is probably from Germany. Then there are the Chinese from the building of their railroad, Japanese, even some black people who once escaped slavery."

"How do you know all that?" Aloisia looked at him with surprise.

"I teach history at the University of Heidelberg. I should know something about my discipline. I'm retiring pretty soon now."

Aloisia was thrilled to have someone so interesting sitting beside her.

"Of course," the professor continued, "Germany has people of all races too. Sweden, for instance, once conquered parts of what's now Germany. In fact I've seen with my own eyes one of their stone markers just outside Bremen."

Aloisia smiled. She was meeting people she would never, ever meet in her village.

"Of course," the professor continued, "The crusaders came across from England and France, even from as far away as Ireland, they came. Yes indeed, when those redheaded Irish got to Bavaria, they liked it so much, they decided to stay and establish homes. Genghis Khan's army had come across from Mongolia and didn't stop until he was near Dresden. Today, there's a little area in that vicinity where the people are shorter and have slanted eyes and high cheekbones. Even their language is different. Then of course, there was Napoleon...."

"Excuse me," Aloisia said, "Did you just say Irish crusaders came down through Germany and some of them stayed in Bavaria?"

"Indeed. They probably thought they had travelled far enough, coming over the Irish Sea, which can be very rough at times, believe you me, not to mention the English Channel. Anyway, most men joined the crusades for other reasons than making the journey safe for those wanting to make pilgrimages to the Holy Land. They mostly went along to get away from poverty at home and maybe make a fortune. Of course, in Ireland there was also pressure exerted by the English. After all, Ireland was completely dominated by them. Still is today, actually."

Aloisia leaned a little closer. "So the red hair," Aloisia hesitated, "The red hair, like mine for instance, might be from the Irish crusaders?"

"Indeed. Once there's red hair in the family it pops up again and again even after generations and generations. Sometimes it appears in families where there has not been red hair since anyone could remember." He looked at her hair. "Who knows, you might be a descendent of one of them. But instead of going east, you're going west." He smiled and continued, not realizing the impact of what he had just said. "Germany is made up of people from all over Europe, and even northern Africa. Some Germans have black hair from when the Romans came north into what is now Germany. And they say the Romans got their black hair from Northern Africa.

Aloisia smiled to herself. Probably that is where Franz got his black hair and Roman nose.

"Well, well, this has been most interesting but I have to get off at the next station." He started to get up but turned towards her again. "I just want to say, that the situation Germany is in today can only lead to future political turbulence. The Treaty of Versailles is a recipe for disaster. How can we ever pay reparations of $33,000,000,000? I want to congratulate you on your decision to leave. Germany is in a very vulnerable situation. Who knows what will happen next?"

Aloisia didn't know what to say except that she enjoyed talking to him.

The train pulled into a station. The professor tilted his hat, put his monocle back in his breast pocket and said good-bye. As the conductor blew his whistle and train lurched forward, Aloisia once again felt confident that immigrating to America was the right decision.

Within a few hours, the terrain became flat. The brick buildings were not plastered over with stucco as they were in Ried. Her train was travelling through the Lunenburg Heath. Dwarf juniper and purple heather in full bloom covered the landscape. She had seen scenes such as this on calendars and in school geography books, but never dreamed of actually seeing them in real life. She quietly recited Goethe's poem about the little rose growing in the heath.

"Little rose, little rose, little red rose, growing on the heath...."

Finally the train reached Hamburg. The first lap of her journey was over without incident. Aloisia had time to purchase a long, grey coat, just as she planned. On several street corners men were grinding music boxes and smiling toothless smiles as people nodded appreciatively. Was employment just as scarce here as in Munich?

The next day, Aloisia firmly holding her passport in her hand, lined up with the other passengers to board the Empress of France. When her turn came, she handed it to an official. Her hair looked good in the photo; she had used her curling iron. There was already an oval stamp on her passport photo, put on by the official in Zusmarshausen. Now this official stamped it again. It said, 'Canada Immigration, Hamburg, May 24, 1927'. He looked at her and nodded. He assured Aloisia that her baggage was safe. "Do you have your receipt? Yes? Well, then, just hold on to it so you can claim it when you arrive. It isn't at all risky. The Canadian Pacific is very reliable."

Aloisia walked up the gangplank. Just over a year ago, Franz had lined up at this very same port to board the Minnedosa, the third largest ship of the Canadian Pacific Steamship Line. The purser led her and some other women to their third class cabin.

## The Making of a Frontier Woman

A whistle blew. Aloisia was on her way. There was no turning back now.

The first few meals on board were poor, but once they reached the foggy English port of Southampton to take on British emigrants, the food improved. Aloisia looked at her new fellow passengers. They seemed to be speaking only with vowels. That was the English language. Where were the consonants?

The Empress of France headed for the open Atlantic. The voyage was rough, heaving waves making almost everyone, including many of the crew, seasick. At times Aloisia felt that the ship would surely crack apart. She reached for her rosary.

> *Hail Mary, full of grace,*
> *The Lord is with thee.*
> *Blessed art thou among women*
> *And blessed is the fruit of thy womb, Jesus.*

Aloisia thought of the Lusitania that sank off this same coast at the beginning of the war. It had been sunk, the German news said, with one torpedo. The second explosion was caused by the detonation of explosives being illegally transported from America to England, the German news said. It was against international rules for passenger ships to carry war materials and apparently the German government had known that not only passengers were being transported. The coils of rope and cable on her decks camouflaged canons and other heavy equipment being delivered to England.

The British and Americans denied this. The second explosion was caused by a second torpedo, making the rescue of more civilians and crew impossible. That is what Franz had told her the British government said. Or was it Schmid who told her? She couldn't remember. She just knew that the controversy raged on, but since Germany lost the war, it also lost the public opinion votes on this debate.

Poor, poor Germany. Aloisia was glad she was leaving.

When icebergs appeared through the mist and fog, she looked down into the leaden water and thought of the Titanic.

*Aloisia*

*Hail Mary full of grace,*
*The Lord is with thee.*
*Blessed art thou among women*
*And blessed is the fruit of the womb, Jesus.*

*Holy Mary, Mother of God,*
*Pray for us sinners,*
*Now, and at the hour of our death, Amen.*

The Titanic had sunk on its maiden voyage in 1912. There were with over a thousand lives lost. If that could happen to rich people on such a ship, how could she expect to be lucky?

## Buffaloes and Silk

The Empress of France finally entered the mouth of the St. Lawrence River and was escorted to the harbour of Quebec City. The voyage had lasted eleven days. The crossing had been made safely!

*Our Father which art in heaven,*
*Hallowed be thy Name.*
*Thy Kingdom come!*
*Thy will be done.*

The stone and brick buildings of the city reminded Aloisia of Munich but she had no time to explore the city. Her ticket included the fare for the Canadian Pacific Railroad. Her passport was stamped again. This time the stamp said 'Dominion Government, Quebec, Immigration Office, June 4 1927.' She and the other immigrants going west were escorted directly to the waiting train, the train going to Montreal.

Once again she inquired about her trunks and crated sewing machine. She shouldn't worry. They were being transferred to a special baggage car on the train even as she spoke. Did she have her receipt? Good. Had she set her watch back? Good.

Everything was so organised. Now she really believed the advertising: 'Go Canadian Pacific, the world's greatest transportation system'. She was on the last lap of her journey. This was Saturday. By next Saturday she would be settled in her new home.

In Montreal Aloisia's group was transferred to another train, the transcontinental. Again the stone and brick buildings reminded her of European cities. French was spoken all around her. Soon the train was westward bound.

With her finger Aloisia traced the route her train was taking on a map. After leaving the outskirts of Montreal, Aloisia's train wound past lakes huge and tiny. Their shores seemed almost barren of fertile soil – or habitation. Grey slabs of

*Saskatchewan grain elevator. Photo courtesy of Bill Stephens.*

rock, many of them larger than the fields around her home in Ried, stretched away from the almost desolate shores. Small evergreens, which had a foothold in some of the crevices, seemed to have a difficult time surviving, let alone growing to any height. They were always stunted with most branches on the windward side ripped off.

Her fellow female immigrants looked at each other in bewilderment. In the morning the same bleak landscape met their eyes. Would the rocks never end?

Maybe Peter had been right. If only Franz could have solved the problems with his father and taken over his family farm. Aloisia could have helped him make a model farm everyone would envy. But, it would never have worked out. His father was still young and scorned the modern ideas Franz had learned at agricultural college. He could live for a long, long time. No, it never would have worked.

The clacking of the train's wheels vibrated through her mind. Keep going, Franz is waiting, keep going, Franz is waiting. Aloisia arranged her hand baggage around her so she would notice if anyone tried to take it. Then she pulled the small camel hair blanket out of its carrying bag and folded it to make a cushion on the wooden bench. As Emma and Maria had said when they gave it to her that last day in Munich, "It was coming in very handy indeed."

Like Germany, Canada had provinces. Aloisia had memorized all the ones she would be crossing: Quebec, Ontario, Manitoba, Saskatchewan (she couldn't get her tongue around that one), Alberta and British Columbia. Manitoba was as different from any province in Germany as could be imagined. The landscape here was big. Big and raw. Yes, those are the words she would use when writing relatives back home.

Then in every direction the land became bleak in a different way. As far as the eye could see it was absolutely flat with a few meandering rivers. Finally, her train passed between innumerable other trains that were standing on tracks beside the one she was on.

"Winnipeg," the conductor announced, "We're coming into Winnipeg."

The train crossed over a wide river. Aloisia was in the main station of Winnipeg. The other immigrants, whom she had befriended on the Empress of France and boarded the train with her in Quebec, said good-bye. Franz had arranged for a priest, a Father Kierdorf, to meet her here and give directions for the last part of her journey. And there he must be! She saw a man in a long, black robe questioning the passengers as they stepped down to the platform. Aloisia took her suitcases, checking that nothing was left behind and stepped down on to the platform. "Father Kierdorf?"

"Guten Tag. Fräulein Schropp?"

His German wasn't the best but still entirely understandable. He asked how conditions were back in Germany. Then he led her to the train she should board to reach her destination of Nelson and assisted her with her luggage. Unfortunately he had to leave quickly. There was a baptism at which he had to officiate. He said good-bye.

Everything was in order. As Aloisia waited for the train to depart, she watched travellers coming and going. A slim young man wearing a cowboy hat was striding up and down the platform. He was wearing high leather boots with spurs. It seemed he was looking for someone.

Suddenly, she spotted a tall man in a bright red uniform and wearing a large brimmed hat. That must be one of those mounted policemen but he wasn't on his horse like the ads in Germany always showed. Instead, he was talking to a man with his black hair in a single braid down the back of his neck. That must be an Indian, a Canadian Indian! One of her brothers had told her that the braid was how you could tell. Or sometimes they had two braids, one on each side. Oh it was so exciting! You see so much when you travel!

The train jolted and started to roll forward out of the city of Winnipeg. Finally, she dozed off to the sound of the train wheels.

"We're in the province of Saskatchewan now," the conductor informed the people as he walked up the aisle.

Aloisia woke to see an elderly gentleman in a train uniform smiling down at her.

"Are you from Germany?" he said, speaking in German.

Aloisia looked up and nodded.

"You're a long way from home. Which city are you from?"

"Ried. It's just a village. Between Munich and Augsburg," she added.

"Ah, Bavaria. What a beautiful area! I love the churches there with their onion shaped steeples. That's where my grandparents came from. Going to meet your husband?"

"Why, yes. How did you know?" Aloisia responded, remembering the steeple of her church and glancing to check that her suitcases were within reach. She had not done any knitting on the train as she remembered that hobos might reach in windows, maybe even climb in. She had to keep her hands free for any emergency.

"Just noticed your suitcases," said the conductor. "Going to Nelson, I see. Nice town, Nelson, really booming, the most cosmopolitan west of Winnipeg. In fact it looks a little European. They even have their own newspaper. You'll like it."

## *The Making of a Frontier Woman*

"Really? My future husband has bought a farm near there. But he spent a few months working somewhere in the middle of Canada when he first came out last summer."

"Well, if this isn't the middle of Canada, I don't know what is. Winnipeg is the gateway to the west. It has one of the largest freight yards in Canada. And a lot of trains go south to the States," he said, putting his thumbs in his side pockets. "Your bridegroom was probably helping with the harvest. That's what most of the men do when they first come – if they're strong and able."

*Train passing over trestle in Canadian Rocky Mountains.
Photo courtesy of Canadian Pacific Archives.*

"That's right, that's what he did," Aloisia smiled. She didn't add that Franz definitely was strong and able.

"Where exactly does he work?"

"I have it right here." Aloisia opened her purse and took out the bundle of Franz's letters tied with blue ribbon. The letters

## Aloisia

were all on different sizes of paper. Some sheets were white, some cream, others rose, some lined, others not. Sometimes the ink Franz wrote with was brown, sometimes black, sometimes even a violet shade. She had been rereading them on this trip and now knew their order and contents almost by heart. "Here it is," she said, holding up the letter for him to see. It was on lined paper. The ink was in dark indigo.

"Hm. Nice handwriting," the conductor said as he examined it. "Ah, he was in Windthorst, I see."

"Do you know it? Could you point it out when we go by?"

He smiled. "No, that's a village, near Weyburn, northeast of Weyburn, to be exact. It's here in Saskatchewan all right but that place is miles away from where we are. It's off the beaten track, you might say. Ha, ha. Well, anyway," he added, 'the Canadian Pacific is laying more track all the time so no farmer has to haul his grain more than five miles."

"Five miles?" Aloisia repeated.

"That's about eight kilometres. Yup, lot's of wheat grown around there. Farming isn't just a job around here. It's a way of life."

Aloisia nodded, though she had never before thought of farming as a way of life. But now that she thought of it, she could hardly imagine herself doing anything else. After all, it was the only life she knew.

The conductor gestured out the window. "Did you notice those tall, red structures we just passed?"

"Yes. I was wondering, what are they for?"

"For storing wheat. Yup, you're going to see lots more of them all across Saskatchewan and Alberta. Right 'til you hit the Rocky Mountains."

"Did you say for storing wheat?" Aloisia thought of the few sacks her family back home brought to the miller from time to time.

"Yup, grain elevators, they're called. And then the grain gets pumped into special boxcars that come along side and away they go to the port of Vancouver where ships are waiting to load it up for the Orient."

## The Making of a Frontier Woman

Aloisia's eyes opened wide. "That much wheat? What a rich country Canada must be to have so much wheat!"

"Yup, we're not called the breadbasket of the world for nothing. And talking about the Orient, my father said we used to pick up bales of silk in Vancouver and load them to come back this way and then on down to Chicago and New York. Our company tries to arrange it so there's always a full load whichever way we're going."

Aloisia shook her head in amazement.

"And the Canadian Pacific is building up-to-date hotels stretching from coast to coast in every major city across Canada. They've just opened a hotel in Regina last month. It's our thirteenth hotel in the chain. What a beauty! Hotel Saskatchewan."

"Sash...Sash...." Aloisia tried to pronounce the name of the Hotel.

"Saskatchewan," he repeated "Everybody has trouble with that name at first. The conductor tipped his hat and started walking up the aisle. Then after a few steps, he apparently changed his mind. He turned back and smiled at Aloisia. "Just thought you'd be interested to know that we're travelling across what used to be called the Great Plains. A virtual ocean of grass in every direction there was. Endless!" Used to be thousands of buffaloes roaming here as far north and south as the eye could see."

"Really?" Aloisia said, glancing out the window. "Thousands of buffaloes?" She thought of her brothers telling her about how in one of Karl May's books he wrote that the Indians would pull buffalo skins over themselves for protection when lightning started prairie fires.

"Sure," he said reaching into his pocket and taking out a small black leather purse. "Hmm," he said peering into it and then emptying some coins into the palm of his hand. "Was going to show you an American nickel but guess I don't have one right now. Anyway," he shrugged, funnelling the loose change back into his purse again, "It has a buffalo on one side. Yes, this here was once the frontier and not that long ago either. Covered wagons, you name it. Of course there are still places around where people are living a frontier life just as primitive today as it was a hundred years ago. By the way, ever heard of Buffalo Bill?"

Aloisia nodded.

"Well this is his country."

"Really?" Aloisia said, looking out the window and then back at him. "Is this where Buffalo Bill used to ride, the Buffalo Bill who toured London and Paris? That one?"

"Yup," the conductor nodded. "And I believe he was in Munich too. Did you see him when he was there? Being so close, I guess you get a chance to see a lot of opera and theatre."

"No," Aloisia answered. The thought of spending money and time to go to the theatre had never crossed her mind. How could he just dream of such an idea? That was for other people, rich people in the city.

"Ah, too bad." I saw Buffalo Bill when he came to Montreal. Actually, he performed mostly down across the line. Chicago, Philadelphia, places like that." He bent down and peered out her window as though he could still see buffaloes, or at least their ghosts. "Yup, when I was just a boy you could see buffalo skeletons right from the train."

Aloisia looked out the window.

The conductor straightened up and looked at Aloisia. "Of course, used to be Indians too camping in their wigwams. Across the border too, in Montana, the Dakotas. It wasn't that long ago there was no border, not that the buffaloes would know the difference." He laughed. "But that was before my time. Anyway," he said, tipping his hat again, "Just thought you might like to know."

Aloisia thanked him. It was all so interesting.

"Yup, used to see buffalo bones all over the place," he said as he turned back up the aisle again. The clattering of the train door signalled his exit to the next wagon.

Aloisia looked out her window at the endless stretches of prairie land. There was no beginning and no end. There were neither fences nor hedgerows. She watched at each isolated station as a few men, women and children struggled with suitcases, trunks and bits of furniture. There was another man wearing cowboots, cowboots with spurs! Once she saw a family of six children each carrying a different part of an iron bed.

Usually there was a grain elevator at each station. A small house, usually with a lean-to tacked on, always seemed to be next to the grain elevator. Often a mother with her little girl or boy would come out and wave at the train passengers. Aloisia always waved back.

Sometimes Aloisia wondered how the huge grain elevators were built inside, what the letters painted on the outside of them meant and what had became of all the buffalo. She also wondered what was happening back home in Germany in the little fields of wheat growing around her village.

One afternoon, Aloisia watched the prairie sky turn ink black while a storm lurked above the bright distant horizon. Thunderbolts flashed and rolled overhead. 'It's just a potato wagon going over a bridge.' Those are the words her brothers used to comfort her with when she was a little girl.

The Canadian sky was so large, not interrupted by trees or hills or church steeples like back home. Once or twice she did see a little wooden structure with a cross on top. The shifting clouds triggered a feeling of powerlessness and desolation in Aloisia's heart. It seemed that she, alone, was travelling to the very end of the earth. The women whom she had befriended on the ship were no longer sitting beside her. They had gotten off in Winnipeg. They were probably already unpacking their trunks.

Aloisia slumped into her seat. Perhaps the warnings of her relatives had been right. No, no, just forget those foolish ideas. It was now definitely too late now for such thoughts. Aloisia straightened herself again. Keep going. If only the war had never been.... If only she could have blinkers for her thoughts like horses had to keep them focused on the path ahead! Anyway, none of the men waiting at the Winnipeg station were half as good looking as Franz.

Gradually, the landscape changed from flat almost treeless

expanses to rolling foothills. The train's locomotive worked harder and harder as it slowly wound its way up steeper and steeper grades. Mountains began to hem the railroad in from both sides.

*The Bonnington on which Aloisia travelled from Arrowhead to Robson, June 1927. Courtesy of Robert D. Turner.*

Would she never get there? Keep going, keep going. Though Aloisia had grown up only about a hundred kilometres from the foothills of the Bavarian Alps, the mountains were only visible on especially clear days. She knew from pictures that Neuschwanstein, the fairy-tale castle King Ludwig had built at exorbitant expense, was in that direction, but she had never seen it. The train climbed into the Rocky Mountains along mountain ridges, skirting deep chasms.

"I believe in God, the Father almighty, creator of heaven and earth...."

She saw the engine of her train coming into view around a bend ahead. It was passing over a deep gulley on a wooden trestle. How could beams be so long? Canada must be a land of giant trees. Did she have to go over that? Yes, she was going over it. She bowed her head and closed her eyes.

"Sacred Heart of Jesus, I place my trust in Thee. Sacred Heart of Jesus, I place my trust in Thee." Finally, she opened her eyes and lifted her head. Her train had passed over the gorge safely. She had survived. The trestle had held. The wood was as strong as iron. Once again, rocks and trees hemmed the train in from both sides.

Soon snow packed mountain peaks and glaciers came into view. She breathed easier. Only God could create scenes so magnificent! Only God could create mountains like that!

A man came around with a tray tied to his waist. It was something like the tray used for spreading lime back home but this was made of wood. The man was selling greeting cards with Canadian landscapes. There was one with a train coming out of a spiral tunnel and another with a train travelling across a high trestle just like the one she had been through. There were several different scenes: a scene of a mountain peak glowing red in the sunset; a train standing beside a tall red granary with golden prairies in the background; a moose with wide antlers and a large sign marking the Great Divide explaining how the water flows both east and west from that point. It seemed everything in Canada was huge! She selected some cards that had several scenes to send home just as soon as she arrived at Broadwater. Opening one of her handbags, she found a safe compartment for them. Her fingers felt something smooth but with an irregular lump on it. What was that? She took out a handkerchief and from it pulled a round burgundy plaque made of pressed cardboard. There it was. She had forgotten for the moment. The words on it, surrounded by painted golden grapes and green leaves, said:

Bewahret
Einander vor Herzeleid.
*Protect each other from heartache.*

Kurz ist die Zeit, die
Ihr beisammen seid.
*Short is the time that you are together.*

Denn ob auch viele Jahre euch vereinen,
*And even if many years bind you together,*

Einst werden wie
Minuten sie euch scheinen.
*One day they will all seem as minutes.*

From it dangled a twisted cord. It was this cord her fingers had touched. It was with this cord she would hang up the plaque in her new home. Aloisia tucked it safely back into the handkerchief again and put it back into her purse.

It was time to freshen up. Aloisia carried one of her suitcases to the washroom. The washroom was so small she could only take one with her. She had to trust that her other belongings would still be there when she got back to her seat. She pulled out the small tin can holding a damp washcloth and a bar of soap. Someone had told her how indispensable these articles would be on a long journey and how true it was!

Then she opened her suitcase and set aside the lavender sachets. She took out fresh undergarments including a lace trimmed petticoat. She unfolded one of the new blouses she had made especially for this trip, the one with the pretty flower print and a slightly oval neckline.

When Aloisia emerged some time later and walked to her seat, other travellers – especially the men – looked up at her in a curious way. Aloisia's hair was still braided and pinned back as before but now it was in two buns pinned side by side on the back of her neck. Perhaps they noticed the scent of lavender wafting by.

The muted green and blue colours in her blouse reflected the colour of her eyes and made a wonderful contrast to her dark red hair. Her hat, now worn at a jaunty angle, bore a bewitching large flower, perhaps a peony, or maybe a rose? Regardless of which, the flower, almost budding into full bloom, picked up the colours in her complexion and her eyes. Certainly, the old saying that clothes makes the person could never have been truer.

# A Fine Network

It was only when Aloisia's train pulled into Revelstoke that the ticket master realised the mistake. Aloisia was not in Nelson, where Franz was expecting her to arrive. When the train finally came to a stop, he told her to stay in the waiting room.

A man in a uniform came to talk to her. He understood German. "I understand you wanted to go to Nelson? You would have had to come across the Crowsnest Pass to get to Nelson."

"Crowsnest Pass?"

"Yes, you've come across the Kicking Horse Pass," he tried to explain but soon realized that though he could understand German, he couldn't really speak the language. "Wait a moment, please." He soon came back and introduced her to a gentleman who spoke German fluently.

"Who told you to get on this train anyway?" the gentleman asked.

"Father Kierdorf. A Father Kierdorf in Winnipeg."

"Who's he?"

"A priest. My future husband said he would give me directions to Nelson. He met me at the Winnipeg station."

"And what made you think he would know where to direct you? Does he work for the Canadian Pacific?"

"No." Aloisia hesitated. "I don't think so."

"Well," the interpreter said in a rather offhanded way, "it was very nice of your priest friend to meet you and all that, but he gave you the wrong advice." He looked Aloisia up and down. "Your bridegroom won't be seeing you today, poor man. You're in the wrong town!"

Aloisia looked around. This would never have happened to her back home. She had long ago acquired the habit of asking questions three times from different people, finding that she always found out more that way. But now, in this strange country, where this habit could have really helped, she had forgotten. Why had she trusted the directions of only one person, even if he were a priest?

"What do I do now?" Aloisia asked the interpreter. "My future husband is waiting for me. Do I have to go all the way back to Winnipeg?"

The interpreter talked to the man in uniform who pointed to a large schedule posted on the wall.

"Not necessary, the Canadian Pacific has a fine network of branch lines and steamers to get people around. Tell her she has to take the train down to Arrowhead. Then she gets on the Bonnington to Nakusp, then another train down to New Denver. Then she has to get on another sternwheeler that goes to Slocan Lake. Then...."

The stationmaster came along. "What's going on here?"

"I'm just explaining for these two," the man in uniform said. "She's lost. That's what happens when the railroad starts bringing in people who can't even speak English. And," he added to the side, "former enemies. I was just telling them...."

"I heard what you said and I don't think it's a joke sending a woman on a wild goose chase. Your idea will take four transfers. I think she's mixed up enough. "Don't worry," he said, turning to Aloisia, "you'll get there." Then realizing she could not understand him, he turned to the interpreter. "Tell her what happened is that at Winnipeg she stayed on the main line which comes here to Revelstoke. She should have transferred at Medicine Hat. It's not the end of the world. It will just take a little longer. We have a very fine network of transportation here in the west."

The interpreter turned to Aloisia. "Don't worry, they're going to figure things out...."

"But my future husband is waiting...."

"Don't worry, Miss. These things always sort themselves out."

The stationmaster continued giving directions, punctuated

## The Making of a Frontier Woman

with interpretations. "The shortest way for her is to take the train down to Arrowhead. It leaves right from this station at 8:15 in the morning, sharp. Explain that she's missed the connection for today so she'll have to overnight here and catch the train first thing in the morning. " He pointed at the clock. "It connects with the steamer Bonnington that goes down the Arrow Lakes. It leaves Arrowhead at 9:40."

Aloisia stood with her hands clasped as more explanations followed.

"So, just to get this straight, tell her when the Bonnington gets to Robson, she disembarks and boards the train headed for Nelson. It'll take her right through to Nelson in just a little over an hour, yessiree. Is this all the luggage she has?"

The interpreter spoke to Aloisia and she reached into her purse and drew out three pieces of paper and held them up for both men to see.

"Aha! The stationmaster said, pointing at the receipts. "It says Nelson right here. All her baggage has gone to Nelson. Your husband will be in a real dilemma when your belongings arrive without you."

Aloisia looked at the interpreter with questioning eyes. "How long will it take to get there. When will I be in Nelson?"

The interpreter talked to the stationmaster again.

"Well, let me see.... From Arrowhead to Nakusp would take three hours if it's smooth sailing. Then it takes about fifteen minutes to get everything unloaded and loaded. Those steamer masters just whip in and out so there can be no sightseeing! But she must not get off the steamer! Tell her that."

Translation.

"Then she's on her way again. The Bonnington might possibly stop somewhere else if it is flagged down, maybe at Renata or Deer Park. But tell the lady she must stay on until she gets to Robson West at 9:45 in the evening. Then she gets off," he stressed the word 'then', "And transfers to the train going east to Nelson."

Aloisia stood apprehensively, waiting for the translation.

## Aloisia

There were people in the train station bustling all around her. She, however, could not remember ever feeling so alone or helpless.

"And explain to her what a transfer is because that's how she got into this mess in the first place. She should have transferred at Medicine Hat instead of staying on the main line."

The translator asked, "She wants to know when she would be in Nelson."

The stationmaster glanced down at his suspenders as though there was some information there. "She'll be in Nelson at 11:00 in the evening. But not this evening. It'll be the day after tomorrow. So right now she'll have to get herself into a hotel. Tell her about the one just around the corner. By the way, I hope you have set your watch back an hour. We're in Mountain Standard Time now."

Aloisia adjusted her watch and looked around. Father Kierdorf's directions had been wrong. How does she know if she was going in the right direction this time? It was all so confusing.

Now the ticketmaster pulled out a small book and wrote something on it. "I'm going to give her free passage. After all it's our fault that we didn't check this all sooner."

"Could you possibly write it down for me," Aloisia asked as the ticket was handed to her.

The interpreter was getting restless. "It's all written down. Just look down the side and you'll see it all. Halycon, Nakusp – that's where you don't get off, Renata, Deer Park." He ran his finger down a narrow column of names. Then he tapped the name, Robson West. "That's where you're going. That's Robson." He took out his watch. "I've really got to get going."

Aloisia, completely confused, realized she was at the point of being deserted. "I have some cigars," Aloisia said, reaching into her purse.

The interpreter and the stationmaster looked approvingly at the cigars and then at each other. "I'll repeat it for you," said the stationmaster to the interpreter, "So you can write it down."

## The Making of a Frontier Woman

This was not the first time on the trip that cigars had come in handy. There were not as many left for Franz as she had hoped.

Someone poked his head out of the office and summoned the stationmaster with his bent index finger.

"Just a moment," the stationmaster said as he disappeared through the door.

The man who spoke some German explained what was going on. The stationmaster had been called away by an urgent telegraph.

The stationmaster came back out into the waiting room in a minute. "May I ask your name?" he said, looking at Aloisia. "There's a man with a heavy German accent bombarding everybody about a missing passenger, a young woman with red hair, slim. Speaks no English...." He looked at Aloisia. "Your name please?"

"Miss Aloisia Schropp."

"Miss Aloisia Schropp?"

Aloisia nodded.

He pointed to the bench on which she was sitting. "Stay there. Your bridegroom is looking for you."

The man translated.

Aloisia smiled with both disbelief and relief. In a minute the stationmaster came out again and explained that he had just telegraphed back to Nelson saying Miss Aloisia Schropp is here in Revelstoke. "Would you like to speak to him? I can arrange a phone call."

Aloisia said yes. "Yes, definitely, if it can be arranged." She had not heard Franz's voice for over a year.

In a few minutes the interpreter came up to Aloisia. He was smiling broadly. "You should come into the stationmaster's office. There is someone who would like to speak to you." He gestured for her to sit down on the chair so she could talk into the speaker.

"Luise?"

It was a miracle. Franz's voice came clearly through the receiver. "Franz? My goodness is that you?"

"What happened? Wasn't Father Kierdorf at the Winnipeg station to direct you?"

"Yes, but...." Aloisia explained the situation and that it would take two days before she would finally reach Nelson. "It won't be today, it won't be tomorrow, it will be June 10, Friday." She nodded as the stationmaster pointed to the schedule he placed in front of her. She repeated the time.

Franz repeated the time. "June 10, eleven o'clock in the evening. Yes, I see it here on a schedule."

"Franz? Have my trunks arrived? I marked them very clearly with your name and Nelson, British Columbia, Canada."

"Yes, they're here."

"Thank God! Both of them? There should be two trunks and also a large crate with my sewing machine."

"Yes, everything is here." There was a pause. "Luise? I think we should get married right away"

"As soon as I get there?"

"Well, not the minute you arrive. We can't get a priest or witnesses at night. But I can arrange for to be married on Saturday."

"But Franz, what about a wedding ring?"

"No problem. There are jewellery stores here. I'll arrange everything. After all, I have two whole days to do it in. Are you well?"

"Yes, just a little nervous, with all this mix-up. Are you well?"

"Don't worry, I'm fine, especially when I hear your voice. So, shouldn't we get married? Don't you think we've waited long enough?"

"Yes, Franz, that would be good."

"Good, I think so too. And Luise," he added, "when you come down onto the station platform? I think it would be better if we didn't kiss. We should just shake hands. That would be more dignified, don't you think, in a public place?"

Aloisia agreed.

"And Luise?" There was a pause. "I love you."

Aloisia looked around. The interpreter was nowhere in sight. The stationmaster was standing there but he couldn't understand German. She put her mouth close to the receiver. "I love you too. I love you too," she repeated.

# People Watching

The next morning, Aloisia was waiting at Arrowheard wharf. She looked at the tree-covered foothills and mountains surrounding the little town. She looked at the boats coming and going. But most of all, she enjoyed watching people.

Some children were skipping rope, their toes making a rhythmic beat on the wooden planks of the wharf.

> *I love coffee.*
> *I love tea.*
> *I love the boys*
> *And the boys love me.*

A dockworker came up beside her and translated. Aloisia thought of her carefree childhood days when her girlfriends got together and giggled while reciting verses like:

Heirat ist kein Pferdekauf
> *Marriage is more than just buying a horse*

Fräulein, Tu die Augen auf!
> *Young lady, open up your eyes!*

The dockworker struck up a conversation and asked about life in Germany these days. His parents lived there.

"Not good." Aloisia explained the inflation, food shortage and unemployment.

"They always say they're fine, not to bother sending anything."

"If you can, send something. Coffee, tea or sugar. Or cigarettes, if your father smokes."

The dockworker nodded. He said he would.

The Bonnington came into

sight. Her beating paddles, her Union Jack fluttering above the bow, the long cloud of black smoke emerging from the smokestack all gave an impression of incomparable strength and beauty. The steamer propelled itself towards the wharf. Finally the Bonnington stood motionless and dropped its gangplank.

Aloisia watched as people of every description walked ashore. They were probably coming from the very place to where she was going.

Among the first that Aloisia noticed was a strange looking man of medium height. His clothes, whatever colour they once were, were now fairly uniform shades of faded grey. His hairline was thinning and the hair he had was streaked with white. He leaned forward; his backpack was large. His forearms were covered with sinews and muscles like roots from an old oak stump. Traces of red streaked his well-trimmed goatee. His eyeglasses were twisted at a crazy angle. Aloisia noticed that the pipe, though in his mouth, wasn't lit. One boot trailed an untied string shoelace.

"Who's that?" Aloisia asked the dockworker.

"That man? He's a prospector."

"What's that?"

"He's looking for silver or maybe gold. See how his eyeglasses are twisted?"

Aloisia nodded.

"Know why?" The dockworker chuckled.

Aloisia shook her head.

"It's from him always referring to that compass and magnifying glass hanging from around his neck. He's always in a rush. A gold rush," the dockworker added with a laugh.

"Really? Has there been some found around here?"

"Oh, there's always rumours and men scurry off here and there to make their fortune."

"And do they?"

"You mean do they actually make a fortune?"

"Yes," Aloisia nodded, "Do they get rich?"

"Maybe one in a hundred – at most." The dockworker pointing his index finger to his head giving the universal sign for insane.

Aloisia turned and followed the prospector with her eyes. The end of a small pickax jutted from the top of his backsack.

A group of ladies and gentlemen now came walking down the gangplank. Aloisia watched as they passed by at a leisurely pace. Two of the women (one with the palest pink face Aloisia had ever seen, was carrying a parasol), were carrying on an animated discussion. They were laughing and excited about the things they were pointing out to each other.

"Those are sightseers just touring around to see the beauty of the area. There are some stunning views around here. We even have artists. They like to paint the shadows falling across the Arrow Lakes as the sun is setting behind the mountains. Those tourists are the ones who have the special menus with caviar, oysters and what not else. Probably going to Ainsworth Hot Springs eventually, if they haven't been there already. Most tourists do."

Hot springs were familiar to Aloisia but she had never been to one, nor had anyone in her family. They would have told her if they had. Now that she was in Canada she might have a chance to go to one. Aloisia followed the tourists with her eyes, noting the styles and the fact that the women's skirts were much shorter than hers. Their ankles were completely visible. Aloisia had noticed before how her hemline was always the longest. She would talk to Franz about maybe altering them once her sewing machine was set up.

There was an unmistakable feeling of excitement in the air. The quiet resignation she had seen in Germany was replaced by lively anticipation. Faces were not drawn. People walked erectly, with confidence and hope. Several men came along carrying boxes and chairs. Their overalls and plaid shirts seemed to be the everyday attire of many men here in Canada. Maybe they were bachelors.

Aloisia spotted a small group of plainly dressed men, women

## The Making of a Frontier Woman

and children. The women wore white kerchiefs on their heads and were talking softly to each other as they went by. Aloisia recognized it as the same language as the Russian prisoners who had been stationed on her farm in Ried. She had often listened to them talk and sing.

"Who are they?" Aloisia asked with a low voice.

"Who?"

"Those people," she said discreetly pointing her finger in the direction of the women and children.

"Ah, those are Doukhobour. Hope they're not buying more land. They're giving us a lot of trouble."

"Trouble? They seem very nice. What's the matter? How are they giving trouble?" Aloisia thought she should ask so she would know what was not acceptable behaviour in this new country. She would not wish to inadvertently do the same thing.

"They refuse to swear allegiance to the crown and join the army. They call themselves conscientious objectors."

"I think if the whole world did that we would be better off. I mean not going to war," Aloisia added quickly when she noticed the shocked look on his face. "Just that part about not going to war," she repeated.

"There's more to it than that. The Doukhobour don't send their children to our schools. Can you believe it? They say the children just learn nationalism. And they don't want to pay taxes to support our schools. They have their own. They refuse to assimilate," he added, shrugging his shoulders. "Our government, at least the provincial one, won't even let them vote anymore. Saskatchewan has troubles with them too."

Aloisia nodded. "Yes, I know Saskatchewan. I went through there."

The dockworker smiled. "Everybody has to go through Saskatchewan or you wouldn't be here! Well, that's where most of them settled. They're vegetarian. Can you imagine that? They don't eat any meat at all and, he lowered his voice and cupped his hand to his mouth, "They don't have any clergy or legal marriages the way we do."

## Aloisia

"Really?" Aloisia watched the small group quietly disappear from sight. "They sure seem harmless enough."

"They keep to themselves." The dockworker seemed happy to have such an attentive listener and continued. "Someone killed their leader, Verigin, a couple of years ago. He was travelling by train. Just a few miles from here too, it happened. He and eight of his followers were travelling along when all of a sudden, boom! His train exploded."

"Who did that?"

"Nobody knows. The case still isn't solved. They keep to themselves. His son is supposed to come out and take over sometime this summer. That's what the papers say, anyway." He looked at Aloisia. "Nobody really knows them that well, but believe you me, they're peculiar."

Aloisia asked no other questions but thought of the delicious beet borscht the Russian prisoners had often shared with her back in Ried. There's always another side to a story....

It was time to board. Aloisia had read about paddlewheelers plying up and down the Mississippi. She had also heard about excursions on the Rhine where fabled old castles faced each other and the legendary Lorelei sat on a high promontory combing her golden hair with her golden comb. Aloisia had, however, never been on such a boat herself. She had never even seen Lake Constance or Chiemsee or Starnbergersee, three of Bavaria's most famous lakes. Aloisia had never even used a ferryboat to transport a hay cart across a small river. That was not required on her family's farm. Those ferries were in Saxony; she had seen pictures in a calendar. No, before crossing the Atlantic, she had never even been on a rowboat. Even the thought had always made her nervous. She couldn't swim.

The Bonnington was a beautiful steamer, painted pure white with bright red trim. She explored the saloon deck where breakfast was ready to be served. Electrically lit chandeliers hung from the ceiling, illuminating the entire area. Oak tables, chairs, sideboards and even a few high chairs were spaced around the room. Silver cutlery was carefully arranged on tables covered with white linen. Matching large folded napkins

## The Making of a Frontier Woman

and arrangements of fresh flowers in the centre of each table completed the elegant scene. Above, a gallery overlooked the area from all four sides.

Aloisia found the stairs to the second deck and looked down on the dining room from that perspective. Aloisia counted place settings for sixty people. What luxury! She would have to write home about that! Aloisia decided to go down and order a small meal. After all, she was almost at her destination, she had a little money left and she was hungry.

Finally, she climbed the stairs to the upper deck. The view of the mountains on either side was magnificent. The sternwheeler's silvery wake, gradually disappearing in the distance, gave Aloisia a dreamlike sensation. A yellow and green tugboat passed in the other direction pulling a barge loaded with cordwood. Some large geese flew low overhead in a narrow wedge formation. She could hear them calling loudly to each other. At one place she saw what appeared to be laburnum trees with their lemon yellow blossoms. What else could give such a show at that distance? There was no settlement. She thought she saw an archway.

The mountain scenery was beautiful, but

*Madden Hotel, Nelson where Aloisia & Franz spent the first few days after their marriage.*
*Photo courtesy of Kootenay Museum Association and Historical Society.*

## *Aloisia*

Aloisia's thoughts kept returning to how clear and strong Franz's voice had sounded on the telephone. Everything was wonderful in Canada. She brushed aside a piece of cinder that landed on her sleeve.

Aloisia disembarked at Robson. The stationmaster at Revelstoke had given her the right directions! She had to wait an hour before beginning the final lap of her trip to Nelson. Nevertheless, she asked two different people if she was on the right spot. Yes, she was standing at the right place. She was boarding the right train, the train for Nelson.

It was almost 10:00 in the evening when the train moved out of Robson. The moon was almost full and Aloisia noticed some large brick homes on the right side of the track. One was three stories high and had over a dozen windows. She had travelled over the Atlantic Ocean, past a desolate, rock enshrouded lakes that almost looked like another ocean, and endless prairies and huge mountains that reached to the sky. Now, so close to Franz, there was civilization again!

# The Scent of Lavender

Aloisia's train pulled into the Nelson station at 11:00 p.m. as was written on her piece of paper. She had already spotted Franz from her window. What a relief! With his erect bearing, Franz had been easy to recognize. It was unbelievable. He was even more handsome than she had remembered.

Franz reached for her hand luggage as she stepped off the train and set it aside on the platform. As prearranged, they did not embrace; they shook hands. But they shook hands for a long time, smiling at each other with disbelief, looking deep into each other's eyes.

"Luiserl, this is the way I've planned things. The wedding is arranged for 10:30 tomorrow morning. We'll buy your ring first. Then we'll stay here in Nelson until Monday because that's when the next boat goes. Right now you must be exhausted."

Aloisia nodded.

"So I'm taking you to the Madden Hotel right now. It's a very decent hotel, run by a Catholic family. They've given me a tiny spare room up in the attic until we get married. That's where I've been staying while waiting for you."

Aloisia nodded again. Her Franz was so smart.

"In the morning we'll pick up the ring. We won't need breakfast because we're having Holy Communion."

Aloisia squeezed Franz's hand, "That would be wonderful. I have everything for the wedding in one suitcase so it won't take me long." She looked at him, still hardly believing he was right by her side. She slipped her hand under Franz's arm and walked with him into the Madden Hotel.

Franz introduced Aloisia to the desk clerk. She spoke to Franz in English. Franz seemed to understand what she was saying. Franz spoke to her in English too! He was so smart!

The clerk nodded and handed Aloisia a key. Again, Franz

said something to her and then shifted the luggage to the foot of the stairs.

"She's going to tap on your door at 8:00 AM."

The clerk nodded and called a young man. He would help carry her luggage up to the room. Franz could now go up to his own little room. He would show his betrothed where the bathroom was, etcetera. His bride to be would be looked after.

Aloisia looked around her room admiring the large light globe hanging from the centre of the ceiling and the lace curtains. There was a crucifix above the bed. It was all very homey. She put her suitcase with the reinforced wooden bands on the table. When she opened it, the scent of lavender filled the room as, one after another, Aloisia took out fresh undergarments she had finely embroidered and crocheted in white. White on white was always the prettiest. She shook out her grey gabardine suit, placed it on a clothes hanger and unfolded the new cream blouse. On each side of the French buttonholes, Aloisia had sewn five tucks. She had also edged the high collar with lace. It was a classic pattern that was always modern. Her brother's wives had the same style when they got married. It made her neck look even longer.

Further down in the suitcase was her prettiest summer nightgown made from fine white cotton and amply gathered above the bodice with smocking. Each cuff was smocked too. The nightgown came right down to her toes. She had never worn it and certainly would not wear it tonight. She draped it over a chair. She could sleep in her old one. It was the one she had worn on the Empress of France that doubled as a housecoat.

The next morning there was a tap at her door. Aloisia checked her watch. It was 8:00 of her wedding day. She quickly went down the hall to the washroom, being sure to lock the door of her room first. Minutes later, she ran back to her room. She hastily put on her blouse and grey suit. She slipped on her grey silk stockings and fastened them to her garter belt. Her new black patent shoes with one single strap across the front (one of the tourists she had seen getting off at Arrowhead was wearing exactly the same style), made her feet look elegant. She leaned towards the mirror. The white lace of the blouse framed her throat nicely.

Finally, she put on the grey coat purchased in Hamburg and adjusted her hat to a jauntier angle. When she pinched her cheeks and earlobes, she didn't look a day over twenty, or twenty-five at the most. Certainly not thirty! She pulled on her grey kid gloves and brushed a little piece of lint from her shoulder.

Oh, one more thing. She had brought some special cigars from Scheufeles. They were sealed in a special little wooden box made for the purpose. Beside the bed, there was a dresser and she placed the box there. These were the last ones left.

Aloisia peeked out the door. Franz was waiting. She came out into the hall.

"You look beautiful! Did you sleep well? I love your hat."

Aloisia smiled. She wasn't used to such a flow of compliments but she had looked at the women passengers on the Bonnington and noticed that her hat was definitely in style, even here in Canada. "Thank you." She looked at his strong face, his Roman nose, his eyes now seemed to be more grey than brown. "You look very healthy, very well."

Franz smiled, showing his white, even teeth. Aloisia had never asked him if he liked dancing but didn't think this was the time. "Did you rest well?" she asked.

"So, so."

Aloisia looked him up and down. "Your suit is very nice."

"Yes," Franz beamed. "It's such good quality. I just got it in a second hand shop here in Nelson. All it needed was a little mending and I could do that myself."

Aloisia quickly looked around. No passerby had heard.

"Luiserl," Franz looked at her affectionately, "the store with wedding rings is just around the corner. It's run by a Swiss man who once worked near Golden as a mountain guide but decided to go into business instead. I think his prices are good."

## *Aloisia*

Aloisia nodded in agreement and linked her arm in his. They passed by shoppers looking at shovels, barrels and many household items in a hardware store window and Aloisia saw many customers within buying merchandise. Then they passed a drug store, grocery store, a lawyer's office and a barbershop. Prosperity and an atmosphere of hope could be sensed everywhere.

"What a beautiful town Nelson is!"

Franz smiled at her excitement. "Yes, there's even a hospital here, and a Catholic School run by the nuns and shipyards and...," he pointed past the waterfront with its piles of lumber. "See the smoke stacks over there? They are smelters for all the silver mines around here."

"Silver?" Aloisia looked up at the forested foothills shouldering the mountains around Nelson.

"Yes, we have just about everything in this country. It's a rich land, like I wrote you. Nelson has its own daily newspaper. Here we are." They were in front of a small store displaying several sizes and shapes of clocks in the window. Franz opened the door and escorted her in. A cuckoo popped out of his Black Forest house and called the half hour as they entered.

"Ah, you're back with your bride!" said the clerk in a Swiss German dialect. "She came after all!"

"Yes," Franz beamed a smile at Aloisia. "This is Miss Aloisia Schropp. We're getting married in two hours."

"Well, then, we had better take a measurement." The clerk took Aloisia's hand and slipped her ring finger through one of the holes in a template. "Perfect! Just the size I thought."

"It's a little loose, isn't it?" Aloisia asked.

"Let's try the next size, if you like," the clerk said, slipping her finger into a smaller hole. "You see, it fits a little too snug. You have to remember, you've been travelling a long time and your fingers are probably just a little smaller. When you start working again, they will probably get larger."

Aloisia looked at her hands. What he said was true. She hadn't milked cows or pumped water or done anything worth mentioning (unless recopying her address book and rereading Franz's letters counted), since she left her home three weeks ago. It was not only her fingers that were smaller; her hands seemed smaller too – softer and more delicate. They didn't seem to belong to her. "Yes, the larger size is better," Franz and Aloisia said, almost in unison.

"So then, let's see what we have here." The man opened the display box and took out a tray of rings. "We have them from eighteen to twenty-two carats. To tell you the truth, my best seller is this one, and I happen to have it in your size. It's eighteen carat solid gold so it will keep the shape and this one is not too wide and not too narrow. It's a classic. You can have it for five dollars."

"Do you like it, Luiserl?"

Aloisia smiled at Franz's endearment of her name. "Yes. It's beautiful, Franzle," she answered, copying his lead.

Franz took five dollar bills out of his small leather purse and placed them on the counter. "No need to wrap it," he said, taking the ring from the clerk. "It will be safe here." He carefully tucked it into his breast pocket and checked with his hand that the ring was really down at the bottom.

"Thank you," Aloisia smiled at Franz as he escorted her out the door.

"That man gave us a good price," Franz confided to Aloisia when they were out on the boardwalk again. "Even from the Eaton's Catalogue, you couldn't get it cheaper. I checked."

Aloisia knew what the Eaton's catalogue was because a woman on the train let her look through her copy. The catalogue had clothes of every size for women and girls, men and boys. There were kerosene lanterns for the house and the barn. There were scythe handles with three blades: a thin, long one for cutting grass, a shorter, broader one for reeds and wheat and the heaviest, shortest one for clearing brush. There were ointments, pots, and cream separators. Really, there was everything one could imagine and many things you couldn't. Someone explained to her, with the help of a pencil and a piece of paper, that every farmer in Canada got such a

## Aloisia

catalogue free several times a year. The paper alone must cost a fortune. What a rich country! What a land of opportunity!

Her Franz was so smart. He thought of everything. She linked her arm in his and they walked along the boardwalk. Any misgivings Aloisia had about coming to Franz when she was in the middle of the Atlantic's rolling waves or the prairie's endless expanses or when she discovered she had arrived at the wrong city, were now completely gone.

"We really have to keep moving," Franz says interrupting her thoughts, "The priest will be waiting."

"Yes," Aloisia agreed. "It's always better to be early than late."

Again, they walked down the boardwalk. This time Franz led her in the direction of the church. Soon they were knocking at the rectory door of The Church of Mary Immaculate. The priest welcomed them and introduced them to another priest and a young woman who had consented to be witnesses. Of course, Aloisia didn't know either of them. Aloisia and Franz walked up to the front pew. There was only one altar on which two candles were flickering.

In a Ried wedding, a multitude of beeswax candles would be softly illuminating the richly engraved gold candelabras, floral arrangements and white starched linen of the main altar. The two side altars, each guarded over by a statue, each statue with a halo encircling the head, would also be decorated with lit candles. Their honey scented aroma would be wafting out over a large congregation and not just a few curious onlookers looking up from saying their rosaries.

After the exchange of vows, the priest ushered Franz, Aloisia and the witnesses into the sacristy. There, under the guidance of the priest, they signed the marriage register.

*Groom: Franz Xavier Baumgartner*

*Residence: Broadwater, B.C.*

*Father: Franz Baumgartner*

*Mother: Karolina Kerl*

*Date of Baptism: May, 1896*

*Place of Baptism: Eggersham, Germany*

## The Making of a Frontier Woman

*Bride: Louisa Schropp*

*Residence: Ried, Germany*

*Father: Josef Schropp*

*Mother: Victoria Voelk*

*Date of Baptism: August 22, 1896*

*Place of Baptism: Ried, Germany*

*Date of Marriage: June 11, 1927*

*Witnesses: Abbie Wall*

*Leo H. Hobson*

Aloisia and Franz looked at their signatures. Everything was correct. They thanked the priest and the witnesses. Franz escorted Aloisia down the street. "Let's go in here and eat," Franz said when a restaurant came into view.

Aloisia followed Franz to a table in the corner. "You know, Franz, it has been eleven years since we sat down in a restaurant together like this."

Franz nodded. "Yes, Mrs. Baumgartner, that was a long time ago and yet now it seems like yesterday."

Aloisia smiled.

Because of having Holy Communion, they had not had breakfast yet but it was now noon and Franz ordered roast beef dinners. Franz said they needed the strength.

This time, when they approached the Madden Hotel, it was daytime and Aloisia saw a cupola above the entrance portion giving the building an almost church effect. The front doors were built into an archway diagonally facing the corner of Baker and Ward Streets. Aloisia and Franz walked in, passing a boy selling the Nelson Daily News.

Next morning when they walked to the Church of Mary Immaculate for Sunday Mass. Mist was rising from the surrounding buildings. The air was fresh and cool but sunshine was quickly warming the boardwalks. Aloisia's steps were short and hardly seemed to touch the ground. After thirty years under the control of others she no longer felt that she was just surviving, she finally knew what life was all about. She felt completely empowered, now starting her own life at her own pace. The whole universe was part of her and she was part of the universe. 'Take it easy, no need to rush,' every part of her body seemed to tell her.

Aloisia reached over and brushed a piece of lint off Franz's shoulder. Yes, Franz was not only close to her, he was hers. And she was his. She could receive communion without confessing her activities during the previous night. She was a married woman!

After mass they had breakfast together. Then Franz lit one of the cigars Aloisia had given him. The aroma was so good and followed them around as Franz explained that Nelson was considered the Queen City of the Kootenays named after the Kootenay River and Kootenay Lake. The Silver King Mine made a fortune on silver and copper. Aloisia looked at the foothills and mountains beyond while curling her thumb under her palm to touch the wedding band, the wedding band that had given her a life of her own.

They stayed in the Madden Hotel until Monday evening, boarding the Kettle Valley train at 9:00 p.m. Aloisia saw her baggage being loaded. Her trunks were in perfect condition. The crate of the sewing machine, except for one board that seemed a little splintered, was also in perfect condition.

The train trip back to Robson passed the brick buildings she had seen a few days before when she was on her way to Nelson.

"What are those buildings?"

"That's Brilliant. One of the main settlements built by the Doukhobour."

"When I was waiting to get on the boat at Arrowhead," Aloisia said excitedly, "I saw some Doukhobour."

"Really? How did you know they were Doukhobour?"

"Someone pointed them out to me. They were wearing kerchiefs and very simple clothes."

"They maybe could have been Mennonites. Were they speaking German?"

## *The Making of a Frontier Woman*

"No, Russian. I heard them speaking Russian."

"Then they probably were Doukhobour. The Mennonites that speak Russian are all on the prairies, Manitoba mostly."

"Franz?" Aloisia hesitated for a just a moment. "Is it true, Franz, what they say about them?"

"What do you mean?"

"That they don't have marriages like we do?"

"I've heard something to that effect. In Canada you'll run into all sorts of religions but to tell the truth, other people's business doesn't interest me too much. We know we have the one true religion. That's all that counts. I've had enough on my plate just getting settled here. How did you find that out, anyway?"

"I was talking to a man when I was waiting at Arrowhead."

"You were talking to a stranger?"

"Well," Aloisia said apologetically, "he spoke German and he was very friendly."

"Not a good idea," said Franz, "not a good idea."

Aloisia said no more. What would Franz think if he knew of how many men she had spoken to on her journey?

From the station they walked down a long gangplank to the waiting steamer. It was the Bonnington, the same steamer she had come down on. Aloisia's trunks and crated Excella were being transferred on a baggage cart. She wondered if the glass face on her little oak and brass clock was still whole. For a moment, the face of the uncle who had given it to her flashed through her mind. What about the cut glass platter with the gold lettering spelling out, 'Give us this day our daily bread'? She used the hand woven cotton duvet covers (one set with red stripes and another with blue), to pack around the silver serving tray with the white porcelain insert painted with blue plums. It had been a farewell gift from her choir. Schmid's face crossed her mind. Thank goodness she was out of that situation.

Franz talked to the purser to make arrangements for disembarking at Broadwater. The purser nodded.

Franz explained to Aloisia that they were now travelling up the

## Aloisia

Arrow Lakes, but not as far as that channel which connects the Lower Arrow Lake to the Upper Arrow Lake.

"Really?" Aloisia gave him a sideways glance. She had seen a few small settlements but mostly all she saw were barren rocky shores. "I passed right by Broadwater?"

"Yes. We'll arrive at 1:30 in the morning if everything goes well, which it usually does."

"1:30 in the morning?" She had never been awake at that time in the morning unless a cow was calving.

"You'll find it's different here. In Germany everything is poor but orderly. Here in Canada, there is more freedom, more flexibility. Getting on or off a steamer in the wee hours of the morning is just taken in stride."

"That's fine," Aloisia said. "I think I've had enough of organized poverty for awhile."

Franz looked at Aloisia and laughed. "Organized poverty is a good way of expressing it. Sometimes I miss the organization but," he said emphatically, "definitely not the poverty. Still," he said, looking up into the evening sky, "it's lucky we have full moon."

Aloisia looked up into the clear sky. She looked around at the moonlit landscape. Truly, it was a beautiful evening, almost as bright as day.

# Bluebird Mountain

Franz placed his arm around Aloisia. He explained some facts about the Bonnington. It belonged to the Canadian Pacific, as had the ships that both he and Aloisia had come to Canada on. "It's steel hulled and 202 feet long," he concluded.

"Feet?"

"Yes, that's how Canadians measure things. Just like the British. Twelve inches equal a foot. The inch is like our German 'zoll'."

A whistle blew and the paddlewheels turned more quickly. The steamer vibrated. Aloisia and Franz went on deck and watched the black plume of smoke billowing from the stack as the captain manoeuvred the Bonnington away from the pier. The intense blackness was from the coal that was burned to create the steam, Franz told her. Cordwood, especially birch, if they could get it, was used to start the massive furnace or to give a bigger head of steam for going through a narrow, difficult place like where the Upper and Lower Arrow Lakes join. But generally, the sternwheelers had converted to coal because so much was mined in the area. Cordwood was now considered to take too much space for the amount of heat it generated. But, you can't start a fire just with coal.

The red, white and blue colours of the Union Jack fluttered overhead as the Bonnington manoeuvred along the east shore of the lake where the current was slacker. Powerful searchlights scanned the shoreline to avoid outcroppings of rocks.

Franz pointed upwards, "Look up at the moon. It has a halo."

Aloisia looked into the indigo sky, "Isn't there some superstition about that?"

"Well, in the Navy we said the narrower the halo the more likelihood of rain. And if you count the number of stars within the halo, it tells how many days it will be until it starts to rain or for how many days the rain will last. There's a little, little star just to the right," Franz said, "do you see it?"

Aloisia put her hand to her brow. "What does it mean, if it's so tiny?"

"In just a half a day, maybe even just a few hours," Franz laughed.

"Is that true though?"

"Sometimes. It rained so much on the North Sea so the halo was never far wrong."

"And what about here?" Aloisia asked, "We had a rainstorm in Nelson just the other day."

"We have had our share," Franz answered enigmatically.

After a while they left the deck for the warmth inside. Music was coming from the dining room. Somebody was sitting at the grand piano and playing some songs she had never heard before. "It's American music," Franz informed her. Because of the late hour the area was quite empty except for a few people enjoying a cup of coffee and some dessert. Franz and Aloisia looked on, having agreed not to waste money. They had made some sandwiches for the trip.

Aloisia admired the luxurious lighting, the furnishings, the size of the dining room, the wood panelling. Sometimes a door of one of the staterooms would open and a passenger or two would come out to lean over the balcony to enjoy the view.

Aloisia continued the conversation where it had left off. "The zoll? Oh, yes, when yard goods come from England it is often marked that way."

Franz looked at Aloisia. He was so lucky to have such a smart wife. "And 5280 feet equals a mile. But also it takes 1760 yards to make a mile."

"Yards?"

"Yes." Franz loved her curiosity. "It takes three feet to make one of those."

Aloisia shook her head in disbelief, "Thank goodness Napoleon introduced the metric system to Europe. It's much more sensible and efficient and easier to learn. A hundred centimetres make a metre and...."

"Sh," Franz put his finger to his lips, "I wouldn't say that in this country." Franz tightened his arm around her and whispered, "Don't forget, we lost the war."

Aloisia looked around. Yes, she was really in a strange land, one that was once an enemy country. Many Canadian soldiers were killed. Adapting to this new country would always have this burden to overcome but she would prove by her actions that Germans were really good people. After all, the common people didn't want the war.

"You'll have to learn the new measurement," Franz said, resuming his normal tone of voice. "And one day, we'll become Canadian Citizens. That will prove our allegiance."

"Yes, that sounds like a good idea. Maybe when we get home you could show me on a ruler. How did you just manage, coming here and not knowing the language? I feel so lost. The English language is so...."

"That's why I learned Esperanto. We need a world language."

"Esperanto? I didn't know you spoke Esperanto."

Franz smiled. "Well, just a little. It sure came handy in Argentina. It uses a lot of Spanish."

Having warmed up, the two went on deck again to watch the moon which dominated the cloudless sky, to watch the powerful search lights bringing the already moonlit shore to dazzling brilliance. Franz pointed to some logs lashed together to make what looked like large floats.

Aloisia looked. "What's that?"

"Booms." Franz explained what log booms were and that he might have cut down some of trees that were in them.

"Aloisia was overwhelmed. "Trees so big? Everything is so big here, and so interesting," was all the Aloisia could think of saying.

The whistle blew.

"We're pulling into Syringa Creek," Franz said.

## Aloisia

The paddles of the Bonnington came almost to a halt. The deckhands threw a large bag to a man on the wharf. They didn't even put the gangplank down.

"That's the mail," Franz said.

"My, oh my! Is that how my letters arrived too?"

"Yes, there weren't enough though," he tightened his arm around her shoulder.

Aloisia leaned closer to him. He would never know just how hesitant she had been to consolidate her belongings and use all her savings to make this trip.

"You know, I was thinking," Aloisia said. "When I was on the boat and then on the train, I had a lot of time to think, and I realized how our families are very similar in a way."

"And what way would that be?" Franz said, giving her shoulder a little squeeze.

"Well, the eldest in my family, Maria, she left to make more room for the others at home. And you gave up your right to the farm so your younger brother, Hans could have it. Both you and Maria were very strong and generous to be able to do that."

"I guess that's one way to look at the situation but I think maybe your sister just had a calling to the Church. As far as I'm concerned, I just didn't get along with my father. Life is too short to put up with all his nonsense."

"Then how will your brother make out?"

"Oh, Hans has a different character than me. He'll manage. My father isn't so down on him."

The steamer turned into Deer Park. The image of a man came into sight. The footplank was let down and the deckhand delivered a box. The steamer departed again as the man disappeared into the shadows of the moonlight.

It crossed the lake to Renata, a settlement where Franz had thought of buying a place before he decided on Broadwater. Some homes, glowing white in the moonlight, were scattered on short lanes branching up from the pier. The deckhands delivered a bag of mail. Then once again, the steamer propelled itself away from the shore and onto the shimmering lake.

Franz continued explaining. "If someone waves a flag, the captain knows he has to turn in."

"Oh! Just like you had to do on Frederick the Great," Aloisia laughed.

Franz smiled. "Well, they don't have to know the alphabet, they just have to wave any white cloth on a stick. Of course when it's foggy or night time they light a bonfire. If there's an emergency they light three. The crew is on the lookout."

"For…. My, oh my," said Aloisia. She just caught her herself from saying "For heaven's sake," an expression which she remembered Franz frowned upon.

Franz took her arm and pointed.

"There's Bluebird Mountain on their right. Broadwater is just around the next bend. We're almost there."

"Bluebird Mountain?" Aloisia peered as the moonlit mountain appeared into view. "What a lovely name!"

Franz described the small, powder blue birds that nested in the area.

Aloisia excused herself. If they were close to her new home she had better freshen up. In the washroom she glanced in the mirror. Never could she remember looking so young. Her skin was glowing from the fresh night air. Her eyes were such a soft shade of green.

Franz was waiting for her when she came out and she took his arm and continued the conversation. "I'm surprised you have blue birds here. At home I've never seen a bird that was blue, of any shade or size. Have you?"

"No, not back home but Canada is a land of surprises. For instance," he gestured along the shore on their right, "much of this area was once owned by a millionaire. I forget the name just now. He and his wife loved the mountains and the lake scenery so much that he bought land and started building a private paradise. He had a wharf built and hired workers to plant fruit trees: apples, peaches, cherries, pears, everything. He had sheep brought in and even gardeners to beautify the landscape with ornamental shrubs."

"Did he have cows too?" Aloisia asked thinking of her favourite cow Goldie back in Ried.

"Yes, a few cows, chickens, just everything you would need for a complete mixed dairy farm. But apparently he had a poor leg and his doctor said the terrain wasn't good for him. And then their son got sunstroke when putting a roof on a guesthouse. He was never the same again. Mentally, that is. So the millionaire sold Broadwater to Mr. Mackereth, who was one of his hired men. For almost nothing. It's Mackereth who told me this all."

"My, oh my. Do they ever come back for a visit?"

"No, they had other places around the world. I think even in Egypt and South America. They just cruised around the world and when they found a really beautiful place, they bought it."

"Really?" Aloisia looked at Franz incredulously.

"I'm not making this up. It's a true story."

Aloisia sighed. "It just shows how important it is to be healthy."

Franz gave her hand a squeeze. "Like us, you mean?"

Aloisia felt her face getting warm. "Who named it Broadwater? It's such a pretty name."

Franz shrugged. "I don't know, I really don't know. It may have been a translation of an old Indian name for the area."

Words from Franz's poem went through her mind. 'I live beside a lake on a mountainside. The area is covered with forest....'

"Are there Indians around here?" Aloisia asked. "I think I saw some on the way out."

"Not right here. By the way, did I tell you what happened to them in Argentina? The white settlers were given a bounty for the scalp of every native, even if it was a fetus."

The whistle blew and the steamer turned into a shallow bay with a small wooden wharf jutting out from massive rocky shore. The sky was still clear. The moon with its halo shone like a magnificent lantern over the water and shoreline.

# Trix

The steamwheeler's searchlight brightened the waves as they slapped and sprayed against gigantic stumps clinging to the shoreline. Gurgling eddies swelled around the small dock. A footplank was lowered. Two deckhands quickly lugged Aloisia's two trunks and crated sewing machine out of the steamer. Aloisia noticed one of them bringing a bag into a small wooden shed on the wharf, going in the door and quickly coming out with a different bag.

"Mail," said Franz, as he and the two men shifted Aloisia's belongings inside the same structure.

Aloisia put her hand baggage down. "What's happening? What's going on?"

"Our place is farther up." Franz pointed up the mountainside. "We're storing your belongings here 'til we can use Mackereth's horse."

The deckhands had already boarded the steamer again. A man's shout, then a loud whistle pierced the night air. The Bonnington moved quickly away from the shore leaving waves rushing and fingering around the grey boulders.

"They'll be safe here," Franz said as the door squeaked shut

Aloisia noticed that there was a latch but no lock.

"I think we won't need this," Franz said putting a makeshift lantern back inside. "It's full moon and we have enough to carry."

"We...we're leaving my things here?" Aloisia asked, when she realised what was happening. She reached into her handbag for the special pouch she had sewn for her keys. Of what good would her diligence be if there were no trunks and sewing machine to unlock? "What if...?" she hesitated, "What if somebody comes by and they...."

"Oh, the steamer only comes by on Thursdays, unless someone lights a fire for an emergency. It's not like back home where little ferries shuttle back and forth several times a day. We're in Canada now."

The situation was incomprehensible to Aloisia. "Are there Indians around here?"

"No. Why do you ask?"

"I was just thinking of names like Arrowhead and Arrow Lake. Are arrows sometimes found around here?"

Franz smiled at Aloisia's curiosity. "I'm told Indians used to come around Broadwater hunting mule deer and picking huckleberries, but not anymore. At least I've never seen any. And even if there were some Indians, they should be probably more wary of us than we should be of them."

Aloisia remembered her brothers quoting from *The Leatherstockings* about Indians, about their noble bearing and their generosity. According to them it was the white men who stole and not the natives.

Franz was already walking off the wharf. Aloisia hesitated only for a second and then was quickly beside him. They crossed the gravelly shore and started walking uphill.

"So they wouldn't steal my trunks?"

"So that's what you're getting at!" Franz laughed. "Not a chance."

She imagined her mother's voice coming from the past, 'Look back. Whenever you are leaving a place, look back to see if you haven't forgotten something. Look back to see if someone is waving or trying to catch up.' She turned around. They were alone. Not a soul could be seen in the shadows of the moonlit night.

Rocks, rocks and more rocks. Rocks of every size and description. Rocks which were large enough to shoulder large trees in their crevices, rocks that jutted out from bunches of grass, small, loose-scattered rocks which moved when you stepped on them, trying to twist your ankle. The foothills had looked majestic and inviting from the water, seeming to welcome the traveller to a leisurely walk on the forested slopes, but that deceptive image now proved false. The pale

## The Making of a Frontier Woman

landscape was tilted sharply against them but Aloisia didn't complain. Later, she would realise that even at this time she had wondered where she was heading. But she was strong and had always been strong, except that one time, back home, when she suffered exhaustion from hauling bricks and mortar for what was supposed to be her parent's retirement house. Instead, as fate would have it, the house was used for prisoners and then as a home for her and Dori. If only the war had not come. Aloisia, was sure the war was the cause of her father's early death.

Back home. What strange words! All her previous life could now be collapsed into those two syllables. But soon she would have her own home here in Canada. And just imagine! It was already paid for! She thought of Franz's last letter where he described the bees preferring his house to Mackereth's because it was warmer. He was such a good writer! That's why she never did destroy his letters, even the one he had explicitly asked her to burn. She had hidden them deep in one of her suitcases before meeting him in Nelson.

A dog's barking broke the night air. A white and black dog bounded towards them. "Hey, there's my Trix! Down, boy, down," Franz yelled. But Trix just kept running around them in circles, whimpering, wiggling and yelping. Even Butsi, the family dog in Ried, could not have been more welcoming.

"The Mackereth's let him off the chain when they heard the steamer pull in. They knew I was home." Trix sniffed at Aloisia's handbag. "Down Trix, I said down," Franz yelled.

"I think he smells that smoked ham I brought," Aloisia laughed. The two of them gave each other knowing glances as they remembered how they had started eating some of it during the previous night.

Aloisia scratched Trix behind his ears. He wagged his tail just as energetically as when she did it to Butsi back home. Back home. What was happening in Ried right now? It seemed impossible that she was so far away. Yet under the same moon her relatives were thinking of her. Of course, it would be already daytime there.

"Where did you get him?" Aloisia asked.

"From the previous owner, the man I bought my land from. He couldn't take him along because he was going off prospecting. So I got him for nothing. He can do tricks, that's how he got his name."

"Tricks? What kind of tricks?"

"Well, he can turn around on his hind legs and even hold a pipe in his mouth while doing it, can't you Trix," Franz said as he patted Trix's head the best he could, considering that he kept running in circles. "I'll get Trix to show you later, when he's not so excited. At first he was a real nuisance, whining all night. He wanted to sleep on my bed like he did with his previous owners. He didn't want to be chained to his doghouse. I think I wrote about that in my last letter."

"Yes, but why couldn't he just be set free? At home, with Butsi...."

"In the daytime it's okay, but at night he's got to be near the house to scare the bears off. They hate the smell of dogs, you know."

Aloisia was shocked. "You've seen bears? Real bears?"

"Naturally. This is bear country and I don't want them to get in the habit of rummaging around my place. They do enough damage at the Mackereth's."

Aloisia was quiet for a moment. "What do they do?"

"For one thing, they take the honey. I've actually seen them lift off the top of a hive, set it aside and take out the frames one by one, just like a human being."

"A real bear eating honey from a bee hive? What would the people back home think about that?"

Franz looked at her. "Don't worry, we have Trix. Maybe he's just a mongrel but is he ever smart! Smarter than any pure bred, I tell you. He's just not obeying now 'cause I've never been away so long and then he's not used to running free at night. It must be quite an adventure for him. And," Franz added, "I have a shotgun too. Anyway, in life I've found out that its people that you have to be more careful of than wild animals. Of course, you can always trust the priests. I don't mean them."

Aloisia wondered how Franz could say that when it was a priest's fault for making her arrival two days late, but said nothing. Trix was zigzagging into the forest shadows on each side and then racing back, wagging his tail energetically and jumping around her.

They had walked uphill for about twenty minutes, when there was a bleating sound. She could make out a few sheep in a pen. There was a one story wooden building with curtains in the windows. A trace of smoke drifted from its small brick chimney.

"Is this...your place?" Aloisia was careful that the tone of her voice did not reveal her apprehension.

"No, no. That's the Mackereth's house, the one that the millionaire built. I'll introduce you to them tomorrow. They're English, but very nice. Their son is going to come down with their horse tomorrow."

Aloisia gave an inward sigh of relief. She certainly had imagined a larger home than that. She had had enough surprises for awhile.

Leaving her belongings on a deserted pier was not a surprise; that was a shock. Aloisia thought of her Excella. Aloisia turned around. Nobody was trying to catch up. Images of her family flashed across her mind.

She noticed a climbing rosebush on a lopsided trellis. It clutched some rosehips from the previous year but seemed ready to bloom again. Nearby some ragged lilac bushes sturdily reached out their withered blossoms.

"They're left over from when Illingsworth lived here. Now I remember the name of the millionaire I was telling you about," Franz explained.

Aloisia put her bundles down, relaxed her shoulders and caught her breath. Though she was a good walker, she had never in her life climbed up such a long continuous slope. She looked behind down through the jagged gap in the moonlit forest towards where her carefully packed possessions, the results of months of careful planning and packing, were stored. She hoped they would be safe and dry if there should be another thunderstorm like the one that swept around their hotel the first night she was in Nelson. She squinted her eyes to look into the tangled wilderness on either side. Bears could be there, wolves and even cougars. Not tigers, of course, like Maria in Africa must have seen.

"Isn't it dangerous here? Can Trix really protect us? Will we soon be home?"

"Not at all! I tell you, the animals are more afraid of us than we are of them! Just last week I met a black bear behind my house and you should've seen him run. Like a shot up the mountain! By the way, I told the Mackereths you knew all about bees. They sure could use a hand."

"Oh Franz, I'm sure you know just as much, if not more." But she was pleased with his compliment.

"There are elk here too, but not many. The cougars get them. Of course if they hear you coming, they get out of the way. They're more scared of us than we are of them."

Aloisia moved closer to Franz. "Will we be there soon?" she ventured to ask in a voice, which she hoped sounded cheerful and energetic, even though her knees felt weak.

"Yes, pretty soon."

A strange uneasiness passed through her. Needles of perspiration, which were no longer cool, covered her back. Good that Franz had told her to wear comfortable shoes. She had been thinking of wearing her patent shoes to make a good impression on neighbours watching her arrival. She felt sticky all over and exhausted. Her lack of sleep on this journey was finally catching up with her.

"Will it be soon now?" She worded her concern a slightly different way.

Before Franz had a chance to answer, a bolt of lightning flashed overhead. A clap of thunder rolled and echoed around them. Franz and Aloisia, their eyes completely adjusted to night, had not realized that clouds had circled the moon. In the same instant, rain poured down on them. Franz grabbed a piece of Aloisia's baggage and ran ahead. "Follow me!" he said, running up some stairs suddenly appearing before them. He quickly unhooked a latch and pushed open the door. With the last ounce of her strength, Aloisia grasped the rough railing and entered.

"Trix, go in your house!" Franz shouted as he snapped a rope on his collar. "Thank goodness, we made it!" Franz lit a coal oil lamp and threw a match into the small stove. He reached for some kindling and pieces of birch from a wood box and added it to the fire. There were two chairs, a small wooden table and a bed. But Aloisia hardly saw them. She was almost dizzy with exhaustion.

"Franz, I just have to lie down," she said, dropping her bags to the floor and stretching out on the bed. Within a few moments, she heard neither the rain nor the crackling of the fire.

# The Fountain of Youth

It was late in the morning when Aloisia awoke. She was not dreaming after all. There actually was a dripping sound. She opened her eyes and looked around.

Franz was moving a couple of pots to catch the drops. He looked over at her. "When the wind blows a certain way, there's the odd leak, but I have the materials to fix that problem now. I added five poles to the top of one wall in order to help with the run off, but it obviously didn't help enough. That was quite a storm!"

Aloisia got up, her hands straightening her clothes as her eyes surveyed the room. There was one door and enough floor space to turn around but not much more. A small kitchen table supported some wooden shelves. Franz's navy chest was butted up against the wall. The photograph she had mailed him was leaning on a small wall bracket.

"But look!" he continued, not noticing Aloisia's open mouth. "The sun is shining. It's stopped raining and it's a beautiful day. I've already been outside and it's hot!" He pointed to the sunlight pouring in through a small window.

Aloisia hardly glanced in that direction. She turned to Franz. "I...I thought that when we ran in here last night this was just...." Aloisia's voice faltered. She looked at a wet rag on the floor. She looked at the rust spot on the tiniest stove she had ever seen. She looked up at the flimsy rafters supporting a roof that could not keep out rain. It comprised of skinny poles, hardly larger than those used to support string beans.

Aloisia looked at Franz, her voice trembling. "This isn't? Is this the house you wrote about in your letter? The place you bought?" She could not believe the calmness of her voice as she noticed several nails in a row behind the door which seemed to serve as hooks.

"Small but tidy," Franz responded, gesturing around him.

"That's what you learn in the Navy!"

Aloisia turned around. The floorboards creaked.

Franz pointed to a blue map tacked to the wall inside the door. It had white survey lines on it. "See? This land all belongs to me." His index finger tapped the upper left corner beneath the number 23. "Lot 23, that's my parcel. Almost thirty-four acres!"

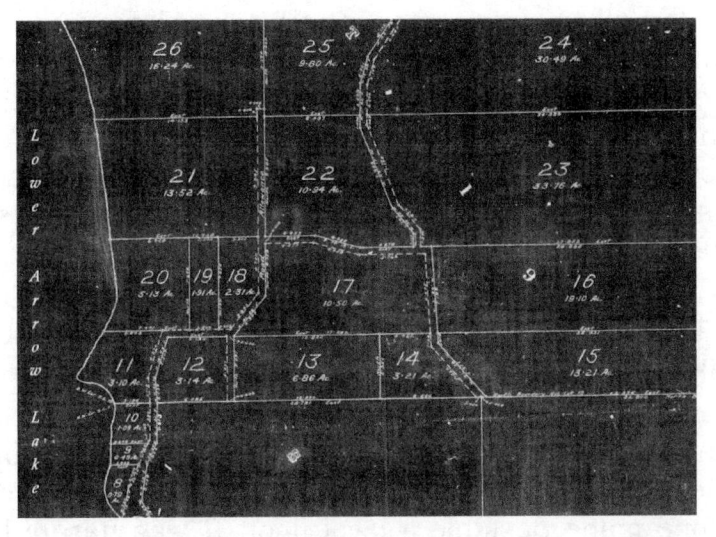

*Survey map showing Franz Baumgartner's property (Block 23, D.L. 5817, Kootenay District, Plan 841). The Columbia River, known as the Lower Arrow Lake, is on left.*

"But Franz, where can I put all the things I've brought? I've more things than there's room."

A furrow appeared on Franz's forehead.

"I mean," Aloisia hastened to say, "Where can I put my sewing machine, my Excella...," her voice dwindled off. Chaotic, muddled thoughts collided in her mind. She peered out the small window. Stumps and brush were hemmed in by wilderness. She looked out the door. There was nothing familiar. She felt completely in an alien world.

Franz put his arm around Aloisia and led her out of the narrow door, "Let's go outside. Nature is so beautiful here!"

She followed him. To the left was a narrow porch with two tin wash tubs. There was not room for anything else. To the right a roll of corrugated sheet metal, which seemed to serve as a chimney, was braced against the wall by a ladder-like structure.

She looked around for comforting visual clues from her past. There was no creaking gristmill with its splashing water wheel, no meadows with grey cattle, no stooks of yellow barley, no deep windowsills holding pots of well tended geraniums, no heavy oak front door, no window shutters painted rich green and no cultivated, undulating fields. There was no outdoor shrine in honour of the Virgin Mary and certainly no Corpus Christi procession winding its way along a well-swept road. No refreshing blue flax fields alternating with the golds and greens on some distant hill. Nothing reminded her of Ried. Nothing. For an instant she thought she heard the sound of a long skirt passing by as she had so often heard in church, but it was only the rustling of some branches.

She turned around. There was the structure in which she had spent the night, hunched against the mountain slope. It was made of thin horizontal poles. Stilts on the downward side of the slope made possible a level floor. It was hardly larger than the hunter's lookout in the forested hill behind her home in Ried. A doghouse was visible under the crawl space. Aloisia did not notice the mountain bluebird darting out of its nest beneath the narrow overhang. Nor did she hear its warble. Firs and cedars stretched like arrows into the azure blue sky, their bases skirted with underbrush. Some trees were dead, leafless, looking like fish skeletons. At home they would have been removed. Aloisia never imagined that Broadwater would look like this.

"Come along!" Franz called cheerfully. "I want to show you everything."

A chipmunk chattered an alarm from somewhere in the dark virgin forest. She saw some stumps with pitch still oozing from them. Aloisia looked at Franz, "Where does one go to the bathroom?"

"There's an outhouse behind there," he said pointing to a

young cedar. "That's the first thing I built. The barn could serve when it's built but I don't approve of using that. Mind you, here in the wilderness an outhouse is really sort of a luxury."

"And..." Aloisia looked around, "...and water?" She saw no sign of a garden either. "The pump for drinking water and washing and cooking and watering the tomato plants in summer?"

"Just a short walk. That's just what I was going to show you." Franz pointed to the faint path on the right that Aloisia had not noticed before. It was covered with russet coloured needles and hemmed in with underbrush.

"It comes from a spring higher up the mountain so it never runs dry. It's the freshest water you've ever tasted. And we'll always have it. You know why?" He didn't wait for an answer. "The spring's on my property too! On that map I showed you, the map in the house, I've marked it in. You can see it clear as day. And there's a pond too, so I can develop a gravity water supply and there's another stream too, but it dries up in summer. We don't need it anyway. We have more water than we could ever use. And believe you me," he said, looking at her intently, "There's nothing more important than a good supply of water."

The sun enveloped Aloisia's shoulders in a gluttonous embrace as she followed Franz along the barely perceptible path winding along the mountain slope. Crickets snapped and ponderous, metallic flies buzzed in low semicircles. A pair of dragonflies, locked in flight, wavered over some tall sweet clover. A droning bumblebee jerked by. Despite the heat, a chill gripped Aloisia's heart.

Franz touched her arm and pointed. A lone eagle soared high up in the clear sky. Aloisia wiped her forehead with her forearm and then, shielding her eyes, looked across the lake to the opposite shore still shaded by mountains, not hot like this side. But of course you need sunshine for farming.

Though she had heard about the existence of virgin forests in her geography classes in school, wilderness like this she could never have imagined. The trees were completely neglected, some had obviously been lying on the ground for years and their branches had not even been removed for firewood. What a waste! There was enough firewood within eyesight to heat her whole village for years.

Flies zoomed around her face. As though celebrating their release from the rainstorm's enforced captivity, dragonflies and butterflies now filled the hillside with busy, crackling noises. Do flying insects ever collide? Swallows and mountain bluebirds were darting through the humid air. Wild daisies and masses of tall, spike-like magenta flowers blazed everywhere between the grey stumps. A bramble caught Aloisia's skirt and she stumbled a little.

Suddenly they came to a clearing and Franz stopped. "Hear that?"

Aloisia stopped and stood still. She heard a gurgling sound and nodded.

Franz walked a few more steps. "Here we are! It's not big, but there's always water. I boxed it in so I could collect the water more easily. See that bee on the edge of the board? She's coming for a drink too! I wrote you how they like my place!"

Aloisia glanced at it and then looked into the surrounding wilderness. "Franz? Where…?" She didn't know how to continue. He was so excited, so enthusiastic about everything….

Franz reached up for a little grey enamel cup hanging from a stick obviously crafted especially for that purpose. "I built it deep enough so a pail can be dipped in and almost filled to the top. I can show you on that map where this is in relation to the spring that feeds it higher up. And what water!"

Aloisia leaned on the stump of a huge cedar tree.

Franz looked at her. "You must be thirsty. I've never tasted such good water, even in the jungles of Argentina," he said, offering her the cup. "Take a sip. It's so refreshing. Like the fountain of youth," he said, smacking his lips. "It never runs dry even on the hottest summer day."

Aloisia drank it in two sips. "It's good, really good."

Franz's piercing grey eyes scanned Aloisia's face. "Are you

feeling alright? You look a little pale." He took the cup from her.

Aloisia anchored her arms across her body. She sighed and looked at the soft moss at her feet. She had the sudden impulse to lie down on it and sleep right there. "It's nothing. I'm okay, maybe a bit tired."

"Are you sure?"

"Franz, just how did you find this place?"

"Oh, that's an interesting story. When I was harvesting in Saskatchewan I saw the ad in the Manitoba Free Press. That's the largest newspaper in western Canada. Mr. Mackereth put in an advertisement for hired help and I was just lucky enough to spot it. I figured it had to be better than having grasshoppers jumping all over and hardly a tree in sight. So I came out. And everything worked out and here we are!" Franz took the empty cup from her. "Delicious, isn't it? Want some more dearest?"

Aloisia nodded and Franz dipped it in the water and handed it to her again. She took a sip and then drank the rest. She wiped her lips with the back of her hand and looked around. "But, Franz, where do you have your vegetable garden? And where are your neighbours? I, I don't see any other farms."

"Neighbours? Well, we have the Mackereth's down the hill. Then across the lake, I keep saying lake but it's a river, there's Renata, that settlement I pointed out from the Bonnington. Some German families live there, actually they're Russian and Swiss, but they speak German. I lived there for awhile and got to know a few people. Nice little community." Seeming to read the question she had on her mind he added, "But this place was cheaper and there's timber here. I can log some cedars for telephone poles. Anyway, we can row over there one morning if the weather's calm. Mackereths have let me use their rowboat before. Have to be careful though, storms come up quickly."

Aloisia thought of log booms and the fact that they were at the broadest part of the Columbia River.

"But we don't need lots of people do we Luiserl?" This was an endearment Franz had started to use for Aloisia. "We have each other." He started to sing. "Holy God we praise thy name. All in heaven above adore Thee."

Aloisia knew this hymn well. In Ried, her choir always sang it at the end of mass after the priest had read the Gospel according to St John: 'In the beginning was the Word, and the Word was with God, and the Word was God.... Born not of blood, nor by the will of flesh.... The will of the flesh....' Aloisia knew what that was about now.

'Thanks be to God.' The end of the reading was the signal for the procession of priests and altar boys to walk into the sacristy. At the same time the organ started the familiar melody and the voices of the choir joined in. Majestic music filled the church while villagers, young and old, agile and decrepit, gradually left their pews, walked down the aisles through the vestibule and out into the churchyard.

Franz had indicated in one of his letters that he wasn't much of a singer, but now he was singing loud and clear. Strange, you could correspond with a man for eleven years and still not know everything about him. She joined in on the last bars, harmonizing in alto.

"...Holy, holy, is Thy Name."

He yodelled across the wilderness. "Listen," he said pointing in the direction where waves of yodelling echoed back from the mountains. "Hear that? I found out that from this spot you can always get an echo." Then, cupping his hands around his mouth and facing the same direction he shouted the cuckoo's call. Again the mountains echoed back the call in repeated waves until the sound became inaudible. "Cuckoo, cuckoo, cuckoo...."

Aloisia smiled up at Franz. "Only God could make mountains like that," she added, repeating what she had said when first sighting them from her train window, but now with much less enthusiasm. She thought of the refrain from Hansel and Gretel:

> Cuckoo, cuckoo, calls from the forest,
> Let us sing and dance....

But Aloisia didn't have the energy or inclination to sing. She didn't feel all that well.

## *The Making of a Frontier Woman*

"Sounds just like the Black Forest, doesn't it?" Franz laughed.

Aloisia had never been to the Black Forest. And now, the tiredness she had felt before, gripped every fibre of her body even more. She could hardly keep awake but tried to continue the conversation. "Do you often hear cuckoos here?"

"No, not unless they're in clocks like we saw at the jewellers in Nelson. They don't have them here in Canada, but we have mountain bluebirds. There's a nest right outside my door. Shh!"

They stood quietly.

"That's him now. Hear that sound? That sort of warble? We don't have them in Bavaria!"

"I hear him." Aloisia said, leaning a little more heavily on the stump. A strand of hair had strayed onto of her neck but she didn't bother to twist it up into her bun.

Once again Franz dipped the black rimmed enamel cup into the holding box, took a sip, smacked his lips and offered it to Aloisia. "You know this cup, the one you're drinking from? It's the very same one I had with me in Argentina. It could tell a lot of stories. And just think, this water here eventually flows right over the border to the United States and into the Pacific Ocean!"

Aloisia looked at the simple cup and handed it back to Franz. His hand disappeared into the holding box and came up with another little cupful of water, "Drink it, drink all you want."

Aloisia drank and looked down at her watch, the white gold watch that had belonged to her mother. What would her mother say now?

Franz stepped closer. "Are you sure you're all right?" He cupped her chin in his hands. "You look a little pale somehow."

Aloisia turned around. Was this a dream? Franz's letters tied together with a blue ribbon and hidden inside the bed linen crossed her mind. She put her hand to her throat.

"You know, Luiserl, you could be pregnant. If everything is in order, you could be."

A smile tried to form on Aloisia's lips. If that were true, she

## Aloisia

really couldn't go back home again – even if she had the money.

Franz smiled, "The water will make you feel better. You know, when I came here last fall there were windfall apples lying around on the ground in the Macareth's orchard, just rotting away. This year I plan to get some before they are too spoiled and make cider. I have a couple of barrels already promised by the priests in Nelson."

Aloisia felt utterly alone. Well, not really, she was married. But somehow nothing seemed real and she felt more isolated in this strange land than she had ever felt in her life.

From somewhere in the surrounding wilderness a breeze sighed into her ear, "There's nothing without work, my dear. Nothing without work...." It was the voice of her mother.

*Aloisia's first washday in Broadwater, May, 1927.*

Aloisia looked down at her hands. They were not swollen. Her fingernails were well-shaped, the cuticles soft. She turned her hands over. There were no calluses. She could never remember having hands like that since she went to Freising for that beekeeping course so long ago.

She looked at Franz. He probably had clothes that needed washing in a sack somewhere. She had soiled laundry too. It had been a long voyage.

Schropp family sayings whispered through her mind. 'Don't put off for tomorrow what you can do today.' 'If you say 'A' you must say 'B'. At least she could start the laundry soaking. Then tomorrow when she hung the wash up on the line, she would give each piece a good shake just as her mother had often told her to do. It saved in the ironing.

She looked at Franz. "Do you have any good soap here for washing? Strong soap for washing clothes?" Aloisia asked hesitantly, "And a wash board?"

# Conclusion

## INTO STRANGER'S HANDS

The Schropp sibling's worst fear after the war, was that the farm they had laboured so hard to build up would fall into strange hands. Because the eldest son, Peter, had no children, Ottiel, a niece of his wife Mina, was adopted. A letter written by Alois Schropp to my mother on August 15, 1934, only seven years after she left for Canada, proved how quickly this concern actually became a reality. In 1935, Peter and Mina, officially adopted Ottiel despite the protests of many of the Schropp family at a court hearing in Zusmarshausen. In 1937 Ottiel married Kaspar Hafner, the hired man working on the Schropp farm. Peter and Mina died. Ottiel and Kaspar inherited the farm, passing it on to their two daughters.

"What would our parents say now?" was the refrain among the Schropp brothers and sisters. "The family farm has fallen into strange hands. If only Aloisia had stayed in Ried."

# Broadwater, The First Time In

Ever since I could understand anything at all, I remember hearing about Broadwater. Broadwater was where my parents homesteaded in the late 1920's. It was in the Rocky Mountain wilderness, somewhere high above the Arrow Lakes. In the Rockies, north of Castlegar, somewhere.

My parents stayed there two years during which time they suffered the cold of winter without proper shelter or food, their homestead surrounded by the howling of wind and wolves.

When my mother was thirty years old, my sister Louise was born on March 15, 1928 in the Nelson hospital, just nine months after they were married. The doctors said being alone in the wilderness was no place to have a first child, especially at that age. Louise did her first crawling on their shack's rough wooden floor.

*My husband, Walter, at the roadsign to Broadwater in 1958*

No matter what the weather Franz and Aloisia logged the tall cedars behind their homestead and cut them into poles of appropriate length for the telephone company. They also sold cordwood for the sternwheeler that was now the only connection between the isolated communities on the Arrow Lakes. My parents made enough money to move away from that rocky, untillable terrain to the fertile Fraser Valley.

## Aloisia

They bought a little farm in Atchlitz just west of Chilliwack, with the railroad passing on one side of the property and what later became the Trans Canada Highway on the other.

My mother was pregnant at the time and Frankie was born shortly after. What had once been a chicken house was turned into a cozy home surrounded by an orchard, well tended vegetable garden, a grape arbour and bee hives. Even from the road people could see Mom's flowers and the neat farmstead with the carefully fenced fields beyond.

They seemed to prosper, but water still had to be pumped for household use and the farm animals. Loosening up the heavy clay soil with cow manure was never ending.

One late spring day, little Frankie who was five years old at the time, drowned in a slough running along the backfield. That tragic evening, instead of going into town for the church's strawberry tea, they had to prepare for his funeral. The sorrow caused my mother to miscarry what would have been their third child.

My parents decided to start fresh. They moved to a larger fifty-five acre farm in East Chilliwack where the peat soil was easy to till and running water was pumped right into the house and barn. I had been born just before the move, to replace the lost son and be company for my sister.

However, the loss of the son and my father's preoccupation with the Second World War propaganda on the radio and in the newspapers destroyed what was left of their marriage. When I was twelve years old my parents separated.

My sister, nine years older than me, had already moved to New Westminster to train as a nurse at Woodlands Psychiatric Hospital. My mother and I also moved to New Westminster where she purchased a house suitable for keeping boarders. She told every newcomer how her husband had tricked her into leaving her wonderful village in Bavaria to live in the cruel, uncivilized wilderness of Canada. One day my mother pointed out an article in a newspaper. It announced that the sternwheeler that had serviced the Arrow Lakes so many years ago had been retired. There was no way to get into Broadwater except by private boat or horseback. For me Broadwater had for so long been a mysterious place and it now beckoned to me.

A boarder mentioned that a road—really only suitable for jeeps, pick-up trucks and vehicles with a four wheel drive—now went through to Broadwater. Perhaps the road was not all that bad. My husband, Walter, had driven our six cylinder '56 Chevrolet across the Cascades before the Rogers Pass was finished. Maybe it could survive another challenging drive. Walter said we would try on our next holiday. The Chev was checked over and the spare tire inspected. Our map (A Sportsman's Map of West Kootenay, British Columbia), showed that we had to get from Castlegar, over the Columbia River to Robson. From Robson a road followed the northeast shore of the River now called the Arrow Lakes because here the river widened considerably. The road, on the other hand, became considerably narrower – and the pavement stopped. It was gravel, one lane, and full of potholes.

After jostling slowly along for over an hour there was a sign that said 'Deer Park'. According to our map, and what Mother had told us, Broadwater would be next. My mother had told us that someone from the Mackereth family, the only neighbour, still lived there. We should look out for their house. If a Mackereth was still there they could point out where the homestead was located.

Slowly we bumped and swerved along the winding road. A mountain rose on our right and the edge of the road dropped steeply down to the lake on the other side. No vehicle came from the opposite direction so we didn't have to back up to some slightly wider part of the road to make space. No tree had fallen blocking the way.

Finally, we arrived at an open space, a clearing that was gradually growing in. There was an old orchard with some sturdy fruit trees well past their prime. Then I saw a bungalow. There was some laundry on a line.

Walter found a suitable place to park. We eased ourselves out of the car and stretched our legs. A well-built man, not past thirty, came out of the building and slowly walked towards us.

"Excuse me," I called out, "Is this the Mackereth place?

We're looking for the old Baumgartner homestead. I'm their daughter and this is my husband."

The man looked us up and down calmly before answering. Our intrusion into his isolated lifestyle didn't seem to bother him. "I'm a Mackereth son," he said in a matter-of-fact voice that did not belie the excitement I felt in hearing the name my mother had repeated so often.

"The Baumgartners?" He thought for a few moments. The silence of the surrounding forest created an overwhelming tension. "That's right, I remember hearing about them. That must have been 'bout thirty years ago."

"Yes, they came here in 1927," I responded, "Mom said their homestead was up the mountain from your place."

"That's right," he nodded casually, "You just have to keep walking straight up." He gestured towards the heavily forested mountain slope beyond the clearing, looking for all the world like a signaller directing traffic around a construction site in the city; a signaller who was sort of bored with his job.

We looked in the direction he indicated. All there was to see were the overgrown remains of another orchard fringed with wilderness beyond.

"Can't miss it," he said a bit more encouragingly, "See that tall group of cedars?" He pointed to the forest beyond. "You'll come to another little clearing. Just keep going straight up." He turned and walked back towards his house. We were on our own.

We started hiking upwards through the tall grasses and brush of the old orchard entering into the forest. I figured if we got lost, it would be simple enough to turn around and go downhill.

After walking about ten minutes, we saw the clearing the Mackereth son had referred to. Grasshoppers snapped and metallic flies buzzed in low, ponderous circles on the long abandoned meadow. Then we saw it! Squatted on the slope before us was a small structure made of thin cedar poles, weathered grey by seasons of rain, sun, wind and snow – my parents first home in Canada! A roll of corrugated sheet metal leaning against one side, must have served as the chimney.

## The Making of a Frontier Woman

A chipmunk chattered alarm. We walked around the back of the structure and squeezed through a thicket of spindly wild cherry trees to reach the narrow wooden door. The latch made a soft clicking sound as my husband pressed it down. The door swung in with barely a creak. We stepped inside. Fine dust, like a grey silk shawl, covered everything. An old, wood-filled apple box was nudged to the side of a sturdy, knee-high cast iron stove. One spindle chair stood against the wall as though waiting to be used. Three forks, soup spoons and knives protruded, like a steel bouquet, from an enamel cup perched on a corner wooden bracket. Everything was exactly as my parents must have left it when they last closed the door.

To the left, behind a narrow partition of boards, was a wall closet barely deep enough for clothes hangers. An ochre coloured *Manitoba Free Press*, lying in the corner, announced a general strike in Winnipeg. Next to it, the brittle remnants of an Eaton's catalogue offered the benefits of corsets, coffee grinders, pickaxes and liniments. It reminded me of cutting out pictures from them for school assignments. In the old days, Eaton's mail order catalogues were sent out free from the Winnipeg head office to every rural household in western Canada.

On the wall to the right were wooden brackets that once supported boards for a bed. A small crucifix gleamed down from the wall where the head of the bed must have been. I took it down and brought it out from behind the partition to get more light. The crucifix was ebony, inlaid with silver.

A ray of sun directed a spotlight onto the floor through the cob web covered windowpane. Cut into the plank was a notch. I knelt down, gripped it and pulled. A door lifted up. I peered in to a dirt crawl space that was completely empty. Nothing but dust.

We went outside to see the barn my parents had built. A potpourri of incense, wafted by some invisible hand, surrounded us. My hands felt the smooth sun warmed handles of an old plough resting among grasses, daisies and thistles. Unbelievably, there still was a trace of the pathway. Walter pointed out a plank door leaning against the mountain slope. "That must have been their root house."

## Aloisia

A pair of dragonflies, locked in flight, wavered and zigzagged over tall wild flowers and seedpods. Dreamlike thoughts permeated the air and mingled with butterflies and mountain bluebirds. Did I hear the voices of my parents talking as they toiled here so long ago? I pictured Mother as she was then, an agile, slender bride, following her husband up the steep wilderness slope to her new home, not yet knowing it would be a hunter's shack.

She told me she had turned around to look back, a habit her mother had instilled in the Old Country. "Look back! Whenever you are leaving a place. Look back to see that you haven't forgotten something, or if someone is waving or trying to catch up." Nobody was waving, nobody was coming, and nobody was trying to catch up. There was only the vanishing trail of black smoke from the sternwheeler, a haze against the distant shore.

Left behind in the storage shed on the pier were the results of months of her careful planning, sewing and packing. Packed in two pine trunks were farewell gifts from her friends in Germany: amongst them a white china serving platter painted with blue fruit given to her by the church choir and a porcelain miniature of the Ulm cathedral. Clothing and linens were used for padding. Aloisia's sewing machine and meat grinder were packed in a crate surrounded by woven cotton floor runners. Her feather beds were pushed into that crate too.

The corridor for skidding raw logs down to the Lower Arrow Lake must be nearby. But we couldn't stay longer. Civilisation was too far away. We made our way back to the car. Mackareth's son did not come out again and we didn't want to intrude by looking for him. Changing hues carried by a cool breeze warned us that dusk was falling.

We had an hour's drive back along the winding dirt road leading to Robson. A motorcyclist coming around a blind corner at top speed, and just as shocked as we were, almost made us swerve off the edge of the road hundreds of feet above the lake.

It all seemed like a dream. "Why didn't Mom want to come along? She could have seen it all!" My husband glanced at me,

"I'm sure she has her reasons."

## Wild Cherries

Back home in New Westminster the following day, I climbed the familiar steps leading to Mom's porch. The smell of freshly baked ginger snap cookies greeted me as I unlatched the screen door and stepped into the kitchen. "Mom! I'm here," I shouted as the door clattered shut behind me.

"Coming, I'm coming," her voice and the sound of shuffling footsteps came up from the basement stairs. Gripping the railing with one hand and an apronful of potatoes with the other, she smiled, "So, so, back from the wilderness?" She tumbled the potatoes into the sink and gave me a hug, "Well, is your curiosity filled now?"

"Mom, it was wonderful!"

"But how was the weather? Walter didn't have trouble with the car, I hope?"

"Butsi, everything was like a dream! It was just like you left it!" 'Butsi' was my mother's nickname. She had once told me that Butsi was the name of the family dog back home in Germany, a very clever dog and Mom had missed her a lot. After that we called Mom "our Butsi" and somehow the name stuck. I always used it with a special intonation when I wanted to share my happiness or coax her to agree with me.

"And the road, dear? How was it?"

"That road was just gravel, but Walter made it in."

Mom walked to the stove and reached for the wire lighter. She gave a spark to the gas element under the coffee pot. "It's amazing that there's a road in at all. We sure didn't have it. Only the ferry once a week. Sometimes we'd go down to see it, just to have some contact with the world. If we'd had a road, it would have been heaven."

"Yes," I nodded sympathetically, "And we also saw your stove! It was so tiny! It would be perfect for a playhouse."

In a few seconds, she deftly arranged the gingersnaps on a plate and set them on the table. "Well it sure wasn't playing when we had to melt snow on it for doing the wash, I can tell you that. And all night those wolves and coyotes howling. The first few nights after I arrived were the worst, but I really never, ever got used to that crying sound, like a woman in trouble." She cupped her hands to her mouth, "Aoo.... Aoo-oo. The crying was all around us. There were so many."

"Really?" Her wolf howls made me smile.

"Really!" And she repeated the howls, "And when your father brought me there for the first time it had rained. Drips were coming through the rafters. I don't know what he was thinking about, bringing me from the middle of a village where we lived next to the church and the village inn was right across the road. You could hear the singing right from our house. And your father brought me to a shack we wouldn't have used for pigs back home and all I had to listen to was howling like some poor woman screaming right outside our wall. And we had to get water from a...."

"Look!" I interrupted. She had told me the story of carrying water from a stream many times before. I took the old Broadwater cutlery from my handbag and spread it on her oilcloth-covered table.

"My, oh my."

"They were left in the corner."

She leaned forward. With fingers made concave from a lifetime of hard work, she gently touched the wooden-handled steel knives, forks and the tarnished silver spoons. "I brought them from the Old Country."

"Why didn't you take them along when you left Broadwater?"

"It was your father's idea," she shrugged. "Yes, he said if there was ever another war, we could go back there and be safe and have something to eat with. I'd forgotten all about that."

It would have been a long way to get there, I thought.

Mother pushed the utensils towards me. "Keep them. I don't need them. They mean more to you."

"Really?" I said, but didn't protest.

I reached into my bag again and handed her a little package wrapped in white tissue paper. "Oh my!" She said, before she had even finished unwrapping. Her features softened. "Here it is. I never thought I'd see this again." She turned the silver and ebony cross over and over in her hands, feeling each angle and contour.

"Whose was it?" I asked. "How did it get there?"

"It was mine. I had brought it because it was small and didn't take up much space. It comes from my oldest sister, Maria, the nun in South Africa. It comes from her, Maria in Africa."

"Mom, how could you leave something so valuable behind in the wilderness? Someone could have come across your homestead and taken it!"

She just sighed. "Your father said that if anyone ever found our place they should know that it had been inhabited by Christians."

"Really? He said that? 'Inhabited by Christians?'"

"That's what your father said. 'Leave it hanging so some stranger will know....'"

We looked at each other. Words failed us.

The coffee started to perk and my mother got up to turn the flame down. "Did you find the root house by any chance?" she asked as she sat down again.

"Yes, and right where you said it would be! But guess what? A huge cedar tree is blocking the entrance."

"The door is blocked? You can't get in?"

"That's right. And anyway, the door is sort of collapsed."

Her head shook in disbelief. "Well, that's almost thirty years ago so that's how things change. I used to be so scared when I opened the root house door. Sometimes I'd jump. I thought a bear would come out at me."

"Did it?"

"No, no. It was only the wind scraping branches or some other thing. It never really happened."

"You've had such an interesting life, Mom. You were a real pioneer!"

She leaned towards me and looked straight into my eyes. "Yes, I think I have that right, to be called a pioneer. I don't think any woman did more work than me."

"That's for sure," I nodded. "And you know the strangest thing of all? Right outside the door, the door to where you lived, there was a virtual forest of wild cherry trees!"

She smiled, tilting her head to one side, the way she sometimes did. "Is that so? Are you sure they weren't birches or alders?"

"No, no. There were still a few cherries the birds had left. They were cherry trees all right!"

"So, so." My mother's concentration shifted to carrying the coffee pot to the table, refilling the sugar bowl from a tin canister on the counter and getting cream from the refrigerator. Finally, she sat down again.

"Mom, wouldn't you like to come next time we go? We would be happy to take you."

"Not really, my dear. You know, I had such bad experiences in Broadwater. I got pregnant the first night I was married and I've told you before I was very sick with my pregnancy. Once I was stung all over by bees. They nailed me to the ground." She always used the expression, 'nailed me to the ground' when she told this story. "And one day I tripped on a root and lay in the hot sun with torn ligaments. I was so thirsty but I couldn't move. Finally, your father came home and carried me inside. I thought I would miscarry! And when winter came, we almost starved to death. The food I brought along from the Old Country was long gone. We were so poor we couldn't even afford postage stamps to write home. My family didn't know if I was alive or dead. That's how bad it was."

"It must have been terrible, Mom. But didn't Dad know how to hunt?"

Mom shook her head. "Your father was no hunter. He had a rifle, but he didn't know how to get anything. He never had any training when he was in the navy, I guess. In the morning, when we opened the door we would see the tracks of deer right by our house. But, when he went out to look for deer he couldn't see any."

"How did you survive then, that first winter?"

"Oh my, oh my. It would be better not to think of it," she took a deep breath and sighed. "A hunter came along, I mean a real hunter. He saved our lives. Somehow he found our place by chance, or maybe he knew it from hunting in the area before. Maybe he even stayed in the hunting shack, I don't know. Your father told him we had nothing to eat. And he just laughed. Laughed out loud! That shocked me."

"You are surrounded by wildlife!" he said and taking his rifle he went out the door. Pretty soon we heard a shot. It wasn't even half an hour. We went out to see what was happening and there he was, coming back. He led us to the edge of our clearing and pointed. "There's an animal waiting for you," he said. We followed him and there was a deer lying, dead, a nice one, under some larches. We couldn't believe our eyes."

Of course we knew what to do then because it's just like butchering a cow. But then we ate venison roast, venison soup and venison hamburger that I ground with my grinder, venison everything, 'til I got sick of it." Mom grimaced. "It was awful, just awful."

"What about the neighbours?" I questioned indignantly. "Didn't they help?"

"Ha! For miles around, there was just the Macareths and they were busy. What could they do? They did what they could. They had a few cows and we got milk in exchange for work your father did. Phew!" She wiped the back of her hand across her mouth. "Sometimes that milk was just awful. I thought they were not milking clean and manure got in. So I asked if I could milk myself, but it didn't help. We found out later that the cows got into the wild parsnips.... Well, we had to live with it. Once, when I opened the cellar door – your father had built a cellar into the floor and once...."

"I saw that! I lifted up the lid!"

## The Making of a Frontier Woman

My excitement made Mom smile. "So, so, you found our cellar. I can tell you a story about that, since you're wanting to collect stories."

I nodded encouragement.

"Your father built it for storage and to keep things cool in the summer. Once when I knelt down and opened that door, there was a dead rat floating in my bucket of milk, face up, looking right up at me! I can stand anything except a mouse or a rat. I don't know why but you've seen it, Ella, when one somehow got in this kitchen here a few years ago."

She was not exaggerating. My strong mother trembled with fear and fled hysterically out of the house that time.

"Well, that really killed my appetite for milk, I tell you. I couldn't even look at milk for a long time after that. And there I was, pregnant." Mother twisted a stray wisp of grey hair into her braided bun (I could never remember her having the red hair that embarrassed her so much as a young woman).

"And remember?" her voice changed to a new intensity, "I told you how we bundled your sister, Louise, in a washtub and carried her up into the forest with us." She placed her elbows on the table and looked at me with those soft green eyes I always envied. "We had to make telephone poles to earn money. The mountain behind our shack was covered with cedars. They don't rot. That was all Broadwater was good for, making telephone poles. We always put Louise in a safe place, far out of the way, but not too far away, so we could keep our eyes on her and she'd be safe from the wild animals. Well, once we were cutting down a giant cedar and it started to fall straight but when it was half way down it twisted in the air. It didn't fall where it was supposed to. It came down almost on top of her."

I shuddered thinking about what had happened so far from any help. I touched Mom's arm.

"Oh my, oh my!" Mom shook her head, "I can still see it today when I think of it. That was a nightmare, I tell you. It just missed Louise by a few feet." She reached for a paper napkin and wiped her forehead. "I tell you, Ella, that was a life. We could have all been killed! And nobody around to help, just all alone in the wilderness. She sighed. "It's best really not to think of it. Really, Ella."

I rested my hand on hers, "It's okay, Mom. It's okay."

Mom's voice relaxed. "The company wanted different lengths, you know. And sometimes we could get three poles from one log, those trees were so tall and straight. Sometimes, when I walk along our street here in New Westminster, I think some of the telephone poles are from us, that we made them. It could be, you know. We sure made enough."

"How did you just manage it all?" I asked.

"I don't really know," she took a long sip of coffee and firmly placed it back on its saucer. "I just know that if I wasn't a pioneer, then nobody was."

"That's for sure, Mom. That's for sure." We sat quietly for a minute, eating gingersnaps. The coffee was hot and sweet. "I just remembered. I saw a doghouse up in the barn rafters."

"Is that so?" Mom's face broke into a smile, "I don't know why we put it there. Yes, yes, we had a dog. He was so cute. Small, but so full of energy. White with black spots, just a mongrel with short hair, but so smart! Now, I can't even remember his name."

"Trix, I think you said once."

"Trix! That was it." She caressed the name with her voice. "He was good company for us. The man who had him before, who lived in the shack before Dad bought it, had taught him some tricks. He could sit up on his hind legs and keep a tobacco pipe in his jaws. But he was really supposed to help against the bears. Bears are afraid of dogs, you know. They hate their smell, but the bears came anyway. Macareths' apples and honey attracted them. You know bears are actually very intelligent, and graceful too, I tell you. I saw them lifting frames of honey from our neighbour's beehives with my own eyes, just like a human, so delicately."

"Really, Mom?" I smiled as she imitated the lifting motion with her fingers.

"Yes, and when the apples got ripe, they would stand on their hind legs and reach up for them and pick them, like a human, so delicately, like a human I tell you! So gracefully!" Mom lifted her arms and pretended to pick imaginary apples. "But coming back to Trix," she dropped her arms again and looked at me intently. "He saved our lives once, from a mad she bear."

"Saved your lives? You never told me that before!"

"Didn't I? Well, I'll tell you. It could have been our end and then there would have been no story to tell for you. We were just coming back from getting water and there were these two little bears, little black bears, sitting right in the pathway, eating blackberries. Dad made some noises but they didn't move so he threw a stick."

"Oh my God! That was a dumb thing to do. Where was the mother?"

Mother raised her hand to silence me. "Let me finish. We were new in the bush. All of a sudden there was the mother bear. She made a snorting noise and her little cubs climbed up a tree so fast you couldn't believe it. The mother bear came at dad but Trix jumped between. He barked and tried to bite the bear from this side and that and the bear was mad, just going round and round him in circles and Trix was yelping but he didn't stop attacking.

Dad shouted, "Get the gun, get the gun!" Then all of a sudden, the mother bear beat off into the bush, just like that. Trix scared her off!"

"But what about Trix? Didn't he get hurt?"

"Yes, yes. Poor Trix. He got some cuts. We had to treat his wounds, but he was okay. One leg we had to bandage. I ripped off a piece of cloth to make a rag." She pretended she was wrapping her wrist. "But that's how smart he was, that Trix!"

"Wow, what a story!"

Mother looked shocked. "That was no story, that was real life!"

"I know, I know Mom. I didn't mean it that way. So what did the little bears do?"

"Nothing. Dad shot them."

"Shot them? The poor things!"

"Well, we didn't need more bears around, that's for sure."

"No, I guess not...."

"Well. It's true life. It's not a fairy tale. I think Dad even got some money for the skins. We sure needed it. Yes, I think, if I remember right, he did. We had to survive."

I shuddered. "Of course, Mom. You had to survive."

We sat there in silence for awhile, just sipping our coffee. My mother pushed her chair back a little from the table and I noticed her lips forming a wistful smile. She was lost in thought. Her eyes softened.

After awhile I asked, "What are you thinking about, Mom?"

"Oh, I'm just remembering something. Your dad got the use of the neighbour's rowboat once. Such a beautiful day it was! He rowed me across the lake."

"Wasn't that a little dangerous, with currents and all? After all it's really a river."

"You have to pick your day and that day the water was calm, just like glass. The sun was shining. Anyway, Dad had been in the navy and there was a little settlement on the other side. Renata it was called. And some of the people spoke German. What a day that was! They asked me to sing and your father even tried his yodel."

"Dad yodelled?"

"Yes," she waved her hand to show this fact was not important. "He learned it when he was in Switzerland that time he was escaping from Hitler."

She leaned forward in her chair and continued in a firmer voice, "We were sure glad when we had enough money to get out of that Broadwater place. Lucky that we could make telephone poles. And then we cut cordwood out of what was left over from the poles and we cut a lot of birches too. We didn't even know at first if we could sell it. We had stacks and stacks of cordwood piled up there in the wilderness. Then one day, we went down and Dad talked to the captain of the ferry and that is a day I'll never forget. The captain motioned with his arm. 'Bring it down, bring it all down'." Mother motioned

## The Making of a Frontier Woman

with her arms imitating the captain. "Bring it down. We'll take it all.' That was like music to our ears and he paid us a good price too. We couldn't believe it."

"What a time that was, Mom."

She nodded and poured another cup of coffee for each of us and pushed the sugar and cream to me. The soft green sheer curtains in the kitchen corner window framed her face. Asparagus and Rabbit's Foot Fern were almost translucent in the afternoon sunshine. Past the veranda, protected by the flickering shade of wisteria vines, were the neat rows of Mom's vegetable garden, a parking area for tenants and a garage with an attached arbour covered with grapes. A bare patch marked where the little old chicken house had been until just recently. The shade of Gravenstein Apple, Italian Prune and Bing Cherry trees dappled the lawn. Beyond were painted fences and her neighbour's homes.

"So, Mom," I said, facing her again, "You don't remember anything about those cherry trees behind your house in Broadwater?"

She shook her head, "To be honest, I don't. Really, Ella, that was all so long ago."

"They must have got there somehow. You didn't plant them there, that's for sure."

"No, no, that's for sure," she said, wiping her hands on a paper napkin. "No place to plant cherry trees, blocking the door."

We both laughed.

She tore the edge off a piece of paper napkin and started twirling it in her fingers to make a small cone. It was a habit she had. "I'm just thinking," she said, "We left Broadwater right after the cherry season because the Mackareths needed help and we could use the money. And of course we could take cherries home to eat and I just guess, when we finally closed the door for the last time to come to the Fraser Valley, there must have been some cherries that we couldn't take along. Or maybe they had started to rot, so I just threw them out."

"That's it! They must have all taken root! The pits all took root!"

"Yes, my dear, they must have all taken root," she shook her head wondering at my excitement.

"Mom, if we go in again, won't you please come along? You know we'd be glad to take you."

"I don't think so, my dear," she looked out her kitchen window. "You may love the wilderness and the mountains but I have to say the only nice time in Broadwater was when spring came. The sun warmed up our shack like a cardboard box put in the sun. In summer it got too hot, like an oven. And in winter...." Her voice trailed off. "Ella, you can love the wilderness and the mountains, but just give me a cleared piece of flat land, neighbours around and running water in the house." She shook her head again. Her features hardened. "I don't want nothing to do with Broadwater," she said firmly. "Nothing draws me to it. Nothing," she added a little louder. "There's just bad memories, hunger, wolves, no person to talk to. We were just lucky to be able to save enough money to get out alive."

I got up and put my arms around her shoulders. "Ah, Butsi. Maybe next time?" Her shoulders relaxed and her face softened, "Well, we'll see. We'll see. Who knows what next year will bring?"

"Come on, Butsi, Broadwater is so interesting."

"Is that so? Ella, you find it so interesting?" Her voice was almost lilting.

"Butsi, it would be wonderful if you could come! You'll see."

"Well, my dear," she sighed. "If it means so much to you.... Maybe I'll come along next time, maybe next year, to see the wild cherries."

# Broadwater: The Last Time In

The first time I saw my parent's Broadwater homestead was 1958, when my husband drove in on a logging road hugging the Lower Arrow Lake. At that time, a son of the Mackereths, who were my parent's only neighbours back in 1927, was still living there. He pointed toward a tall stand of cedars on the forested slope above their acreage and said to just keep walking in that direction.

We found the homestead – completely intact. We did, however, have to squeeze through a stand of wild cherry trees almost blocking the door of the shack my mother once had to call 'home'. A cedar tree growing right in front of the root house made it difficult to reach the door.

The second time into Broadwater it was the mid 1960's. We took our two children along; I so wanted them to see this part of their heritage. The logging road didn't go through anymore, so we drove to the newly completed Keenleyside Dam and then launched our fourteen foot motorised sail boat. It was quite a challenge and slow going as we had to manoeuvre around floating logs, stumps, branches and debris of every size and description caused by the flooding of the dam. We couldn't make it to Broadwater before nightfall so we pulled the boat ashore at a place called Deer Park and camped overnight. A deserted shack served as our shelter. After our picnic dinner and before we went to sleep we lay on huge logs for hours and watched showers of shooting stars. They looked like falling diamonds in a clear and soundless night sky. I found out later that this happened every August and is called the Perseids meteor shower. The next morning, after having bacon and eggs around a campfire, we were told by a squatter in the area that during the night our shelter had been surrounded by coyotes or wolves – or both.

Our little family continued north along the east shore of

the Lower Arrow Lake until my husband located the desolate Broadwater beach. He carefully tied our boat to a huge stump still firmly rooted to the bank. Then he led us up the mountain on what seemed to be an old skid area for logs. After about half a mile we found patches of fireweeds and daisies which marked the spot where Mackereth's homestead once stood before B.C. Hydro bought it and burned all structures down to the ground, a measure they said was essential to prevent liabilities.

We kept hiking upwards and found the homestead. Bullet holes had shattered the two little windows. Beer cans were lying here and there on the floor. Fortunately, I had taken the cutlery and the silver crucifix when we were there the first time.

The third time in it was the 1970's. This time we were able to drive in from the north end of the lake. Rain had entered our parent's home through the broken windows. The roof had collapsed. Somebody had removed the little stove my mother used for cooking, baking bread and heating water. The pioneer home was only a tumbledown shack now. I only wish that somehow, some way we could have taken out the little stove the last time we were in. The woodshed was also ready to fall down and the once sturdy two storey barn stood at a precarious angle.

There were two other times when we tried to show the Broadwater homestead to friends and a relatives visiting from Europe. We tried to drive in from Robson again, as we had done in 1958. Each time, however, to our disappointment, we had to turn back. The road was a winding pile of rocks, the mountain on one side was trying to push us off into the river far below us on the other. We managed to back up to a space in the road wide enough so we could turn around and gave a sigh of relief.

After those trips I never thought I would be able to see Broadwater again. However, in the spring of 2000, my sister Louise informed me that she had been in contact with Bunty, a Mackereth son, now retired in Castlegar. The road was better, it had been fixed up. Bunty knew the way in and had, in fact, even offered to drive us in his truck right to my parent's homestead.

Time was passing and now Bunty, in his mid seventies, had some serious health problems. If we didn't take the opportunity this year, it might be too late. None of us were getting any younger and the strain of such a trip might soon prove too much for any of us. My sister suggested we could try for the beginning of June, taking the bus from New Westminster to Castlegar. Perhaps Bunty would be able to pick us up at the station, take us to a motel and the next day drive us into Broadwater.

So at 6:00 AM one morning in early June we boarded the Greyhound bus to try again to reach Broadwater. It rained, as we expected, all the way, the windshield wipers slapping unevenly as we tried to make ourselves comfortable on the thirteen hour ride. But everything went as scheduled. Bunty was waiting for us at the bus station when we arrived and drove us to the Sandman Inn. We were not surprised that the radio forecasted more of the same weather.

Next morning, as planned, Bunty met us in the lobby. We could hardly believe that the rain had stopped. It was a warm, sunny morning with only a few cumulous clouds resting high in an azure blue sky. A new weather report forecasted a warm sunny day.

"How did you get Bunty for a name?" I asked as we headed for his reassuringly sturdy half ton 1983 Ford truck.

"It's really a nickname. My older brother and sister called me that after the nursery rhyme they sang when my mother brought me home to Broadwater from the hospital. Somehow the name stuck.

We chorused out the rhyme:
> Bye, baby bunting,
> Your daddy's gone ahunting
> To get a little rabbit skin,
> To wrap his baby bunting in.

"Our mother always called you Bunty," I said. "You were only a baby when she and dad left Broadwater in 1929. What should we call you Arthur or Bunty?"

"Well, Arthur is my real name. My name is really Arthur."

As we climbed into the truck I saw a chainsaw lying in the back. Bunty, or should I say Arthur, since he seemed to prefer that name, noticed my observation. "Just in case, just in case there's tree in the way or somethin'." Arthur drove over to Robson and the paved road soon turned into gravel. "It's called the Broadwater Road now," he said as we slowly bumped along. Despite the long wet spring, the road wasn't bad. The edges of the road were fringed with blue lupins, white thimble berries, Oregon grapes, fox glove and sweet clover. Pushing them to the road's edge was a dark forest of pines, Douglas firs, larches, birches and cedars. When, occasionally, the truck bounced across narrow wooden bridges, Arthur pointed out the local creeks: Syringa, Tulip, Big Cayuse, and Little Cayuse. Finally we came to Deer Creek, the place where my husband, our two children and I had camped overnight on our way to Broadwater many years before.

Arthur stopped the truck at a view point to point out a patch of white empty shoreline across the lake. "That's the last of the Renata settlement, after the building of the Arrow Lakes Dam in the sixties." Ahead, Bluebird Mountain (named, I presumed, after the small powder blue mountain bluebirds that lived in the area) gently rose on a peninsula jutting out from the east shore. Behind Bluebird Mountain lay Broadwater. Arthur explained he had shot thirty bears in the area during his years of homesteading. "You can't just scare them off. You get them or they get you. There's no in between. Shot a couple of cougars too and so many wolves and coyotes I couldn't count, maybe a hundred. They're hard on the livestock. You can't just scare them off. They come back."

I remember my mother saying, "The wolves and cougars would get the Mackereth's sheep by the throat. They wouldn't even eat the whole animal, just left them lying around."

During the trip, Arthur entertained us with more stories about the area. One was about a young red-haired woman whose husband had been killed a few years before. He had been drinking and driving on one of the local roads. Recently

## *The Making of a Frontier Woman*

Katy–that was her name–had bought land in Broadwater and sometimes came out to live in her mobile home there. Now she had a partner; he was a carpenter. Arthur said he was a good choice because she needed lots of help trying to establish her vacation home there in the wilderness.

It took us one and a half hours to make the twenty-six mile drive in. Arthur pointed to the scattered clearings that indicated where his family once homesteaded, swung his truck around and parked in a wedge of wilderness. We stiffly lifted ourselves out of the truck. It felt as though my vertebrae had become disconnected.

Some young families were camping a little way down the slope on some acreage they had bought. Yes, land was beginning to sell around Broadwater – after all these years. Arthur explained that he had given a parcel of land to his son. He, in turn, had sold it because paying almost a thousand dollars a year in taxes for a few acres of land did not make sense to him. He got thirty-five thousand for it.

Louise and I walked down to get a better view of the lake and see what the new owners were up to. They had campers, folding chairs and fishing poles. Their first permanent structure was an outhouse. They were trying to bring water into their campsite by digging a trench towards a small stream.

Arthur, in the meantime, walked over to find Katy. He thought she must be around somewhere because her four wheel drive was parked next to her small mobile home. He wondered if she would like to see our parent's homestead too. In a few minutes he came back up the slope with Katy and her dog. The three of us started to hike up the mountainside. Katy told us that she had once come across the homestead while exploring with her dog and someone had told her that it had been a trapper's cabin. She was thrilled to discover the true history of the place, and even meet the daughters of those pioneers who once lived in that shack so many years ago.

"Don't veer to the right," Arthur's voice interjected our conversation, "The homestead is straight up." We continued the climb until we came to an overgrown clearing.

"There it is," Arthur pointed out a log foundation crowded in by ferns and young cedars. Thin logs–or should I say, poles–were scattered around the site. They obviously had once been part of the homestead's walls and rafters. A window frame leaned against a large cedar stump, the glass panes broken and scattered about among the brush and weeds. Traces of white paint indicated that it had once been salvaged from some other building and carried in to complete the hunting cabin. It seemed somebody had started to take it away, along with the many other parts of the building now missing. They obviously decided against it.

Louise stayed on the downward side of the log foundation. What was left of the floor, came up level to her chest. The back entrance was at ground level. I say entrance, but there was no sign of the door frame or door. I knew where it had been from previous visits. My dad had once given me the keys to the buildings here, had carefully sewn them on a piece of cardboard. I'm sure he knew, even at the time he gave them to me, that they would never find a matching keyhole again.

We did find two wooden brackets with a thick wire dangling between them. This had obviously been crafted to hold a curtain. By the length of the wire, it could have been for covering the clothes closet. Louise and I pulled out the wire and we each took one bracket.

For some reason I now thought of the Catholic priest who once said mass on their combination cupboard table and I thought of the freshly baked bread which mother served him after. He was the person who advised my parents that this was no place to farm and they would be much better off moving to the Fraser Valley.

"Exactly how big was the cabin?" Louise asked. "I often wondered."

Arthur figured, using the seven inch span from his thumb to his middle finger as a guide, that the cabin was 10' by 16'. On this little floor, my sister learned to crawl, and stand and walk.

We looked at the mountain slope immediately behind the cabin for the remains of the root house. It was hardly noticeable; two giant cedars almost entirely concealed the

## The Making of a Frontier Woman

sagging steps, which led to a caved in wooden door. The gable roof, once jutting smartly out from the slope to protect the entrance from the elements, now shrugged lopsidedly among grasses and underbrush. We walked a few steps further and came to what Arthur said was once the woodshed. Here, again, there was no trace of a door; the area was strewn with logs. My sister found an old scythe blade. Rust had made it fragile, almost lace-like in places. The handle was nowhere to be seen.

We continued along the ridge, climbed over branches and loose-scattered rocks to see what was left of the barn. It was difficult to make out where the walls once were; any traces of a door, windows or door frames of this once sturdy building, were missing. That there was once a second story and a hayloft, where the doghouse was stored years ago, was hard to imagine. Scavengers had taken most of the material away.

My sister was being very quiet.

"How are you doing, Louise?"

"Not that good," came her quick reply. "I'm thinking about poor Mom being 'way up here alone in the wilderness. It makes me sick."

"Let me show you the creek," Arthur said, pointing further along the ridge.

Dad had made a point of telling me that his Broadwater property had its own source of water from a spring-fed creek and I was looking forward to finally seeing it. After a minute or two, we came upon an idyllic scene: a quiet bubbling brook, moss-covered rocks and fern-covered banks. From high above sunshine filtered down creating bright, kaleidoscopic

*The author (left) and her sister, Louise, at the remains of the Broadwater homestead*

flecks of colour on the forest floor.

The brook was narrow and we stepped across it to the other side to have a closer look at the stumps left standing from my parent's logging days. Katy took pictures of Louise and me standing between them. The sound of the cross cut saw and their voices, the smell of cedar sawdust, seemed to still fill the air.

"Dad said he built a box to catch the water and make it easier to dip out," I said. "Do you think we can still see anything...."

"No, there's nothin' to see, been no trace of that for years. Can't get to it now anyway. There's been too much rain lately. It's too mushy without boots. Anyway there's nothin' to see."

I would have liked to have looked, however Arthur pointed out a 1 ½ inch pipe, evidence that Dad had channelled water closer to the homestead – something I never remember hearing about – and led us away. Maybe he was getting tired, maybe he remembered that he didn't have his rifle with him.

We wandered around the remains of the homestead again. I lifted a large, smooth rock, a slab really, which must have been the step into the barn. Small rocks placed underneath made it level, even after all these years. I could sense my father's pleasure so long ago when he found out how well that rock served the purpose. Another piece of water pipe jutted out of the debris around the woodshed. Perhaps Dad got the water this far. Maybe Mom rinsed the laundry in the woodshed and hung it there to dry if the weather was too wet. Maybe....There were a lot of unanswered questions.

Once again, reaching the back of what had been the cabin, rays of sunshine high lighted some long cedar stakes leaning against a tree. "Look! Bean poles!"

"No. Those are what's left of your Dad's fence 'round his propagation area. They had to be higher, much higher."

"Propagation area? You mean fruit trees?" I said unbelievably.

"Sure. He was startin' them from seed but you have to keep things like that fenced in up here. The deer, you know. See there?" Arthur pointed to a few spindly trees, the branches and leaves of which only started high over head as they struggled through the encroaching evergreens. "Those are pear trees. That's all what's left of your Dad's propagation area. They must have grown quite a bit before the fence collapsed or the deer would have got 'em. See over there?" Arthur pointed at a cedar post lying on the ground next to the hole out of which it had toppled. "That post marked the corner of it. And over here," he said pointing to a slight depression which was barely noticeable, "Goin' along side where the fence was, is where your father used to skid the telephone poles."

"Really? Right past their cabin?"

"Yup, right past their cabin and down to the water."

"Did the horse walk beside the trench or in it?" I wondered half aloud.

"In it," Arthur answered, "In it. It was the horse pullin' the logs that made the trench. The horse pulled the cart too."

"Cart? They had a cart?"

"Sure, just a two wheeled cart for bringin' things up and down from the lake."

"Really? Mom never mentioned having a cart. What do you call a two wheeled cart, anyway?"

"A two wheeled cart, I think," Arthur answered. "A two wheeled cart."

My sister and I looked at each other and laughed.

The weather was sunny and the breezes balmy, but it was time to think of going back. Rosie, a friend of Arthur's who was a local historian in Castlegar had tea and sandwiches waiting for us. She had invited a lady whose parents once lived in the community of Renata and met my parents in 1927.

We walked back down to the truck and Katy, thanking us and waving good bye, started down the slope towards where she and her partner were camping. Her dog had already headed for 'home'. Arthur said she had built an outdoor oven in which she made the most delicious bread, buns and cake.

"You might be gettin' hungry," Arthur smiled as he

flipped down the back door of his truck to make what he called a chesterfield. He offered us Pepsi or Orange Crush and opened a large, black lunch pail containing cheese sandwiches, bananas, apples and rolled oat cookies he had baked himself. He said his mother called them Aggression Cookies because if you were feeling angry or frustrated you could get rid of your mood by working on this dough. They were delicious and we asked for the recipe. I called them 'Broadwater Cookies'.

**Cookies**

3 cups butter

3 cups light brown sugar

3 cups white flour

6 cups fine rolled oats

1 tablespoon baking soda

Mix and form into small round balls.

Place balls on cookie sheets and press with bottom of a glass dipped in white sugar.

Bake for 10-12 minutes in preheated oven of 375 degrees.

*Aloisia showing how she could handle bees, just before she got stung*

What a picnic we had! The heat of the sun had released the sweet fragrance of wild roses. Breezes mingled their aroma with the wilderness air. From this spot we could see the lake about a half a mile below. A cast iron leg of a stove protruded from a hump of earth. Whoever took the tiny stove from the cabin must have stumbled going over this rough spot and lost this leg. It joined my collection of nails, a plough blade and a piece of 1½" galvanized pipe that Dad had repaired with some wire.

While we ate, Arthur pointed out the direction of the six-mile trail that winds behind Bluebird Mountain to Deer Park. He smiled, "That's the old Indian trail your Dad took to purchase his horse. He called the horse Cherry; his real name was Jerry. But your Dad knew the name 'cherry' from picking them so he thought the horse had that name." This story must have been passed down to Arthur by his parents or older siblings. Arthur was still 'Baby Bunty' at the time these events took place. Arthur also knew the story about Dad getting sprayed by a skunk when Trix was exploring under a log bridge. Arthur's parents must have pointed out the skid for the logs, the propagation area and the boxed in stream too.

When we were finished our picnic lunch, we put the remainders back into the truck again. As if reading our thoughts, or maybe because he was tired too, Arthur said, "I'm going to drive you down to the place where the dock used to be. You don't have to walk."

He drove his truck carefully past all that indicated his parents had once pioneered on this mountainside: the gnarled remains of apricot, peach, pear and apple trees. There was no longer any trace of the black currants or raspberries which Arthur's family had once picked and sold.

"Mom said you used to have bees."

"Yes, yes. Had them mainly for the fruit trees. Did you hear 'bout when your mother first arrived and she was showin' how to hold a frame full of bees in her bare hands? And we took a picture and then right after some got caught in her stockings and got mad and stung her all over?"

"Yes," I said, "Actually I have a photo of that." Here was another anecdote handed down in their family.

The campers with the folding chairs were still there and Arthur gave a little chuckle. "That stream they're diggin' towards always runs dry in the summer."

"Aren't you going to tell them?" Louise asked.

"Ah, they'll find out soon enough. Anyways, they never asked my opinion. They'll find out." Arthur continued giving explanations as he held on to the steering wheel and concentrated on the best way to get his truck down to the shore. "Did you know about the millionaire who opened up this area?"

Mom had mentioned that the Broadwater area was first owned by a man called Illingsworth who cut an estate out of the wilderness around 1900. He brought everything in by barge and sternwheeler to establish a get-away place. Apparently he was very rich and had other places in Egypt, and India.

"Illingsworth," Arthur continued, "That's what his name was. He had everythin' from logging and farming equipment to cows and sheep and everythin'. He even hired people to plant flower gardens. He even had roses planted–all kinds–and had pathways and archways and trellises too. Then he put an ad in the Winnipeg Free Press–it was actually called the Manitoba Free Press then–and hired my Dad as his chief foreman. That was about 1913. Illingsworth called his land 'rolling', which was a joke if ever I heard one. Then Illingsworth's doctor said the uneven land wasn't good for his legs–he walked with a limp for some reason. And then his only son got brain damage from sun stroke when he was roofin' the guesthouse. So Illingsworth decided to sell the whole fruit ranch–that's what they liked to call it–to my Dad for a very reasonable price. Anyway, they say Illingsworth liked exotic places and had other properties in India and Egypt."

I knew from my parents that Mackereth had got their place for a song. That is what I remember my mother saying, anyway. It really wasn't worth that much anyway. Too isolated and steep. Rocks all over the place. And some years later, in 1926 my dad answered Mackereth's ad in the same newspaper looking for hired help.

"It must have really looked like a wild paradise when Dad first came on the scene," I said. "The roses and archways and everything must have still been there." That was when Dad learned about the thirty-three acres for sale up from Mackereth's with the hunting cabin on it.

## The Making of a Frontier Woman

"Yes," Arthur nodded. He didn't elaborate. Perhaps he was thinking about the hard time he had growing up there in the wilderness. My sister said nothing. "There's Ella romanticising again," she probably was thinking. Katy was taking it all in.

I tried another question. "Didn't the teacher that came to teach in your area board with your parents? Didn't she have to sleep in the same bed as your sister?"

"Yes," Again, no elaboration.

Now we were at the water's edge, trying to imagine what my mother thought when she disembarked from the Minto in 1927. We climbed out of the truck and looked at the spectacular view across the lake. Louise and I collected pebbles from the shore. Each handful was an assortment of different hues and textures. Did mother walk here? Lilac bushes and wild roses quivered in the sunny breeze. The laburnums, right at their peak, added thousands of bright yellow splashes to the other colours.

We climbed into Arthur's truck again, girding ourselves for the trip back to Castlegar. We chatted about this and that, Arthur again naming the streams as we crossed the little wooden bridges, now in reverse order. Deer Park, Little Cayuse...."

"How many bears and coyotes did you say you killed?" I asked.

"Well, there was wild life everywhere. Actually shot and killed two cougars. And coyotes? Maybe ten, but trapped a lot more, 18 coyotes just in one year. Bears, I would shoot about six every year. If you don't, they just come back. There's still lots of wildlife here today, for that matter. You said the B.C. Hydro has turned your parents thirty-three acres into a reserve for ungulates? Well, that's one thing that's hardly left. The cougars got them all. Lots of cougars around here now. They've taken over."

Suddenly, I was very glad that we didn't look for that boxed in spring. Who knows what animals drank there? And poor Mom! No wonder she was afraid to go into that root house with all those wild animals prowling around. I remembered how frightened she said she was when the wolves howled around their cabin at night. And then there was the time my parents were coming along the path with buckets of water and two bear cubs were sitting in the way. And how Mom used to say that Broadwater was not a fairytale, it was real life. And that if she wasn't a pioneer then, nobody was. No wonder she never wanted to see it again.

We were now on the road winding back along the Arrow Lakes towards Castlegar. Louise suggested I take a picture and I did. Before long Arthur again pointed out the Keenleyside Dam, named after the head of B.C. Hydro at the time and we were driving into Castlegar again.

Arthur parked his truck on the street in front of Rosie's home. Rosie was eighty-nine years old and lived alone. The yard had signs of recent gardening and potted plants on her little porch were waiting to find a home somewhere in the already filled beds. We arrived later than expected and Rosie was out in her back yard with Clara, the woman whose parents met Mom and Dad back in 1928. Clara beamed when she saw us and told the story of how my parents would row across the lake from Broadwater to visit her parents in Renata. Clara was only eleven years old at the time but even after all this time could never forget my parents name, Baumgartner, and the entertaining afternoon of singing associated with it in their isolated community. My mother had a beautiful singing voice, she said, and my father did some yodelling.

While picking raspberries my mother used to sing alto as I sang the melody to such favourites as 'Clementine', 'The Lorelei', 'Old Black Joe', 'I'll Take You Home Again, Kathleen' and the all time favourite which we never tired of:

> *You are my sunshine, my only sunshine.*
>
> *You make me happy when skies are grey.*
>
> *You'll never know dear, how much I love you.*
>
> *Oh, please don't take my sunshine away.*

So I knew my mother had a lovely voice which magically complimented any song I sang from my little repertoire learned at school. I had forgotten that Dad could yodel. Now, however, I faintly remembered hearing him once when I was a child. I think we were at the front of the farmhouse where he wouldn't frighten the cows; he certainly wasn't professional by any stretch of the imagination. He just tried to amuse me.

We entered Rosie's back door and to our surprise instead of preparing tea and sandwiches, she had cooked a roast beef dinner with all the trimmings: mashed potatoes, gravy, whole onions and a green salad. We ate while Rosie served. She explained that ever since her husband died that's the way she did it.

"Did you see the golden chains?" she asked. "I guess they were all quite a sight this time of year."

Arthur nodded. Louise and I gave each other blank looks and shook our heads. What was Rosie talking about?

"Golden chains." Rosie repeated, puzzled that we didn't understand what she was referring to. "You know, golden chains. They're yellow. Must have been blooming everywhere along the water at Broadwater this time of year."

"Oh, you mean laburnums?" Louise and I chorused in unison.

Arthur nodded and smiled.

"Yes, yes. They were everywhere down around the Mackereth's and the beach too. They must have all seeded themselves from Illingsworth's garden."

On the way back home Louise and I agreed that this would be the last time we would travel to Broadwater. It was just too far. And the homestead was gradually deteriorating as it returned to the embrace of the wilderness from which it was once hewn. Soon it would be impossible to find.

Of course, even if every trace of the Broadwater homestead finally disappeared, if you came in by boat in the month of June you could see the yellow laburnums blooming right from the water.

# Epilogue

Time has passed. Our children, Celena and Eric, have both found my parent's homestead or I should say, what remains of it. Eric located the door of the root house and brought it home to me. It serves as an entrance to the path that goes down to the ravine garden. Celena brought home a bouquet of wild flowers from the meadow clearing that still decorates a mantle with other objects picked up on our previous trips. In the kitchen a jar is constantly re-filled with cookies made from the recipe given to me on our last trip to Broadwater.

# LOGGING AN ESCAPE FROM THE WILDERNESS

## A Comparison to the Pioneer Life of Susanna Moodie

During the history of Canada many women emigrated from Europe hoping for an improved economic situation. Instead, they often found themselves in isolated shacks surrounded by wilderness and wild animals, their dreams turning into a bewildering nightmare of despair. This desperation, however, often fueled a grim determination to survive their gruelling hardships in the face of apparently insurmountable odds. *Roughing it in the Bush* [1] is Susanna Moodie's written testament to her ingenuity in helping her family escape their lonely pioneer homesteads and move closer to civilisation. She rightfully deserves her place in Canadian history and Canadian literature.

Many other women, however, were also pivotal in helping their families escape the wilderness and remain unsung heroes. Aloisia Baumgartner, my mother, who arrived in the Kootenays of British Columbia in 1927, was surely one of these pioneer women. Though she arrived almost one hundred years later (Moodie arrived in the wilderness of eastern Ontario in 1832), both had very similar experiences.

For each of these women Canada represented an alternative to the despair of a known future in their homelands of England and Germany. Moodie's father had suffered severe financial losses and her husband received the poor income of a low ranking officer. They "...possessed all that the world can bestow of good – but wealth." [2]

In my mother's case, the hardships caused by the Treaty of Versailles, the devaluation of currency and the subsequent

---

[1]  Susanna Moodie, Roughing it in the Bush, (Toronto, McClelland and Stewart, 1962)

[2]  Moodie, p.36.

## Aloisia

depression forced her suitor to accept an arranged marriage which included a farm as a means of livelihood. Her former suitor, now unhappily married, kept trying to make contact with her.

Aloisia, in the meantime, had been in correspondence with Franz Baumgartner, who had immigrated to Canada. He wrote that food was plentiful and the wages were high. She decided join him as his bride in 1927.[3] Surely life in Canada would be better than in her homeland.

Among their fellow immigrants, both Moodie and my mother travelled farthest west. Moodie wrote that her party was the last to leave the boat on its westward voyage beyond Quebec.[4] One hundred years later, after a misdirection to Revelstoke which delayed her arrival in Nelson by two days, my mother was the last to get off the train among all her fellow travellers who boarded in Quebec.

As they travelled, both found the beauty of the landscape overpowering. When Moodie saw the St. Lawrence for the first time she exclaimed, "What wonderful combinations of beauty, and grandeur, and power, at every winding of that noble river! How the mind expands with the sublimity of the spectacle, and soars upward in gratitude and adoration to the Author of all ...."[5] When my mother saw the grandeur of the Rocky Mountains she exclaimed more simply but with the same emotion, "God Almighty created mountains like that. I enjoyed it!" Moodie was as impressed with the European appearance of Quebec as my mother was with the Doukhobor brick homes in British Columbia.[6]

Their praise for Canada's natural grandeur, however, turned to shock when they saw where they were expected to live. Neither Moodie's dwelling in the dense bush north of Peterborough, Ontario, nor my mother's on the mountain wilderness one mile above the Columbia River, could compare with the solid, many roomed homes of their childhood. Nor were these dwellings quaint and cosy log structures seen in

---

3    Baumgartner, Franz. Letter to Aloisia Schropp. 14 August 1926.
4    Moodie, p. 36.
5    Moodie, p. 28.
6    Aloisia Baumgartner, personal interviews, 1940-1983. All subsequent information regarding Aloisia Baumgartners life experiences come from this source.

advertisements. Both women could identify with Old Thomas's sermon in *Roughing it in the Bush*: "The farther in the bush, say I, the farther from God, and the nearer to h_l."[7] Moodie compared her homestead in the backwoods of Ontario to a pig sty. "I could only stare at the place, with my eyes swimming in tears...."[8] My mother said her shack would not even be used as a woodshed back home because the roof leaked. A roll of corrugated sheet metal propped against an outside wall served as a chimney. Even decades after leaving her homestead, she refused every opportunity to visit it saying emphatically, "Broadwater was hell. I don't want *anything* to do with it!"

Both women were the youngest of large families and grew up surrounded by a highly organised society. In Moodie's parlour oriented life in Suffolk, England writing, reading, drawing and the art of conversing were considered essential. The character Tom Wilson in *Roughing it in the Bush* points out just how unqualified she and her husband were for pioneering. "The refined habits in which you were brought up and your unfortunate literary propensities ... will make you an object of mistrust and envy to those who cannot appreciate them, and will be a source of constant mortification and disappointment to yourself."[9] For Moodie, the dilemma of having no agricultural skills was made a little more merciful by her complete ignorance of the absurdity of her initial pioneering attempts.

My mother grew up in the heart of a Bavarian village. Her home was adjacent to the most beautiful church in the district and within a few steps of the local community centre and school. She sang alto in the church choir and taught sewing and fine needlework to the local women. On Saturdays she polished the brass knocker on the front door in preparation for Sunday when relatives and friends from miles around came to attend mass, socialise and visit their family.

But she also learned all the skills essential for running a farm: seeding grain, helping a cow calve, harvesting, getting bee hives ready for winter.... Nothing, however, could have prepared her for logging a virgin forest, surrounded by sighing

---
7   Moodie, p. 159.
8   Moodie, p. 69.
9   Moodie, p. 54

trees and lurking beasts. Though my mother was familiar with virtually all aspects of agrarian life, the move to the Canadian wilderness was both a physical and cultural catastrophe as there was no assistance from a reservoir of a family or community infrastructure to which she was accustomed.

Lack of roads into their remote homesteads also caused severe hardships. In fact, Moodie and her children had to wait until after the first snowfall before they could move out of the bush to Belleville because their only means of getting out was by horse and sled. One hundred years later and two thousand miles farther west, my mother's baggage could only be brought up the rocky slope above the Lower Arrow Lake (simply a broadening of the Columbia River), to her homestead by using a horse and skid.

Virgin forests with bears, cougars and wolves were completely alien to emigrants from Europe where wildlife in the often park-like forests consisted of a few deer, rabbits and birds. My mother never got used to her first night's experience in the wilderness, coyotes and wolves wailing just inches away through the thin walls of her wilderness shack. In later years she often said that the sound (probably intensified by her own feelings of despair), was like that of women sobbing. Unfortunately, though my father had been educated both in an agricultural college and in the navy, hunting was never part of his curriculum. Moodie complained of being tormented by mosquitoes, black flies and rodents.

Hunger was a constant concern for both women. The innards and head of a cow obtained from the only other homesteader for miles around, as well as a deer shot by a sympathetic hunter who stumbled across their wilderness shelter, helped my parents survive the first winter. For Moodie, accomplishments such as learning how to skin a squirrel and make it into an edible meal, would shock rather than impress relatives and friends in their homeland.

Humiliation prevented my mother from writing her relatives that she had fallen into more destitute circumstances than

## The Making of a Frontier Woman

those she had left behind. A letter from her favourite niece one month after my mother's arrival in Broadwater starts with the words: "I was very disappointed to hear nothing at all about you and your situation except your address from which I learned you are already married."[10] Besides shame, the grind of day to day survival and the lack of money for postage stamps were other deterrents from trying to explain her situation. In *Roughing it in the Bush*, Moodie wrote: "...but for the clothing sent us by our friends from home, who were not aware of our real difficulties, we should have been badly off indeed."[11] When this book was published in Great Britain in 1852, the candid description of Moodie's early wilderness experiences embarrassed her British relatives, who had given the impression to their social acquaintances that Susanna was fairing quite well in Canada.[12]

It was not until my mother's first trip back to visit her relatives in 1957, that she fully explained her pioneering experiences, including the freezing of one of her toes. In winter the heat from the little stove could not always melt the ice in the water buckets stored in the corner of the shack. She often said, "Broadwater was *hell*. There was no hope and no *nothing*. There was *no* pioneer life in this country if that wasn't it."

Escape. Escape from the wilderness was the burning desire of both women. Moodie used her composition skills to write the Lieutenant Governor asking him to allow her husband continued employment in the militia so he could pay off their debts. This written request finally resulted in her husband's appointment as sheriff, which meant the family's final release from their desperate financial situation and the opportunity to move to the more established area of Belleville.

According to Moodie's sister, Catherine Parr Trail, in Canada it was not considered a woman's job to be involved with the labour of felling trees.[13] My mother, however, had some experience in looking after her family's small forest in Bavaria. My father trudged through four miles of virgin forest

---

10   Kraus, Maria. Letter to Aloisia Baumgartner. 5 July 1927.
11   Moodie, p. 218
12   Charlotte Gray, *Sisters in the Wilderness: The Lives of Susanna Moodie and Catherine Parr Trail*, (Toronto, Penguin, 1999), p. 214 – 219.
13   Catherine Parr Trail, *The Canadia Settler's Guide*, (Toronto, McClelland and Stewart,1969), p. 57-58.

(the trail was barely visible), to purchase a workhorse from another homesteader. Then he and my mother logged side by side. When their first child arrived nine months later they tucked it into a galvanised wash tub and carried it to their work site. Once there the tub was placed close enough to be safe from wild animals yet far enough away not to be in line of falling timbers. My mother worked hand in hand with my father to cut cedars into telephone poles of various required lengths. They cut birch trees into cordwood. Finally, through logging, they earned enough money was made to move out of the wilderness to the Fraser Valley.

It is a sad irony that when life for each of these women was getting easier, each lost a healthy, beloved son in drowning accidents. Both boys were five years old when they died. Only after these tragedies, in which their adopted land was christened with a part of themselves, could they emotionally accept the country of their exile as their home. How could they leave the land which held the graves of their sons? They must begin to call Canada their home.

Regardless of their different country of origin, dates of arrival, or their pioneering destinations in Canada, Susanna Moodie and Aloisia Baumgartner grappled bravely with the disappointment of finding themselves in such alien, primitive circumstances. Both endured gruelling physical hardships, loneliness, hunger, and homesickness for the irretrievable past – and survived. Though they did not conquer the wilderness, they did not let the wilderness conquer them. Each turned their bewilderment, misery and regret into a fierce determination to escape to a better life.

Had they an opportunity to meet and speak freely with each other as kindred spirits, one might overhear the following conversation:

"What went through your mind, dear Aloisia, when you first saw your new home in Broadwater?"

"Home? I thought it vas a shack for smoking meat. But then my husband opened the door and I realised...."

"Door? Your door was on? We found ours behind some bushes around the back. Fortunately the hinges were still on...."

## The Making of a Frontier Woman

"Oh my, oh my. In my village where I come from we wouldn't have stored wood in a shack like mine. It leaked! It vas just a hunter's cabin propped up on one side so it would have a level floor. Level. Ha! And can you imagine trying to fit my sewing machine in *and* my trunks with all my nice belongings from the Old Country, into a space where there was hardly enough room to turn 'round?"

"My porcelain teapot, all decorated with gold leaves and blue ribbons, broke. And black flies.... Everywhere!"

"My coffee and tea pots were nice too, of deep blue enamel. My children have them.... But, Susanna, you had *flat* land. You can *farm* on flat land. A hay wagon can't tip over.... All we had was rocks and wild forest. Just lucky I could work so hard to make telephone poles out of those cedar trees. Cedar don't rot and that's what the telephone company paid money for, we found out. And we had them right behind our cabin, some so tall you could get three different lengths out of one tree. And what was left over we made into cordwood. We had rows and rows of it piled up there in the forest. I never forget the day when the captain, the captain of the stern wheeler, smiled at us and said, 'Bring it down, bring it down. I'll take it all.' That's what he said. And he gave us good money. And from the birch trees we made cordwood too. Have *you* ever used a crosscut saw, Susanna?"

"No, but I know what it is. My pen is what sawed us out of our misery, if you know what I mean. And then I wrote a book about all my experiences. It was very popular and I made money too. Maybe some day someone will write your story, Aloisia, about how you logged to get out of the wilderness."

"My story? By the way, did I tell you my mother was named Victoria, after Queen Victoria?"

"Really? Well, my dear Aloisia, you never can tell. Maybe one day somebody will write down your story. After all, when I think of it, writing is a bit like logging, in more ways than one."

"Writing is like logging?"

"Yes, my dear. It would make quite an analogy, if one just

thinks about it.... And then there's the polishing at the end."

"I, I .... Did I tell you about the time I opened up the trap door in the floor where sometimes I stored food and there was a drowned rat staring up at me, face up? In my only pail of milk! I didn't want to drink milk after that. And I was pregnant! I thought I should miscarry.... Oh my, oh my. But what's the use of remembering all those bad memories? Is better to forget. We should talk about nice things, Susanna. You know, once my husband rowed me across the lake to a little settlement called Renata where some people spoke German and I could understand them and talk to them. What a beautiful day that was! The sun was shining; the water was like glass...."

"We made a trip like that once too!"

"Really Susanna? Well, as I was going to say, those people in Renata were so nice. I sang some German folksongs for them. And my husband tried his yodelling that day.... Oh my, I guess it wasn't *all* bad. We had our golden moments...."

# Bibliography

Atwood, Margaret. <u>The Journals of Susanna Moodie</u>. Toronto, Oxford Press, 1970.

Bowman, Bob. <u>Dateline: Canada</u>. Toronto, Holt, Rinehart and Winston, 1967.

Chisholm, Patricia. "Dogged Ladies of Upper Canada." <u>Maclean's</u>, 31 Jan., 2000.

Gray, Charlotte. <u>Sisters in the Wilderness: The Lives of Susanna Moodie and Catherine Parr Trail</u>. Penguin, 1999.

Klink, C.F. <u>A Literary History of Canada</u>. Toronto, University of Toronto Press, 1965.

Mandel, Eli. <u>Contexts of Canadian Criticism</u>. Chicago, University of Chicago Press, 1971.

Moodie, Susanna. <u>Life in the Clearings</u>. Toronto, Macmillan, 1959.

Moodie, Susanna. <u>Roughing It in the Bush</u>. Toronto, McClelland and Stewart, 1962.

Moss, John. <u>Patterns of Isolation</u>. Toronto, McClelland and Stewart, 1974.

Story, Norah. <u>The Oxford Companion to Canadian History and Literature</u>, Toronto, Oxford Press, 1967.

# About the Author

Ella Benndorf was born in 1936 of German immigrants on a Fraser Valley homestead near Chilliwack. When she was two years old her family moved to a large 55 acre dairy farm on Prairie Central Road. At the age of thirteen she moved to New Westminster with her mother. After completing high school she married and had a daughter and a son.

In 1970 she and her husband built a home in an old growth forest overlooking Stoney Creek in Oakdale, Coquitlam. She completed her Bachelor of Education at the University of British Columbia and her Master of Education Degree at Simon Fraser University.

After her retirement from her position as a teacher/librarian, she traveled extensively with her husband and became a member of New West Writers. Part of her master's thesis was published in the prestigious German-Canadian Year book as was her illustrated *Logging and Escape from the Wilderness: A Comparison to the Pioneer Life of Susanna Moodie*. She also has been published in both international and national magazines. Her publications include: *For Every Bee There is a Reason* and *Gateways to Shared Secrets*. Her research on North Road, one of British Columbia's oldest roads, as well as other articles, has been published in local community newspapers. She has also written a multicultural cookbook called *Mom's Soup for You*.

In 2001, the author's enthusiasm for the environment and gardening won her several nature garden awards. Her watercolour paintings often reflect the wilderness and vestiges of pioneer life. She named two creeks in Oakdale: *Harmony* and *Consultation,* and was a founding member of Salmonoid Enhancement Program in Coquitlam. Her nomination for the YWCA Women of Distinction was due mainly to work in her community of Oakdale and multiculturalism.

She became a Baha'i in 1969 and since then has been very active in working for the oneness of mankind.

The author's discovery of her father's letters dating from the middle of World War I until her mother left Bavaria for Canada in 1927 proved to be the catalyst for research into the social history of those times. Her parents met at a bee-keeping course where a priest pointed out Aloisia as being a very suitable prospect for marriage. Though initially reluctant, she was finally persuaded to correspond with him. He wrote letters from his ship even when it was anchored at Scapa Flow. He wrote from his family farm, from Argentina and finally from the prairies and wilderness of the Canadian Rockies. To Aloisia's shock, an isolated hunting shack virtually hanging from a mountainside became her new home. *Aloisia, the making of a Pioneer Woman* reveals gripping dilemmas including the universal challenges intrinsic to human nature: love, betrayal, hope, and those qualities every settler to the New World requires in full measure—courage and determination.

*Author at door of Broadwater homestead, 1958.*

CPSIA information can be obtained
at www.ICGtesting.com
Printed in the USA
LVHW051245061019
633322LV00012B/372/P